WITHDRAWAL

Learning to Lead in the Secondary School

Learning to Lead in the Secondary School is designed to meet the needs of subject leaders and heads of department in secondary schools, offering practical advice and guidance to teachers taking on these demanding roles.

This highly informative book is structured around six sections that address all of the key areas in leading a department. Areas covered include:

- Becoming a subject leader
- Managing effective teaching and learning
- Leading and managing people
- The strategic direction and development of a department
- The deployment of staff and resources
- Managing your own performance and development.

This book will be invaluable to middle managers in schools, subject leaders and heads of departments. It will also be of interest to teachers and managers at all levels and will be useful to those undertaking research or further qualifications in educational leadership and management.

Mark Brundrett has taught in secondary, middle and primary schools and was a headteacher for a number of years. He is currently Professor of Educational Leadership at the University of Hull and Visiting Professor of Education at the University of Hertfordshire.

Ian Terrell taught in schools for a number of years before going on to teach in higher education. He is currently Principal Lecturer at Ultralab, which is part of Anglia Polytechnic University.

Learning to Lead in the Secondary School

Becoming an Effective Head of Department

Edited by
Mark Brundrett and Ian Terrell

 RoutledgeFalmer
Taylor & Francis Group

LONDON AND NEW YORK

First published 2004
by RoutledgeFalmer
11 New Fetter Lane, London EC4P 4EE

Simultaneously published in the USA and Canada
by RoutledgeFalmer
29 West 35th Street, New York, NY10001

RoutledgeFalmer is an imprint of the Taylor & Francis Group

Typeset in Bembo by
HWA Text and Data Management, Tunbridge Wells
Printed and bound in Great Britain by
TJ International Ltd, Padstow, Cornwall

British Library Cataloguing in Publication Data
A catalogue record for this book is available from the British Library

Library of Congress Cataloging in Publication Data
Learning to lead in the secondary school : becoming an effective head of
   department / [edited by] Mark Brundrett and Ian Terrell.
      p. cm.
   Includes bibliographical references and index.
   1. High schools–Great Britain–Departments–Management.
   2. Educational leadership–Great Britain. 3. High school teachers–
   Professional relationships–Great Britain. I. Brundrett, Mark.
   II. Terrell, Ian, 1954–
   LB2822.3 L43 2003
   373.2´011´0941–dc21   2003046558

ISBN 0–415–27782–5

Contents

Section 6: Managing Your Own Performance and Development

Illustrations

Figures

Tables

Contributors

Rob Bollington taught in secondary schools and has been engaged in management training for a number of years. He is an adviser in Bedfordshire.

Mark Brundrett is a former headteacher and has taught in three institutions of higher education. He is Professor of Educational Leadership at the University of Hull.

Neil Burton has taught in schools, at college and at university level. He currently teaches in a secondary school in Northampton.

Hugh Busher taught in schools and has extensive experience of teaching in higher education. He is a Senior Lecturer in Education at the University of Leicester.

Chris Comber is a lecturer in education at the University of Leicester where his research interests focus especially on the use of ICT in schools.

Diane Duncan is a former headteacher and she has taught in three higher education institutions. She is a Senior Lecturer in Education at the University of Hertfordshire.

Geraint Lang is a Principal Facilitator at Ultralab, which is part of Anglia Polytechnic University.

Tony Lawson is a lecturer in education at the University of Leicester. He has extensive research interests, especially in the area of the use of ICT in education.

Mark Penny teaches at Burnt Mill School in Essex.

Ed Powell is a Senior Lecturer in Education at Anglia Polytechnic University.

Stephen Powell is a Principal Facilitator at Ultralab, which is part of Anglia Polytechnic University.

Lesley Saunders joined the General Teaching Council (England) as Policy Adviser for Research at its inception in September 2000 and is now engaged in developing and implementing a research strategy for the GTC.

Bob Smith has taught in higher education for many years. He is a lecturer in educational management at the University of Leicester.

Howard Stevenson taught in secondary schools for a number of years. He is a lecturer in educational management at the University of Leicester.

Ian Terrell taught in schools for a number of years before going on to teach in higher education and to conduct a wide range of research projects. He is currently a Principal Lecturer at Ultralab, which is part of Anglia Polytechnic University.

Kathryn Terrell is currently a headteacher. She has published widely on educational management issues.

Acknowledgements

Learning to Lead in the Secondary School was originally to be edited by three people and not the two who completed the construction of the text. These three originators were Mark Brundrett, Marilyn Leask and Ian Terrell. Indeed the two final editors would readily admit that the credit for the inception of the book and much of the essential initial negotiation with publishers should go to Dr Leask. Sadly changes in post and weight of duties prevented Dr Leask from continuing with work on the text. The remaining editors would, however, readily acknowledge the debt that they owe to their colleague who remained a valued advisor in the latter stages of the development of this work.

Thanks are also offered to all of the contributors to the text whose names are enumerated on the contributors pages. It was envisaged right from the outset that this should not be a work that was confined to the imagination and academic knowledge of the editors, both of whom have considerable experience in schools but have now worked in higher education institutions for some time. The editors are aware that the contributors to the text all lead extremely busy and demanding lives, whatever part of the education sector they work in. For this reason the editors would like to praise the contributors for giving of their time unstintingly in order to ensure that the final work met that initial aim of producing something that had close contacts with the work of schools and their partner organisations.

Finally the editors would like to thank their families. Once again these families not only tolerated the fact that many hours of time were spent on developing the text but also contributed to its completion. In the case of Kathryn Terrell this was by drawing on her own considerable experience as a teacher and headteacher in order to contribute to the text. In the case of Pat Brundrett this was by offering help, advice and tolerance during the production of yet another book.

Abbreviations

DES	Department of Education and Science
DFEE	Department for Education and Employment
DFES	Department for Education and Skills
HEADLAMP	Headteachers' Leadership and Management Programme
HEI	Higher Education Institution
HMI	Her Majesty's Inspector
INSET	Inservice Education and Training
LEA	Local Education Authority
LMS	Local Management of Schools
LPSH	Leadership Programme for Serving Headteachers
NC	National Curriculum
NCSL	National College for School Leadership
NFER	National Foundation for Educational Research
NPQH	National Professional Qualification for Headship
OECD	Organisation for Economic Co-operation and Development
OFSTED	Office for Standards in Education
PRP	Performance Related Pay
SMT	Senior Management Team
TTA	Teacher Training Agency

Introduction

It has become one of the great truisms of education that the level of outcomes in schools will have a direct relationship with the quality of leadership in the institution. Much of the work of the school effectiveness and the allied school improvement movements have affirmed time and again that high quality leadership is the key to high quality schooling. It is partly for this reason that there now exists a plethora of texts on leading schools.

Many, if not most, of these texts have focused especially on the role of the headteacher in school development, although one has to admit that there has been an increasing interest in the work of deputy headteachers and the whole School Management Team. In recent times this interest has extended to the role of Heads of Department and there is even a sense in which a view has developed that can best be described as the notion that 'we are all managers now'.

The reasons for the development of this idea of ever increasing delegation of management functions are, like most other things in schools, at one and the same time both complex and simple. Undoubtedly the movement, which began transnationally in the 1980s, which was best summarised as Local Management of Schools, has meant that individual institutions have been required to carry out a wide variety of management functions that would, hitherto, have fallen within the remit of local or national government. Added to this, the pervading culture of accountability in all aspects of life, combined with a most laudable desire to drive up standards of public services, has meant that many new pressures have fallen on schools as well as other public sector organisations. In this sense there is simply much more management to be done than was ever the case in the past.

It is thus logical that no one person, or small team of people, can take on all the management functions that are now a necessary and inevitable part of school life. There is a more subtle and in many ways commendable set of developments that have been witnessed in recent years that have contributed to devolved management structures. It overstates the case greatly to say that we have seen a radical democratisation of schools take place in recent years and there is an argument which runs that effective schools can never be true democracies. There has, nonetheless, been a commitment in both theory and practice to the notion that power and responsibility should be spread throughout organisations thus legitimating decision-making processes. As a very desirable bye-product it is held quite commonly that such organisations have become more effective than they might have been had they remained monolithic top-down structures.

It was with these things in mind that *Learning to Lead in the Secondary School* came into being but the text is not aimed solely at middle managers in secondary schools since it is hoped that readers from many levels in schools will find what it contains to be useful. In fact, to return to the notion that all staff are managers in some form, all teaching staff in schools, from those who are newly qualified to the headteacher, should find items of utility in these pages.

From the outset the decision was taken that the text should not be an academic piece of work that was packed with references but did not reflect the daily life of schools. The editors and contributors have, rather, attempted to keep a balance between providing a work that is of practical use to colleagues in schools but is also backed up by reference to leading contemporary theory. In fact one central commitment of the editors, in all aspects of their professional life, is that the academic and the practical should be interconnected as closely as possible.

For this reason the text is not formed in traditional chapters that march along to some inevitable conclusion that suggests that the writers have all the answers to becoming a leader in school. Instead the text is structured in 'Sections' and 'Units' with the aim that these should form a structured whole that can either be read in entirety or can be dipped into when readers need to find out more about a particular topic.

Section 1 commences the text by looking at the overall issues of leadership and the relationship between the ever expanding knowledge base on school effectiveness and improvement and leadership. There is an increasing commitment to the idea that all good leadership should flow from an ethical and moral base and Hugh Busher, a very well known figure in the field of studies into middle management in schools, offers a strong defence of values driven leadership. The ubiquity of accountability as a phenomenon in education and other services has already been commented on and so, positioned very early in the text, Diane Duncan discusses issues of accountability to the various stakeholders in education.

In Section 2 the text addresses the issues that are at the heart of schools: effective teaching and learning. Ian Terrell and Ed Powell outline the problems of planning in order to be an effective practitioner and reflect on models of teaching and learning. In the last unit of this section Ian Terrell and Stephen Powell provide their perspectives on the ever-increasing importance of ICT in developing learning.

One of the greatest challenges that any school leader faces, whether they are middle managers or members of a senior management team, is leading staff. In Section 3 Ian and Kathryn Terrell discuss how best to lead and manage people in education and how to create the learning department and the learning organisation. This, in turn, is related to the recent developments in interconnecting staff development and performance management.

In Section 4 the overarching strategic direction of schools and departments is addressed through a series of units which commence with a detailed overview of leadership concepts, especially as they relate to middle managers, provided by Rob Bollington. Bob Smith outlines how long term vision is implemented into practice through development planning and Chris Comber and Tony Lawson offer a detailed exegesis of their work on the importance of ICT in leadership. The section is completed by a contribution from Lesley Saunders, a senior member of staff at the General Teaching Council, who discusses the ever-increasing importance of the use of statistical performance data.

In Section 5 Neil Burton addresses the best use of finance and resources and Howard Stevenson discusses recruitment and deployment of staff and health and safety in schools with special reference to managing stress.

In the final section Ian Terrell, Geraint Lang and Kathryn Terrell draw together some of the key issues underlying the text by reflecting on self management for the subject leader, online communities for professional development, and moving towards senior management.

The contributors to the text are drawn from a wide range of backgrounds and all have a wealth of experience in schools. Some, like the editors, are professional academics who enjoyed many years of work in schools prior to moving into higher education; others are teachers, advisors, and senior members of professional organisations. Whatever their background, all share a common commitment to enhancing the quality of experience in schools for all members of the school community whether that be students, staff or other adults.

Readers may wish to note that this text has drawn heavily on the various 'standards' for school leaders that have been developed in recent years. The standards for subject leaders and headteachers in England and Wales can be found in the 'Teachers' Standards Framework' developed by the DfES (see http://www.teachernet.gov.uk/standards_framework/index.cfm). The Scottish 'Standard for Headship' can be found in 'The General Teaching Council for Scotland Standard for Headship' (see http://www.gtcs.org.uk).

Becoming a Subject Leader: Roles, Values and Accountability

1.1 The Role of the Subject Leader

Mark Brundrett

INTRODUCTION

OBJECTIVES

By the end of this Unit you should:

- Know about the discoveries in the school effectiveness and improvement movements that have emphasised the importance of leadership in enhancing school outcomes;
- Be able to conceptualise clearly the role of the middle manager or subject leader in schools;
- Have a clear understanding of the developing national framework of standards for teachers and school leaders;
- Be aware of the development of training opportunities for middle managers and subject leaders.

The school effectiveness and improvement movements have become an international phenomenon that has begun to reveal some of the key issues in enhancing school performance. A generation of such studies had emphasised and re-emphasised the vital importance of school leadership in developing schools in order to ensure that pupils and students gain as much as possible from their educational experiences. The early research studies in these movements tended to focus on the importance of the school headteacher or principal in managing change in order to drive up standards in education but, more recently, there has been an increasing realisation of the vital role that is played by middle managers or subject leaders in developing schools and colleges. This reinvigoration of the middle manager's role has been recognised and embraced both in higher education institutions and at the highest levels in government and a number of programmes have now developed, tailored to meet the needs of those heads of department or subject leaders.

THE IMPORTANCE OF GOOD LEADERSHIP IN SCHOOL EFFECTIVENESS AND IMPROVEMENT

Over the period of a generation, leading educational researchers have attempted to discover the factors that can enhance school effectiveness. In particular the work of Rutter *et al.* (1979) and Mortimore *et al.* (1988) have come to be seen as seminal empirical studies that revealed that some schools were more effective than others, even when the social background of students was taken into account. Rutter *et al.* famously identified a number of key features as being associated with success (Rutter *et al.*, 1979), amongst which was noted the requirement for a combination of firm leadership and teacher involvement. The equally celebrated work of Mortimore *et al.* was also able to suggest a group of nodal factors that can lead to effective schooling including: purposeful leadership of the staff by the headteacher; involvement of the deputy head; and involvement of teachers (Mortimore *et al.*, 1988: 250).

Such findings have been replicated and extended in North America, the UK, the Netherlands and Australia. Teddlie and Reynolds (2000: 4) point out that there have been numerous summaries of the research on school effectiveness stretching over a period of a generation of researchers. This plethora of international research has been undertaken using increasingly sophisticated techniques but the factors observed by Rutter and Mortimore and their researchers have continued to emerge with tantalising consistency. Research in the UK itself has, for instance, produced startlingly similar lists of conditions upon which high quality teaching and learning appears to be contingent amongst which effective leadership seems to be one ubiquitous, indeed universal, feature (see, for instance, the work of Alexander, 1992; Sammons *et al.*, 1995; Barber *et al.*, 1995). Indeed the most compelling feature of school effectiveness research is its remarkable consistency of findings over time and across different cultural contexts.

The problem with such findings, especially those which provide lists of desirable features of school management and organisation, is, however, that they tend to be both descriptive and normative (Ouston, 1999). It is of little surprise that good schools have good leaders and that the staff of successful schools work together; the problem appears to lie in devising the methods by which institutions can ensure that they select the best staff and enhance the skills of those already appointed. It is, perhaps, partly as a response to this central criticism of the school effectiveness movement that many researchers have chosen to pursue the related but divergent path of school improvement. Whereas school effectivess attempts to define the *what* of change, school improvement is the *how* of change (Stoll and Fink, 1996). The distinctive difference in the 'improvement' definitions lies in their emphasis on the relationship between *change* and educational outcomes (Duncan, 1999). In the formulation set out by Hopkins *et al.* (1994), for instance, the stress is on the importance of assessing the outcomes of improvement for the pupils, the aim being to bring about a much closer link between the school and the classroom. This postulation of the complex relationship between institutional constructs and learning processes can be seen as a seminal feature of much of recent influential work in the UK (see, for instance, Stoll and Fink, 1996;

MacGilchrist *et al.*, 1997). Gray *et al.* (1996) have noted, however, that the gap between the two traditions of effectiveness and improvement is now beginning to close and increasingly researchers are drawing on both fields of research for insights on how to help schools make desirable changes (Mortimore, 1998; Teddlie and Reynolds, 2000). It seems evident from both traditions that high quality education can be developed within schools and that such development is essentially derived from the production of a supportive nexus of connections amongst staff, pupils, parents and other stakeholders within school communities in order to develop a positive, learning-centred culture. Within this nexus good leadership is a feature that seems to be universally recognised. In their major study of the field Teddlie and Reynolds have stated that:

> We do not know of a study that has not shown that leadership is important within effective schools ... Indeed leadership is now centrally synonymous with school effectiveness for many, including many operating within the school improvement paradigm ...
>
> (Teddlie and Reynolds, 2000: 141)

It is notable, however, that Teddlie and Reynolds indicate that this leadership is usually seen as being provided by the headteacher or principal. It is the central contention of this text that this investment of leadership in one overarching super-ordinate is an insufficient and inadequate description of leadership in schools.

THE INCREASING REALISATION OF THE IMPORTANCE OF THE MIDDLE MANAGER IN SCHOOLS

Recent governmental emphases have focused on notions of excellence defined in terms of achievable targets both in the UK and in the international context. This notion of effectiveness can be viewed as both a challenge and burden for school leaders in that it clearly delineates goals for achievement but is susceptible to the critique that it offers a debased and instrumental depiction of education. One thing that has become abundantly clear from the effectiveness and improvement studies is, however, that good leadership plays a vital role in creating the culture that enhances learning in schools. It is therefore of no great surprise that 'leadership' has become one of the areas of greatest interest in educational research and writing in recent years. Even a brief exemplification of the literature in the field would reveal that there is a large and growing range of texts focusing on 'leadership'. Within these texts a number of themes have emerged which include the efficacy of centralised versus distributed notions of leadership; the contrast between competency and academic models of leadership development; and the contradistinction between functionalist and democratic models of leadership.

More recently there has been an increasing realisation that schools cannot reach their full potential unless all the staff are involved in developing the school. Both governments and academics have argued consistently for an innovative restructuring of school leadership in order to enhance school-based management (Dimmock, 2000). With the development of local management of schools there is really just too much to do in a school that involves leadership, management and administration for this to be the preserve of one person or even a small group of senior staff. This has led some commentators to suggest that what is needed is a complete reconceptualisation of what we mean by leadership in schools. One way of expressing this new notion of leadership is that it should be distributed throughout the school rather than focused in any one person or small group of individuals (Gronn, 2000) and a number of studies have now shown that in most effective schools leadership extends beyond the senior management team (Harris, 1999; Busher and Harris, 2000).

One of the most important groups within this distributed leadership is at the middle management or subject leadership level (Harris *et al.*, 2003: 131). Those working at this level in schools inevitably carry with them a wealth of personal experience which it is vital for the school to key into if the organisation is to achieve its goals. Subject leaders will have mastered the craft of teaching and will be expert in developing the learning of children and students; they will also be at a level in the organisation which enables them, possibly uniquely, to act as a fulcrum between those working in the classroom and the senior management team of the school. National and local government, parents, governors, headteachers and senior managers may set the agenda for school development but this can only be enacted successfully if those who work with children on a day-to-day, minute-by-minute basis are informed, consulted and empowered to do so. The subject leader is frequently the figure who interprets, nego- tiates and enacts the policy and may, indeed, write the relevant policy document for the initiative for their subject or subjects. In this way middle managers are the glue that holds together schools since they are frequently the ones to turn policy into action.

Sadly research shows that subject leaders are poorly catered for in terms of training (Adey, 2000) and few higher education institutions or Local Education Authorities have developed comprehensive specialist courses for middle managers (Harris *et al.*, 2003: 134). It is to be hoped that the recent development of national programmes for school leadership, outlined below, may eventually rectify this situation.

THE ROLE OF MIDDLE MANAGERS IN HELPING SCHOOLS TO MEET THEIR GOALS AND THE NEED FOR TRAINING.

The development of 'national programmes' for school leadership in the UK and internationally has revealed that those in authority in many countries, particularly in the West, realise the importance of well trained leaders in schools (Brundrett, 2000). These national programmes are often based on an adapted 'competency' or 'standards' framework such as that for subject leaders. These standards-based qualifications can contrast with the academic qualifications in school leadership and management, usually at master's degree level, that have been provided by institutions of higher education for a number of years. There is a danger of 'political control' and increasing 'bureau- cratisation' of national qualifications but the commitment to school leadership shown by these developments is greatly to be applauded and many higher education insti- tutions have increasingly tried to ensure that the national standards framework is reflected in the content of higher degree programmes.

One such example of this governmental commitment to school leadership is shown in the development of the National College for School Leadership which was established at Nottingham, England, in 2000 in order to 'provide a single national focus for leadership development and research' (DfEE, 1999). The College has been responsible for the continued development of a national network of school leadership development which provides a ladder of opportunity and qualifications for school leaders including the National Professional Qualification for Headship (NPQH) for those aspiring to headship, the Headteachers Leadership and Management Programme (HEADLAMP) for those recently appointed to headship and the Leadership Programme for Serving Headteachers (LPSH) for experienced school leaders. It is clear from this list that the major commitment in the early years of the development of these programmes has been to the enhancement of the knowledge and skills of the most senior management in schools but, happily, there are increasing signs that there is a growing commitment to the development of leadership throughout schools.

The National Standards for Subject Leaders were originally published in 1998 by the Teacher Training Agency as part of an attempt to define a professional development framework for teachers at all levels in schools. The standards are cross-phase and are structured in four sections:

- Strategic direction and development of the subject;
- Teaching and learning;
- Leading and managing staff;
- Efficient and effective deployment of staff and resources.

(TTA, 1998)

The standards give official imprimatur to the importance of the subject leader in schools:

> While the headteacher and governors carry responsibility for overall school improvement, a subject leader has responsibility for securing high standards in teaching and learning in their subject as well as playing a major role in the development of school policy and practice. Throughout their work, a subject leader ensures that practices improve the quality of education provided, meet the needs and aspirations of all pupils, and raise standards of achievement in the school.
>
> (TTA, 1998: 4)

Few statements could convey so decisively the centrality of the middle manager or subject leader. Such statements are re-echoed in the Teaching Standards Framework published by the DfES in 2001 where it is stated that:

> Subject leaders provide professional leadership and management for a subject to secure high quality teaching, effective use of resources and improved standards of learning and achievement of all pupils.
>
> (DfES, 2001)

With the introduction of performance management and performance related pay schemes the responsibilities of subject leaders have, if anything, been increased. The task of monitoring and supporting staff in any but the smaller schools is too large for the headteacher to undertake on his or her own and the role of assessment and monitoring will thus inevitably fall onto the capable if already burdened shoulders of middle managers (Harris *et al.*, 2003: 132). The amplitude of this vital and ever more demanding role indicates that subject leaders deserve better and more systematic training and development for their rewarding but arduous task. Research funded by the Teacher Training Agency (Harris *et al.*, 1999) has begun to identify some of the key components that such training should contain, within which three key issues were identified. First, the importance of the partnership approach with an emphasis on reflection on learning was highlighted. Second, it was found that external agents, such as mentors, critical friends, advisors or higher education tutors, were powerful elements in assisting the individual to evaluate the outcomes of implementing change. Third, it was discovered that there is a critical linkage between 'workshop and workplace'; in other words training and development is of little use if it is divorced from the practicalities of school and classroom life (Harris *et al.*, 2003: 140). Models of such approaches already exist in the increasingly sophisticated methodologies employed in national programmes, such as NPQH, and higher education programmes and specific qualifications focusing on leadership for learning are already coming into existence. In order to prepare to make the best use of such programmes as they emerge it is essential that subject leaders are encouraged to reflect on their own practice, to enhance their skills in as systematic a way as possible, and to share their skills with others.

Action point

- Look carefully at the National Standards for Subject Leaders and the Standards Framework. Consider which of the standards you feel your level of training and experience enables you to fulfil with confidence. Then make a list of those standards about which you feel less confident. Think carefully how you might find opportunities to gain the knowledge and skills to become more expert in these areas. This might be through informal, personally guided activities or might involve discussions with a mentor, manager or appraiser in order to secure more formal training activities or greater experience.

- Look carefully at the list of websites in the Appendix. This is a lengthy but by no means exhaustive list of websites of organisations involved in school leadership development. Visit those sites that you feel are particularly relevant to your own stage of professional development and professional context. Many of these sites offer useful links to other organisations. Begin to build up a list of key sites and 'favourite' sites of interest. Many teachers find that such internet based sources increasingly provide an invaluable source of reference and guidance.

CONCLUSION

Evidence from a large number of research studies has suggested that one of the key issues in improving educational provision is the quality of leadership that is provided to staff and students. In fact, of course, we do not need complex research to reveal that high quality leadership is important. The anecdotal evidence and simple common sense of teachers in schools not just suggests but very strongly affirms that high quality leadership and management are vital components in making life better for all in education.

Educational research and public policy has, in the past, tended to concentrate on the leadership role of a few senior managers in the highest positions of authority in schools. More recently it has been realised that if a school is to function to its fullest potential the leadership capabilities of teachers throughout schools, especially subject leaders and middle managers, must be tapped. Such teachers play a crucial role in schools and are situated in the middle and at the heart of schools. Policy may be made by senior managers, frequently under the influence of other groups of stakeholders, but it is often middle managers who ensure that the policy is successfully enacted by small teams of staff in classrooms. Moreover, the policies which subject leaders and middle managers are required to put into practice are now often related to staff development or performance management, not just to curriculum matters.

The development of standards frameworks, including those for subject leaders, carries with it dangers but is, on the whole, to be welcomed in that it provides a clear basis for role definition and for training and development. There are now signs that more carefully structured development opportunities for middle managers are beginning to emerge and this is to be welcomed wholeheartedly. It is hoped that this text provides one element in that beneficial progression.

REFERENCES

Adey, K. (2000) 'Professional development priorities: the views of middle managers in secondary schools', *Educational Management and Administration*, 28: 419.

Alexander, R. (1992) *Policy and Practice in Primary Education*, London: Routledge.

Barber, M., Stoll, L., Mortimore, P. and Hillman, J. (1995) *Governing Bodies and Effective Schools*, London: DfEE.

Brundrett, M. (2000) *Beyond Competence: The Challenge for Educational Management*, Dereham: Peter Francis Publishers.

Busher, H. and Harris, A. (2000) *Leading Subject Areas: Improving Schools*, London: Paul Chapman.

DfEE (1999) *National College for School Leadership: A Prospectus*, London: DfEE.

DfES (2001) *The Standards Framework*, http://www.teachernet.gov.uk/standards_framework/frmwork-stp2.cfm?position=sl

Dimmock, C. (2000) *Designing and Leading the Future School: A Cross-Cultural Perpective*, London: Falmer Press.

Duncan, D. (1999) 'School effectiveness and improvement', in M. Brundrett (ed.) *Principles of School Leadership*, Dereham: Peter Francis Publishers.

Gray, J., Reynolds, D., Fitz-Gibbon, C. and Jesson, D. (eds) (1996) *Merging Traditions: The Future of Research on School Effectiveness and School Improvement*, London: Cassell.

Gronn, P. (2000) 'Distributed properties: a new architecture for leadership', *Educational Management and Administration*, 28, 3: 317–38.

Harris, A. (1999) *Effective Subject Leadership: A Handbook of Staff Development Activities*, London: David Fulton Press.

Harris, A., Busher, H. and Wise, C. (1999) *Interim Report to the TTA on the Effective Training of Subject Leaders*, Nottingham: University of Nottingham, School of Education.

Harris, A., Busher, H. and Wise, C. (2003) 'Effective training for subject leaders', in N. Bennett, M. Crawford and M. Cartwright (eds) *Effective Educational Leadership*, London: Open University Press/Paul Chapman Publishing.

Hopkins, D., Ainscow, M. and West, M. (1994) *School Improvement in an Era of Change*, London: Cassell.

MacGilchrist, B., Myers, K. and Read, J. (1997) *The Intelligent School*, London: Paul Chapman Publishing.

Mortimore, P. (1998) *The Road to Improvement*, Lisse: Swets and Zeitlinger.

Mortimore, P., Sammons, P., Stoll, L., Lewis, D. and Ecob, R. (1988) *School Matters: The Junior Years*, Somerset: Open Books Publishing.

Ouston, J. (1999) 'School effectiveness and school improvement: critique of a movement', in T. Bush, L. Bell, R. Bolam, R. Glatter and R. Ribbins (eds) *Educational Management: Redefining Theory, Policy and Practice*, London: Paul Chapman Publishing.

Rutter, M., Maughan, B., Mortimore, P. and Ouston, J. (1979) *Fifteen Thousand Hours: Secondary Schools and Their Effects on Children*, Somerset: Open Books Publications.

Sammons, P., Hillman, J. and Mortimore, P. (1995) *Key Characteristics of Effective Schools: A Review of School Effectiveness Research*, Report Commissioned by the Office for Standards in Education, Institute of Education.

Stoll, L. and Fink, D. (1996) *Changing Our Schools: Linking School Effectiveness and School Improvement*, Buckingham: Open University Press.

Teacher Training Agency (TTA) (1998) *National Standards for Subject Leaders*, London: HMSO.

Teddlie, C. and Reynolds, D. (2000) *The International Handbook of School Effectiveness Research*, London: Falmer Press.

FURTHER READING

Bennett, N., Crawford, M. and Cartwright, M. (2003) *Effective Educational Leadership*, London: The Open University/Paul Chapman Publishing.

Brundrett, M., Burton, N. and Smith, R. (2003) *Leadership in Education*, London: RoutledgeFalmer.

Busher, H. and Harris, A. (2000) *Subject Leadership and School Improvement*, London: Paul Chapman Publishing.

Kydd, L., Anderson, L. and Newton, W. (2003) *Leading People and Teams in Education*, London: The Open University/Paul Chapman Publishing.

Preedy, M., Glatter, R. and Wise, C. (2003) *Strategic Leadership and Education Improvement*, London: The Open University/Paul Chapman Publishing.

Teacher Training Agency (TTA) (1998) *National Standards for Subject Leaders*, London: HMSO.

1.2 Value Driven Leadership

Hugh Busher

INTRODUCTION

OBJECTIVES

By the end of this Unit you should:

- Understand the key values required by middle managers in schools;
- Have a clear knowledge of where these values come from;
- Be more able to articulate your own values in relation to students, teachers and curriculum subjects.

Rational/functionalist discourses of leadership focus on what leaders do and offer explanations for the efficacy of their actions. Micro-political discourses offer insights into how leaders negotiate their aims and objectives. Ethical and moral discourses offer explanations for why leaders choose to act in certain ways. Ribbins (1999: 2) points out that values explain the why of the human enterprise. They also offer explanations for why people prefer to resist some directions in which leaders choose to take institutions, whether under pressure from external agencies or of their own volition. These three discourses interact around and through the agency of the leader as person.

In focusing on the third of these this Unit attempts to make sense of what lies at the core of people's actions in this fragmented post-modern world. Schools in England and Wales face and serve pluralist communities in a pluralist society. Consequently ethical issues are involved in every decision that is taken by leaders, be they teachers or school principals, as they struggle to meet the competing demands on them. Greenfield (1993) talks about the moral complexity that flows inevitably through administrative action and sees the central realities of educational administration being human values. Values lead to action in both everyday life and in educational administration.

In this post-modern world, Harrison (1994) asserts the need to have a critical ethical perspective on educational management rather than a narrowly economic one. Leaders have to be concerned with issues of personal dignity and equality when developing practical social codes to build communities as well as with economic imperatives. In this view persons, not systems, are perceived as the centres of knowing and the constructors of meaning (Harrison, 1994: 177). So institutions and communities like schools (Sergiovanni, 1994) are built through processes of debate, dialogue and interaction between individuals and between individuals and collectivities, leading to the implementation of some values and perspectives rather than others. This process is a moral and a political one because it involves the creating, organising, managing, monitoring and resolving of value conflicts, where values are defined as concepts of the desirable (Hodgkinson, 1999: 7) and power is used to implement some values rather than others (Ribbins, 1999).

As social and cultural diversity increases, equity for a wider diversity of students becomes a greater social priority for school leaders. This requires them to look not only to the internal processes of schools but also to their schools' relationships with people in the residential communities that they serve. It is only in this way that school disaffection can be tackled effectively (Riley *et al.*, 2000). However, such diversity places school leaders in a quandary when what appears an equitable solution to one community may seem prejudicial to another. Determining how to balance and pursue alternative value laden paths for efficiency, equity, effectiveness, excellence (Stout *et al.*, 1994) and the personal growth and development of staff and students is a moral quagmire for school leaders at every level from principal to classroom teacher.

School leaders at all levels do not work in institutional vacuums. They are influenced by values and policy pressures in the external contexts of their schools. Stout *et al.* (1994: 5) assert that values underpin all aspects of education: who should go to school; what are the purposes of schooling; what should children be taught; who should decide issues of school direction and policy; who should pay for schools; and how are divergent values and belief systems brought to bear in the politics of education – i.e. within the political systems through which education is provided.

At a regional level, Riley *et al.* (2000) consider the quality of LEA (local authority) leadership is important as well as the values that are emphasised and expressed through its policies and its approaches to strategic management; the cultures it fosters among its schools; and the networks it develops to engage teachers and facilitate school improvement.

The internal policies of schools that are constructed by senior management serve as policy contexts for middle leaders and their colleagues in academic and pastoral departments. The histories of institutions also enshrine values which influence how leaders at all levels in a school can work. Stout *et al.* (1994: 7) discuss how these histories affected the values enshrined in schools in the New England states of the USA and how these values changed through time.

The pilot study, from which extracts in this Unit are taken, gives evidence of multi-level (West *et al.*, 2000) or distributed leadership (Gronn, 2000) in some secondary schools in England and of the values held by seven middle ranking leaders in particular school social and policy contexts. It shows how the values they held affected the ways in which they interacted with and tried to influence their colleagues and the extant educational systems and social structures. Middle leaders were chosen opportunistically from pastoral and academic departments of different sizes, but several of which were linked into faculties. Snowball sampling was then used to find the middle leaders' 15 subordinate and superordinate colleagues. Data was collected through semi-structured interviews that focused on middle leaders' relationships, actions and values; through observation of a day in each middle leader's work that was interpolated with conversations to explicate some of the events of the day; and through documentary materials such as departmental handbooks. Ribbins (1997) points out that it is only by listening to people's voices that one really finds out what it is like to be and to work in institutions like schools. To attempt to generalise these findings to broader contexts or different macro-cultures would be unwise, given the differences that exist between different macro-cultures that, in some cases, have been shown to inhibit the implementation of Western leadership and management practices in them (Lok, 2001; Kazmi, 1998).

WHERE LEADERS' VALUES COME FROM: SHAPING THEIR WORK-RELATED IDENTITIES

An important aspect to being a middle leader is the bundle of personal values and qualities that he/she has constructed. Who people are, the personhoods they have developed (Aubrey *et al.*, 2000), affects how they act in their formal and informal roles in their institutions. Through their lived experiences and interactions with other people and social and institutional structures, people construct values. In the pilot study, middle leaders reported that their work-related values came from various sources, such as their home/childhood experiences:

> I try my best to treat people as equally as possible and as fairly as possible. I think I get that from my Dad. He was a realistic Christian. He puts a lot of standing on justice and how you should treat other people and how you get it in return.
>
> (Young male head of RE)

They also came through positive experiences of school and personal interests:

> I loved school. I thought it was great because I did everything and I got into everything … It was more my whole school experience – being with other people, and doing stuff … we had outdoor pursuits … which I thought was fab. Geology [at university] involved a lot of field courses a lot of working outside … and doing things as a team.
>
> (Young female head of Geography)

and of teachers:

> I had a very good geography teacher throughout my secondary school … I found the way that he taught lessons … made learning so much easier and so much fun … [He] just seemed to know what he was talking about … and he enthused about it … And that in turn made us want to learn about it more. What made us learn successfully was that our books were always marked.
>
> (Young male head of RE)

especially those who were prepared to reach out to their students as people:

> She [English teacher] … was interested in you as an individual … She was interested in everyone but I felt that I had a link with her. As well she was very caring. She was very interested in what you were going to get at 'A' level. She made sure that she went the extra mile with us as a group.
>
> (Established female head of faculty)

Negative experiences of school also influenced their current values:

> I think we can all remember that [bad experience]. I can remember public humiliations that were not meant cruelly but were … my book being held up and Miss Hxxx saying 'your disciples look like glamorous women'. And they did. It was a very funny comment, actually, but not funny to me as a seven-year-old … I don't think it [should be] part of [any] teacher's style. I suppose we all do use a bit of sarcasm. But I would not want to put people through anything like that … kind of public humiliation.
>
> (Established teacher, but new head of Sixth form)

Other sources of values, they claimed were their lecturers in higher education, former colleagues in teaching, and contacts with institutions and persons external to their schools. These values became embedded in the work-related identities they constructed for themselves through the interplay of their personal histories with their institutional contexts and job descriptions. It led them to focus their work on eight functions:

- Working with recalcitrant students
- Acting as the go-between for senior staff and subject area colleagues
- Supporting subject colleagues
- Supervising the work of subject colleagues
- Advocacy: promoting the interests of the subject area
- Doing the 'admin.' and providing the resources
- Providing expert knowledge
- Providing the vision for their area.

BEING EXPLICIT ABOUT VALUES: SHAPING LEADERS' PRACTICES

Values lie at the core of how leaders build relationships with their colleagues and students. Hodgkinson (1991: 164) talked about educational leaders being in an area of ethical excitement. Leaders who want to build an emancipatory organisational culture that encourages collaborative learning or professional learning communities focus on encouraging staff and caring for students, encouraging dialogue, encouraging openness and risk-taking, and maintain relationships while wrestling with ambiguity and professional disagreements. This, claim West et al. (2000: 40), 'builds up a consensus around high order values that members of the school community can relate to and believe in' and sustains school improvement. The central importance of values led Begley (1999: 2) to consider that the first responsibility of leaders is to reflect on and make explicit their own values, then to consider other people's values and finally to engage in dialogue with other people to resolve values conflicts.

The middle leaders in the pilot study made explicit values statements about:

- pupils/students;
- teachers and teaching;
- the importance of their subject area;
- the allocation of resources to students;
- working cultures in their subject area.

Students are important actors in the process of school improvement and have clear insights into what constitutes effective teaching and learning for them (Ruddock *et al.*, 1996). Starratt (1999) argues that advances in the cognitive sciences suggest that learning is much more an active process than a consumerist one. He argues that it is students not teachers who have 'the work of sense making, of producing knowledge suggested by the curriculum, of performing that knowledge in a variety of assessable products, of explaining how those performances and productions reveal their understanding' (p. 23) and incorporating new knowledge into previous knowledge frameworks.

Middle leaders' values for pupils focused on pupils being happy and enjoying their lessons:

> You can't actually educate students, people, when they are unhappy or disturbed or there are things going on in their background. We still tend to ignore that ... I am reminded when students are having difficulties, of how difficult it can be if you are alone or unhappy ... and [yet] we expect students just to come in and perform.
>
> (Established teacher, but new head of Sixth form)

having a sense of achievement whatever assessment grades they gained:

> We want to give them an appreciation of the subject. We want them to fulfil their potential. We want them to go out as far as they can to be critically aware, and to appreciate the subject even if they don't continue with it.
>
> (Long established male head of History)

and having a sense that teachers cared for them so that they cared about their lessons, too:

> [It is] caring in a kind of impersonal way ... it is not whether they like you or not, which is the common thing – oh, I must be a teacher and they must like me – but caring about whether they respect what you are trying to do is very, very important, and how you go about doing that.
>
> (Young female head of Geography)

They wanted students to respect themselves and:

> build up self-esteem. If you [a student] succeed at whatever level you are capable of, it will help to prepare you for whatever you go on to, into work, into further education, into your relationship to others ... People are pleased if they get good results, but it is the process of getting that and hopefully the personal and intellectual skills that they develop through that.
>
> (Long established male head of History)

To do this some middle leaders thought:

> You need to talk to the [students] about what it means to be human, really. [Teach] trust, responsibility. We all feel that students are people who know what their rights are but are less aware of their responsibilities.
>
> (Established teacher, but new head of Sixth form)

The values that middle leaders held on teaching were clear too:

> To get [teachers] to be varied [in their approaches to teaching]. To get them to try to catch the kids interests … I want them to … teach in a dynamic way.
>
> (Young female head of Geography)

> Any teacher would think it important that you had a very good subject knowledge … I believe that we have a duty to educate … all young people and that the education should be suitable to them.
>
> (Established teacher, but new head of Sixth form)

as was the importance they attached to their subjects. For example:

> Geography is everything. You can't do anything without geography. You can't go anywhere without geography. You can't make anything without geography … It teaches [students] to question what they are doing … it teaches them enquiry.
>
> (Young female head of Geography)

The subject leader in RE emphasised the importance of teaching students tolerance and understanding and acceptance of difference.

Middle leaders in the pilot study claimed they allocated resources on a principled basis, supporting Simkins' (1997) view that resource allocation in schools is a value-laden activity. Resources were allocated to try to meet students' needs equitably within the budgetary frameworks available:

> If one group of students doesn't get the resources one year, we will make sure it does the next year … if there are gaps [in curriculum resourcing] we will work together to try to fill them by preparing our own resources using our own materials. In terms of timetable we try to allocate it as fairly as possible.
>
> (Long established male head of History)

Middle leaders considered it important to sustain and enhance their colleagues' and students' performances, even if their colleagues did not entirely welcome this or the government instituted package in which it came:

> Quite a lot of people are not very happy about doing performance management but recognise that … it is a hoop that they have to jump through. I think it is quite a positive and productive thing … If you do it every so often it makes you think a little bit more about what you are doing. Then you get back into the habit of doing it. That has a knock-on effect on the rest of your teaching.
>
> (Young female head of Geography)

Responsibility for enhancing professional learning helped the middle leaders to project values of setting challenging standards of performance to all students in their area, which were linked to national curriculum age-related levels of performance, and of monitoring carefully the quality of their performance against those standards.

CONSTRUCTING PARTICULAR SCHOOL AND DEPARTMENTAL WORK-RELATED CULTURES

Cultures are social structures (Giddens, 1984), made up of beliefs, values, rituals and ceremonies, and language that help their members and outsiders to sustain particular identities and recognise the boundaries of particular social and institutional entities (Schein, 1992). The cultures of a school and its related but differentiated departmental and year group or Key Stage sub-cultures are shaped by leaders' values, social factors such as the gender, ethnicity and SES of the members of the group, and the school's histories and the socio-political contexts in which it is situated (Busher and Barker, 2003).

Middle leaders in the pilot study preferred to develop positive interpersonal relationships based on shared values as these helped to construct a sense of community, as Sergiovanni (1992, 2001) expected, which helped to enhance the quality of learning and teaching. This was most clearly demonstrated in one faculty, where professional disagreements appeared not to breach the sense of social cohesion:

> Sometimes we have blazing rows … over something professional. It is not personal … But socially as a team, although we are so diverse, we chat in the staff room. At the end of term we have a faculty meal either in school or we go out. Some of the faculty go to the pub on a Friday, not every week … As a faculty we have a bit of a laugh and a joke … We wouldn't want to go out with each other all the time, and certainly not with all the faculty, but I make a point of doing something at the end of each term as a faculty.
>
> (Established female head of faculty)

Middle leaders' values for working with staff colleagues emphasised collaborative, rather than collegial, cultures:

> Within your subject area it has to be a team. It is the team that works together. I have always seen my role within the department within which I have worked as taking a lead in terms of developing schemes of work, of monitoring standards, and discussing ideas within the team. The team contribute to that rather than the leader [being directive]. The subject leader gives suggestions as to what should happen… maybe draws upon what they have gained from other experiences to bring to the team so the team can share that and have ownership of that.
>
> (Long established male head of History)

However, middle leaders acknowledged the unequal distribution of power in their academic and pastoral departments (Foucault, 1990), recognising that they were accountable to their senior staff as well as responsible to their students for what happened in it. Ultimately, some thought, they had to use their delegated authority to implement policies required by senior staff even if their colleagues did not like them. None the less they thought it important to negotiate with colleagues how those policies were implemented and to convey their colleagues' views to senior staff if necessary. Busher and Harris with Wise (2000) elaborate on what this process of bridging and brokering entails.

Middle leaders were closely concerned with the values that were projected through the cultures of their departments, not surprisingly as these profoundly affect the ability of people to work together. The core values that middle leaders in the pilot study projected were trust of staff and, to a certain extent, students; positively valuing and offering support to colleagues; finding means for engaging staff in dialogue and decision-making; and acknowledging differences between colleagues:

> I think the fact that we have this trust in the [Sixth formers] to time manage and always be on top of their work, I think that comes from the way that [head of Sixth form] is with them, sort of trusting in them, but being there if there is a problem, and being stricter with them if necessary to sort something out. He is fair. And he is the same with staff. He is very fair, but if there were a problem he would want to sort it out.
>
> (Established female admin. assistant to the Sixth form)

Staff were given a positive view of themselves by middle leaders as some of their colleagues acknowledged:

> He is very supportive of what we do and tries to give us that sense of our importance in the whole system, and that we are valued. And that is something he does very well and the SMT [before] the new chap [headteacher] came in did not do very well at all. People need to feel valued for what they do. They need to feel when they are not doing it right that they are accountable but none the less valued and supported …
>
> (Established female teacher of History)

and supported practically:

> I am there in terms of discipline, in terms of advice, in terms of providing assessments, instructions and so on. To make sure that it is all supportive, and that [staff] feel confident. Because if you feel confident you are going to feel happy and if you feel happy you will teach better and then you will get better results.
>
> (Young female head of Geography)

The middle leaders engaged staff in decision-making formally and informally, to generate a sense of ownership of departmental policies and practices among staff:

> We have a formal briefing every Thursday morning and then we have a faculty meeting once every four or five weeks on a Monday afternoon after school for an hour. But the actual real running takes place constantly throughout the day, breaks, lunchtimes and during lessons … We as a faculty get on so well that it is done informally through conversations in here [humanities office]. We are confident enough to wander into each other's lessons without fear of upsetting anyone, and pass on information in that way … It does not need to be strict.
>
> (Young male head of RE)

However, middle leaders also recognised that their colleagues held values, too, as a result of their different professional life experiences, and they needed to take account of these perspectives when taking decisions in their subject or pastoral area.

> People have different backgrounds, different experiences, different expectations of what they want. Often if you are trying to get somewhere, you have all these different people wanting to do it in different directions. I think it is my job to make sure that we are all going in the same direction. We may get there at different times but we will get there. I think that is probably the hardest part of my job, managing the different characters in my department … You have to know the character of the department. Sometimes things don't go down very well at all. You have to listen to what they are saying, and sometimes that is fine because it could be about workload, which is a real issue … but I am still getting pressure from above … so sometimes it is a matter of saying sorry, this is what we are doing.
>
> (Established female head of faculty)

These different and sometimes conflicting values that are legitimately held by teachers – they are linked to their views of myths and experiences of successful teaching and learning – underpin resistance to change. Van der Westhuizen (1996) argued that resistance is a normal not a pathological part of community or institutional life. Value conflicts may arise at different levels from that of personal preferences to that of cultural imperatives (Hodgkinson, 1991). The more that such conflicts are handled at the lowest level the more likely it is that a compromise can be negotiated.

Individuals live in tension with the cultural frameworks of their civil societies and institutions because their personal values systems are only partially formed by these entities. They also survive in asymmetrical power relationships (Giddens, 1984) with these entities, being relatively powerless as individuals (Foucault, 1990). In schools they are constrained by the histories of their institutions; by the other people around them (students, parents, support staff, and academic colleagues and senior staff) with more and less power than themselves (Foucault, 1990); and by the demands on them from their social and macro-policy contexts, such as National Curriculum guidelines. Leaders wield more power than others as they try to implement their vision and values of successful teaching and learning and organisational practice. However, non-promoted staff, support staff and students also wield power in pursuit of their visions of schooling (Hoyle, 1981) especially if they collaborate to project their shared values through coordinated action (Busher, 2001). Sometimes the collective views of members of a department can compel middle leaders to alter the ways in which they implement their preferred values:

> Within the department I would like it run as a sort of co-operative … A few of my department wanted to be told 'this is what you must do, and I'll be checking that you have done it'. They wanted … definite boundaries.
>
> (Long established male head of English)

CONSTRUCTING VALUES DRIVEN LEADERSHIP

West *et al.* (2000) perceived school improvement being brought about by multi-level leadership that is built around values. Their view is that successful leadership is not hierarchical but federal (or distributed) and is tight on values and focuses on the purposes of the school, but encourages participants other than the designated leaders to take initiatives. This leadership is set in external and internal social and policy contexts.

Like all institutional leaders, middle leaders of academic and pastoral departments have to respond to the external socio-political contexts in which their departments and schools are set and by the implicit and imposed values from those contexts. Moos (2000) points out the impact on schooling and education of globalisation; of the OECD emphasising in the 1980s decentralised finances; and of models of New Public Management (NPM) emphasising systems thinking, personal mastery and tight hands-on management, explicit standards and measures of performance. Woods (1996: 15) complained that a narrow and 'distorted view of consumerism, that can only be found in the unreal world of the perfect market, has dominated the rhetoric and shaped the educational debates' of the last two decades of the twentieth century in the UK. Kazmi (1998: 86) points out that there are similar problems and tensions in India between 'the demands of materialistic values imitated from western societies' and his own cultural heritage. In the pilot study, middle leaders perceived these sources of pressures and values being the National Curriculum and other influential curriculum frameworks in the macro-policy context, OFSTED inspections, Key Stage Three strategies and performance management. These macro-policy contexts are also active at local or regional level (Riley *et al.,* 2000; Busher and Barker, 2003), sometimes called the mesosphere, and include the impact of schools' residential communities on the curriculum and on staff, student and parent relationships. The internal policy contexts, the microsphere of the school, are established by a school's senior management team. These affect how middle leaders work, as participants in the pilot study acknowledged.

Leaders have to mediate the values from all these contexts to their colleagues and to their students to make teaching and learning relevant and appropriately differentiated, as Krechevsky and Stork (2000) found, as well as compliant with internal and external policy-makers' demands. Making choices about values and actions involves leaders and their colleagues in moral decisions about the nature of the learning community they want to construct. It means that values are central to the field of educational administration (Willower, 1992:). Ribbins (1999) remarked that privileging some values over others is a political act – applying power to sustain some actions in preference to others.

As leaders are always facing dilemmas of people, resources and power, MacBeath and MacDonald (2000) suggest that ethical decision-making is key to how school leaders use power. They suggested that leaders use different types of authority but argued that moral authority was most likely to promote social cohesion. Sergiovanni (1992) listed five types of authority, sometimes described as legitimate power: bureaucratic – based on rules and regulations; psychological – expert human relations; technical-rational – based on knowledge of topic and system; professional – norms and standards; moral – explicit values and shared norms in the community.

Middle leaders in the pilot study offered leadership to their colleagues and students through using a range of social, symbolic and material resources as sources of power and authority to try to shape their colleagues' actions – Giddens (1984) talks about this as controlling other people's actions. Values emerged through the use of these sources of power as certain principles and practices were privileged over others. The sources of power can be summarised as:

- Offering systemic resources to sustain colleagues; use of authority to support colleagues; and acting as an advocate for the team with senior staff, students and parents.
- Offering symbolic resources, such as a vision for the subject area which incorporates core values for staff and students, as well as how the department fits into school plans for development.
- Offering material resources to help colleagues and to project their vision of effective teaching, learning and departmental organisation. This took one of three forms: first, the knowledge that the middle leaders valued and transmitted to colleagues, which privileged some actions and not others, focused on knowledge of systems; of students and how to work with them; of substantive subjects; of subject pedagogy. Second, the middle leaders helped to sustain and transform the curriculum through the creation and application of physical resources. Third, middle leaders organised the subject or pastoral area emphasising team work and collaboration.
- Offering social resources: making the department a pleasant place in which to work; enhancing social cohesion.

The cultures of departments are shaped by middle leaders asserting certain values, indicating the social and practice norms to which people are expected to adhere. These norms are often presented as codes of practice and public morality. In the pilot study, departmental codes were clearly displayed in every classroom, and teachers drew students' attention to them. These codes encourage pupils to work in certain ways and relate to people in certain ways. Mary Gray (1997) reported how students helped to build such codes of practice with the teachers in her school and how this engaged them with a positive approach to their behaviour that was based on intrinsic understanding of values rather than extrinsic rewards and punishments.

Such codes might enshrine 'empathy, tolerance for diversity, and commitment to justice' (Ghosn, 1998) in a school or department committed to inclusivity and social justice. In one school outside the pilot study, the school code was the acronym TRUST, which emphasised 'R'espect for others and 'S'tandards of work as well as 'T'ruthfulness and 'T'rust in each other. However, in some schools a gap emerges between the rhetoric of the moral codes and vision statements and the relationships modelled by staff not only in their interactions with students but in their interactions with each other, many of which are quite visible to students. Such divisions encourage cynicism amongst students and staff alike, and make difficult the maintenance of cohesive teams and departments.

The relationships that are encouraged between students and teachers, as well as between students, by particular approaches to pedagogy powerfully convey values. Middle leaders in the pilot study were keen to sustain particular ways of teaching that promoted: active learning; meeting all students' learning needs (differentiated curriculum); celebrating excellent achievement at whatever level of performance; enjoyment of studying. Ghosn (1998: 68) suggested that teaching needs to focus on particular skills of 'listening, critical thinking, cooperation, conflict resolution, and problem solving' if teachers want to promote social justice and inclusivity.

How time is used by leaders, be it in the timetabling of lessons or the sequencing of activities within a lesson, be it in timetabling meetings or scheduling social activities, projects values to other participants. Giddens (1984) discusses how control of time by some people imposes values on others. Lafleur (1999) points out that the designation of time for certain activities disempowers people from engaging in others. For example, students are expected to attend lessons, or give an explanation for non-attendance. To overturn such designations of time is an assertion not only of that teacher's authority but of the importance (privileged value) of the reason for doing that. In the pilot study, middle leaders took students out of other teachers' lessons when they had to arrange detentions with them for previous misdemeanours, thus asserting the importance of moral behaviour by students: i.e. of compliance with the school's norms and codes of practice.

The use of space in a department and the layout of that space (e.g. the arrangement of classroom furniture, or the allocation of rooms to particular staff or subject areas) also offer powerful symbolism through which values are projected. It was noticeable in one department in the pilot study that teachers moved comfortably in and out of each other's rooms during lessons, not only to get resources but also to speak with each other without disturbing the lesson in progress. The same department shared a resource room, which all teachers used when necessary. The head of department did not have a separate office, although she did have her own teaching room, like all the other teachers in her department. This easy collaboration portrayed a value of departmental cohesion, of which teachers in the department whose rooms were located outside the department suite felt they were less of a part.

Resolving value conflicts is at the heart of leadership, but this cannot be achieved without access to power, and becomes itself a projection of power: projecting a coherent set of values which privilege a certain approach to education inevitably means that other values and approaches to education are marginalized. Ribbins (1999) argues that value conflicts need to be resolved in a particular direction to create successful teaching and learning through collaboration. But the construction of successful teaching and learning has to take account of the macro-cultural and political demands that are imposed on education as well as of the professional education values held by leaders from classroom to whole-school level, and of the values held by students. It is the responsibility of leaders at all levels in a school to enable this by facilitating an effective working environment through developing positive working relationships with all parties involved.

REFERENCES

Aubrey, C., David, T., Godfrey, R. and Thompson, L. (2000) *Early Childhood Educational Research: Issues in Methodology and Ethics*, London: RoutledgeFalmer.

Begley, P.T. (1999) 'Academic and practitioner perspectives on values', in P.T. Begley and P.E. Leonard (eds) *The Values of Educational Administration*, London: Falmer Press

Busher, H. (2001) 'The micro-politics of change, improvement and effectiveness in schools', in A. Harris and N. Bennett (eds) *School Effectiveness and School Improvement: Alternative Perspectives*, London: Continuum.

Busher, H. and Barker, B. (2003) 'The crux of leadership: shaping school culture by contesting the policy contexts and practices of teaching and learning', *Educational Management and Administration*, 31, 1: 51–65.

Busher, H. and Harris, A. with Wise, C. (2000) *Subject Leaders and School Improvement*, London: Paul Chapman.

Foucault, M. (1990) 'Foucault on education', in S. Ball (ed) *Foucault on Education*, London: Routledge.

Ghosn, I. (1998) 'Connecting to classroom realities: curriculum, methods and the hidden curriculum as agents of peace', in I. Ghosn and E. Samia (eds) *Weaving the Fabric of Peace: Tolerance, Justice and the Child*, Byblos: Lebanese American University, Centre for Peace and Justice Education.

Giddens, A. (1984) *The Constitution of Society*, Cambridge: Polity Press.

Gray, M. (1997) 'Conversation with Agnes McMahon', in P. Ribbins (ed.) *Leaders and Leadership in the School, College and University*, London: Cassell.

Greenfield. T. (1993) 'Wither and whence cometh the phoenix', in T. Greenfield and P. Ribbins (eds) *Greenfield on Educational Administration*, London: Routledge.

Gronn, P. (2000) 'Distributed properties: a new architecture for leadership', *Educational Management and Administration*, 28, 3: 317–38.

Harrison, B.T. (1994) 'Applying critical ethics to educational management', *Educational Management and Administration*, 22, 3: 175–83.

Hodgkinson, C. (1991) *Educational Leadership: The Moral Art*, Albany: State University of New York Press.

Hodgkinson, C. (1999) 'The triumph of the will: an exploration of certain fundamental problematics in administrative philosophy', in P.T. Begley and P.E. Leonard (eds) *The Values of Educational Administration*, London: Falmer Press.

Hoyle, E. (1981) 'Managerial processes in schools, Block 3, E323', *Management and the School*, Milton Keynes: Open University.

Kazmi, A. (1998) 'Ethics and professional values in business and industry in India', *Paradigm*, 1, 2: 86–93.

Krechevsky, M. and Stork, J. (2000) 'Challenging educational assumptions', *Cambridge Journal of Education*, 30, 1: 57–74.

Lafleur, C. (1999) 'The meaning of time', in P.T. Begley and P.E. Leonard (eds) *The Values of Educational Administration*, London: Falmer Press.

Lok, C.L. (2001) 'The impact of competence-based management development programme for Chinese managers in Hong Kong', Doctoral thesis, Leicester: University of Leicester.

MacBeath, J. and MacDonald, A. (2000) 'Four dilemmas, three heresies and a matrix', in K.A. Riley and K.S. Louis (eds) *Leadership for Change and School Reform*, London: RoutledgeFalmer.

Moos, L. (2000) 'Global and national perspectives on leadership', in K.A. Riley and K.S. Louis (eds) *Leadership for Change and School Reform*, London: RoutledgeFalmer.

Ribbins, P. (1997) *Leaders and Leadership in the School, College and University*, London: Cassell.

Ribbins, P. (1999) 'Foreword', in P.T. Begley and P.E. Leonard (eds) *The Values of Educational Administration*, London: Falmer Press.

Riley, K.A., Docking, J. and Rowles, D. (2000) 'Caught between local education authorities: making a difference through their leadership', in K.A. Riley and K.S. Louis (eds) *Leadership for Change and School Reform*, London: RoutledgeFalmer.

Ruddock, J., Wallace, G. and Chaplain, R. (1996) *School Improvement: What Can Pupils Tell Us?*, London: David Fulton.

Schein, E. (1992) *Organisational Culture and Leadership*, 2nd edn, San Francisco: Jossey-Bass.

Sergiovanni, T.J. (1992) *Moral Leadership: Getting to the Heart of School Improvement*, San Francisco: Jossey-Bass.

Sergiovanni, T. (1994) *Building Community in Schools*, San Francisco: Jossey-Bass.

Sergiovanni, T. (2001) *Leadership, What's in it for Schools?*, London: RoutledgeFalmer.

Simkins, T. (1997) 'Managing resources', in H. Tomlinson (ed) *Managing Continual Professional Development in Schools*, London: Paul Chapman.

Starratt, R.J. (1999) 'Moral dimensions of leadership', in P.T. Begley and P.E. Leonard (eds) *The Values of Educational Administration*, London: Falmer Press.

Stout, R.T., Tallerico, M. and Scribner, K.P. (1994) 'Values: the "what?" of the politics of education', *Politics of Education Association Yearbook 1994*, London: Taylor and Francis.

Van der Westhuizen, P. (1996) 'Resistance to change in educational organisations', paper given at the Fifth Quadrennial Research Conference of the British Educational Management and Administration Society, Cambridge University, UK.

West, M., Jackson, D., Harris, A. and Hopkins, D. (2000) 'Learning through leadership, leadership through learning', in K.A. Riley and K.S. Louis (eds) *Leadership for Change and School Reform*, London: RoutledgeFalmer.

Willower, D. 'Educational administration: intellectual trends', in *Encyclopedia of Educational Research*, 6th edn, Toronto: Macmillan.

Woods, P. (1996) 'Beyond consumerism – the idea of consumer-citizenship', *Management in Education*, 10, 3: 15–16.

FURTHER READING

Begley, P.T. (ed) (1999) *Values and Educational Leadership*, New York: State University of New York Press.

Begley, P.T. and Leonard, P.E. (eds) (1999) *The Values of Educational Administration*, London: Falmer Press.

Sergiovanni, T.J. (1992) *Moral Leadership: Getting to the Heart of School Improvement*, San Francisco: Jossey-Bass.

1.3 Subject Leader Accountability

Diane Duncan

INTRODUCTION: WHAT DOES SUBJECT LEADER ACCOUNTABILITY MEAN?

OBJECTIVES

By the end of this Unit you should:

- Be aware of the changing context of education which has led to increased accountability in schools;
- Be able to identify the factors which have led to the particular model of accountability which subject leaders now have to work to;
- Have a clear understanding of the way in which accountability relates to issues in teaching and learning.

Historically, secondary school headteachers have always recognised subject leaders or heads of department as key players in their school's success. This is because they are the drivers of standards of performance in terms of examination results and school improvement. Strong subject departments are often the basis on which parents choose the school in the first place. Parental choice, based upon academic performance and high standards of teaching, did not suddenly appear with the advent of league tables: middle class parents have traditionally evaluated schools on their academic performance in both the independent and state sectors. Subject leaders have consequently always played a major role in determining the success of the school as a whole. In this sense subject leaders have long been accountable to heads, parents and pupils but the accountability was essentially private and internal to the institution. What is different in all sectors of state education today is that accountability demands have been increased both within and outside the school. Accountability now embraces a wider range of stakeholders: moreover it is public, sharp-edged and carries with it punitive measures if its statutory requirements are not met. Punitive measures may include a less than satisfactory Ofsted report, 'naming and shaming' underperforming schools, and parents choosing other schools for their children. They are what Bush (1999: 9) refers to as 'sanctions' because they provide the 'teeth' for those wanting answers about a school's performance. The historical basis from which this particular model of accountability developed will be discussed later on. For now, the discussion will focus on the following questions: what does a subject leader have to do which is different in terms of responsibility from class teachers? To whom is s/he accountable and why? The role of subject leader or head of department generally occupies a middle management position within the secondary school's hierarchical structure because they have additional responsibilities to those of the classroom teacher and are accountable both above and below their position in the school's overall management structure. In this sense they are a 'layer' of management between the senior management team and those at the chalkface (Fleming and Amesbury, 2001: 2). Typically, in a traditional management model, subject leaders are positioned between classroom teachers and the head and senior management team. They play a key role in helping to move a school forward in terms of its improvement plans, strategic development, overall goals and mission statement. They are also expected to ensure the smooth day-to-day running of the school's business and to monitor the progress of pupils and those staff within their department or subject team. Internally, subject leaders are accountable upwards to the head and SMT and downwards to the teachers in their subject team and the pupils they teach. They are also externally accountable to school governors, parents and less directly to education policy makers and politicians. These external accountability groupings are sometimes referred to as *stakeholders*, a term which is often used loosely to categorise 'all those who have a legitimate interest in the continuing effectiveness and success of an institution' (Waring, 1999: 180). However, the term could be equally well applied to pupils, departmental staff and key personnel higher up the chain of command, all of whom are internal to the institution and each of which has a legitimate interest in the effectiveness and success of an institution. A more helpful grouping recognises that there are different interests and value systems depending on whether you are a pupil, a parent or a politician. For example, Becher *et al.* (1979) recognise that a teacher has three kinds of accountability: moral (to pupils and parents as clients); professional (to one's colleagues); and contractual (to the school governing body and political masters). An emerging further type is market accountability, which is where clients have a choice of the institution they might attend. More importantly, differing models of accountability are underpinned by particular ways of conceptualising what goes on in schools and different sets of interests. In other words accountability, like knowledge, is seldom value free. For example, parents will want their children to succeed and do well in their chosen subjects so that they are able to compete in the higher education and the job market. Professional colleagues will want to work in a subject department which is run efficiently and which makes it possible for them to do a professionally rewarding job of work. Headteachers and school governors want their school to do well in league tables in comparison to other schools, to improve their performance over time and to secure a favourable reputation in the local community. The interests of politicians and policy makers are shaped by the political agenda of the day, which is driven at the moment by an imperative to drive up standards of pupil performance in England and Wales. As to the question of *why* subject leaders are accountable, the answer is double-edged: they both *have* to be and *ought* to be. On the one hand, they are constrained by powerful pressures to do so since failure to comply risks the application of punitive sanctions. On the other hand, they have a moral and professional obligation to lead and manage their subject so that opportunities for pupils to succeed are maximised, as are colleague teachers' chances to teach to the best of their ability. It is the complex range and scale of both internal and external accountability which makes the role of subject leader both challenging and intensely problematic in today's secondary schools.

CHANGING CONTEXTS OF ACCOUNTABILITY

In order to understand why things are the way they are now, it is necessary to understand the historical changes which have taken place in education over the last few decades. The most significant milestone halfway through the twentieth century was the 1944 Butler Education Act. The principles and values upon which the Act rested have since been referred to as visionary and far-reaching by many educational historians. A key part of this vision was the establishment of a democratic partnership between the State, Local Education Authorities and the teaching profession where decisions about schooling and its organisation were made at the local level.

The Act achieved a consensus, seldom achieved before or since, about how education should be controlled, financed and organised, which lasted for almost forty years. During this time the teaching profession was not considered to be accountable to the government for the content of the curriculum, nor was it required to justify its decisions to policy makers or parents (Scott, 1999). One of the hallmarks of the post-war consensus was that the government of the day did not intervene in local decisions about the organisation, teaching or management of educational provision. Trust in the expertise of the professionals was by and large assumed and rarely challenged. However, whilst relatively independent from governmental and parental pressures, schools were in fact accountable to Local Education Authorities and to Her Majesty's Inspectorate, albeit that such inspections were infrequent and of a wholly different kind to those now conducted by Ofsted. The accountability ethic during this period was therefore of the professional kind and a long way from the invasive accountability systems in operation at the present time. The 1988 Education Reform Act replaced the principles of universalism and social equality enshrined in the 1944 Act with the ideology of the market via individualism, public choice and accountability. Central to the Act was a National Curriculum which was imposed on primary and secondary sectors of state education and schools were required to teach or, to use the discourse of the day, *deliver* a prescribed curriculum.

For a while the *ways* in which teachers taught were one of the few areas of control and independence left to their professional judgement. Ten years later this too became a focus for change and intervention with the launch of the National Literacy Strategy in primary schools. This was quickly followed by the National Numeracy Strategy in 1999 and 2002 saw the implementation in secondary schools of the National Literacy Strategy at Key Stage 3.

Under the 1988 Act, power was wrested away from Local Education Authorities by devolving funding and financial control directly to schools. The rhetoric of parent power, greater choice and a market forces approach to education replaced social democracy with consumer democracy. As LEAs gradually lost much of their control over schools, accountability pressures shifted from education authorities to central government and the consumers. One of the core values of what became known as the politics of the *New Right*, was that the education system should be built upon the principles of public choice and accountability. Educationalists, including teachers, were no longer the sole guardians of expertise and for a time during the 1980s and early 1990s they were rarely consulted during the swathe of new legislation, which was designed to have far-reaching implications for schools and the education system as a whole. Within this new educational orthodoxy, there was to be direct accountability between the producer and the consumer.

The current 'accountability-with-teeth' culture is not, of course, restricted to education. It has penetrated most public institutions including the health service, social services and local government. Indeed, in the 2002 Reith Lecture, Onora O'Neill pointed to the complex protocols and detailed procedures of most accountability systems as evidence of a 'crisis of trust' in public sector institutions. The scale and scope of its labyrinthine systems are such that she compared the current drive for greater accountability to 'great draughts of Heineken's, reaching parts that supposedly less developed forms of accountability did not reach' (O'Neill, 2002). Accountability is also an international phenomenon within education and Boyd (1997: 12–13) points out that in many nations, including the USA, Australia and Canada, 'schools are under a kind of scrutiny unknown in the past, as the demand for better results and more efficient use of resources keeps intensifying'.

This section has brought together some of the key features of historical change in the accountability systems which now operate in state secondary schools. Accountability is not a stable and immutable concept. As different values and principles come to the fore, depending on the political imperatives of the time, the particular nature and emphasis of accountability changes. So how does the process *work* in practice and what does it involve as far as the responsibilities of the subject leader are concerned? This will be the focus of the next section.

MODELS, MECHANISMS AND PROCESSES OF ACCOUNTABILITY

An attempt to understand the complex and sometimes conflicting nature of accountability has been achieved by describing its salient features in a series of ideal models. These descriptions help to point up the particular emphases which are in the ascendancy in differing accountability relationships. Halstead (1994) suggests six different models:

- the central control model (contractual, employer dominant)
- the self-accounting model (contractual, professional dominant)
- the consumerist model (contractual, consumer dominant)
- the chain of responsibility model (responsive, employer dominant)
- the professional model (responsive, professional dominant)
- the partnership model (responsive, consumer dominant).

Two of these models, the professional and the consumerist, have already been mentioned in the previous section of this Unit. Scott (1999) draws on the work of

Halstead and considers five models of accountability. It is worth reading Scott's definitions and analyses of these models in Chapter 2 of *Managing External Relations in Schools and Colleges* by J. Lumby and N. Foskett (eds). One of these, *the evaluative state model* (Scott, 1999), is particularly applicable to state primary and secondary schools at the current time. Here, the state gives over the precise implementation of policy to semi-independent bodies such as Ofsted which, whilst accountable to government ministers, overrides existing forms of accountability such as LEA-school relations. In this model, the inspection process itself becomes the means by which schools comply with government policy (p. 27). With its regular cycle of inspections and severe sanctions for failing and underperforming schools, Ofsted has been granted significant powers to compel schools to conform to government prescriptions on its behalf. In this accountability system the responsibility for failure shifts from the government to quasi-governmental bodies and the school itself. However, it is important to remember no particular model of accountability is static or immutable. Systems of accountability are value-laden and can change, depending on the particular historical and political circumstances of the time. Of particular importance to subject leaders is Scott's (1999: 30) claim that 'systems of accountability … can never be imposed absolutely. There is, in other words, space within any imposed model for local initiative'. This means that school managers can be proactive, and influence the types of accountability in which they find themselves. For example, since the beginning of the Ofsted account-ability regime, many schools have learned to find ways of managing and controlling the inspection process in ways which better serve the interests of school staff, parents and pupils. Such schools have learned to use external accountability systems to their advantage as well as to improve and develop themselves.

CORE PRINCIPLES

So, what are the mechanisms and processes of accountability which subject leaders have to direct and manage in order to fulfil their responsibilities? Whatever paper systems and planning formats are used, certain fundamental principles should remain sacrosanct and these essentially concern the pupils, staff, parents and the school as a whole. The point of any accountability system must be to tell the truth simply, clearly and in an open and transparent way. This applies equally to subject leader accountability as it does to a hospital and its patients or a finance company and its shareholders. This means that pupils are taught well, know what they need to do in order to improve, are prepared well for examinations and are enthusiastic about the subject. It means that parents are well informed about their children's achievements, know what is being done to help them if they are having difficulties and how they can support what the school is doing. As far as the subject team or department is concerned, it means ensuring that everyone works together as a team, knows and understands the broad and smaller picture in terms of the subject's development and has a clear sense of direction. Moreover, each individual's effort is recognised and valued and the team is kept up to date and fully informed of changes and new external initiatives. This collective endeavour needs then to be carefully aligned with the school's aims and mission statement so that policy is translated into practice within the context of the school's overall planning hierarchy.

THE NATIONAL STANDARDS FOR SUBJECT LEADERS

In 1998 the Teacher Training Agency published a set of generic national standards for leadership which emphasise the importance placed upon middle management in the drive to improve achievement in schools. There are five parts to the standards: the core purpose of the subject leader; key outcomes of subject leadership; professional knowledge and understanding; skills and attributes; and key areas of subject leadership. These standards set out comprehensively what subject leaders are expected to work towards and, if an overview of what is expected of subject leaders is required in preparation for an interview for example, they are a useful source of information. They are also a valuable checkpoint for more experienced subject leaders and, in order to ensure that aspects of the role are not being advantaged at the expense of others, should be referred to from time to time.

THE PLANNING AND DEVELOPMENT CYCLE

The planning and development process is dealt with in greater detail in the section on strategic direction and development (Section 4) so this section will confine itself to a summary of its key features and broad structure of organisation. The key point to keep in mind about this process is that it should *not* simply be a bureaucratic exercise. If it is managed well it is a means of ensuring that the actual process of accountability is systematised and ordered. This then makes it possible for the complex business of a particular subject's improvement, development and action to be understood within a framework and common language which is easily understood by diverse audiences both within and outside the school.

Development planning is now well established in many schools and subject leaders, as the school's middle managers, have a pivotal role to play in its construction and implementation. The key to its success is the extent to which it provides a clear sense of direction which everyone in the subject and senior management team can follow and understand. Planning at the level of the subject or department means thinking about long-term and short-term issues and goals. The long-term goals will be defined by a broader sweep of desirable aspirations and achievements whilst the short-term goals will be specific, focused and achievable within a prescribed time limit. The standard structure and organisation for what has become known as the planning cycle, involves the following key stages: *audit, vision, construction, implementation and evaluation*. This cyclical process helps to provide subject leaders with answers to several important questions which Fleming amd Amesbury (2001: 120) have developed:

- Where are we now? (*audit*)
- Where do we want the developing subject/department to be in five years time? (*vision*)
- What changes do we need to make? (*construction*)
- How shall we manage these changes? (*implementation*)
- How shall we know whether our management of change has been successful? (*evaluation*)

The broad outline of this process normally follows the six-stage pattern set out below (adapted from Fleming and Amesbury, 2001):

- Audit
- Strategic plan
- Subject development plan
- Improvement plan
- Key Stage, year, subject and programme plans
- Action plans

WHAT IS SUCCESSFUL SUBJECT LEADER ACCOUNTABILITY?

One of the points in the preceding sections has been to show that accountability systems are influenced by prevailing values and belief systems and, as such, can change and *be* changed. What schools are facing today is part of a new culture of accountability, which is affecting most of the public sector. It demands increasing amounts of information, comparative data and target-setting without necessarily helping professionals to account for their practices and achievement in ways which parents, pupils and school governors might find interesting and helpful. At their worst the current trend for what O'Neill (2002) refers to as 'ever more perfect accountability', can 'damage rather than repair trust' and create 'a culture of suspicion'. What is needed she argues is '*intelligent* accountability' (p. 5). What might this include from the perspective of the subject leader?

One of the things which successful schools have done in recent years is to learn to control and manage accountability in ways which serve the interests of teachers, pupils and parents as well as the school community as a whole. It therefore matters that teacher managers do not blindly acquiesce to its prescriptions as though they were mere technicians. Their professional knowledge, experience and wisdom needs to inform every stage of the process because this is an important source of informed 'truth' which makes accountability of any kind make sense. Following on from this, one of the key requirements of subject leaders is to adopt an attitude and mindset which ensures that they control the process without letting it control them.

Action point

Identify the key groups of stakeholders that relate to your school and department then:
- Consider the different needs and requirements of these groups or individuals;
- Consider to what extent these needs are complementary or clashing;
- Identify the methods, both formal and informal, by which these groups or individuals are informed and consulted about developments in your subject area and consider how these could be enhanced.

INCLUSION

The most self-evidently important task for subject leaders is to ensure that the quality of teaching and learning is constantly monitored with clear signs of progress and an upward trend of achievement for *all* pupils. Whatever demands are made upon subject teams with respect to accountability, the central focus must remain firmly on teaching and learning since this is the key to successful subject teams and departments. However, there is now a new emphasis on the importance of all schools becoming *inclusive* schools. Since 2001, Ofsted school inspectors have received additional training to ensure that procedures for monitoring and inspecting entitlement for *all* pupils are tightened up. This not only means that there need to be robust systems in place to ensure that pupils with special educational needs have full access to the curriculum but that the progress and well-being of pupils is not impeded or negatively affected by incidents of bullying and racism. This matters as much for the particular subject as it does for the school as a whole. Indeed, there is an important reference in the *National Standards for Subject Leaders* (TTA, 1998) which mentions the need for high expectations and success with pupils with special educational needs and linguistic needs as well as the requirement to ensure that teachers of the subject know how to recognise and deal with racial stereotyping (5. B vii, xi, p. 11). To underscore the point more strongly, some high achieving schools with respect to pupil progress and standards of achievement, could find themselves judged by Ofsted to be in 'special measures' because of findings of bullying and racism not sufficiently held in check by school policies or practices. Subject leaders therefore need to ensure that inclusion features as an important part of their development planning and accountability system. If there are issues of concern, subject leaders will need to confront them openly with their subject teams. One of the means by which subject leaders are, or are not, successful in this area of accountability will be dependent on the degree to which they are able to offer a strong lead, a determination to secure improvement and an ability to handle both the issue and their subject staff with sensitivity and tact.

To be successful at accountability subject leaders need to be strong on paper systems and to be able to produce spreadsheets and data sources as a matter of course. If manageable, user-friendly ways of dealing with the paper work can be found, it then becomes easier to focus on the more important aspects of the task. These include being proactive and ahead of the game so that new initiatives and demands can be anticipated without becoming yet another burden. New developments and improvements needed for the subject need to be made with an eye on the strategy, mission, aims and vision of the whole school. Most important of all is the team itself which needs to feel a collective ownership of the vision and the direction in which the subject is moving. This means that individual members of the team need to be given specific areas of responsibility which draw upon their respective strengths and qualities. The concept of *distributive leadership* is an important concept in the more recent literature on schools facing challenging contexts (see especially, Harris, 2002; Gray, 2000). Quite simply, this means that responsibility is devolved throughout the school so that there are many rather than a few leaders. The power of praise, involving others in decision making and giving professional autonomy to individual teachers are some examples of its most effective strategies. This approach to leadership can be equally well applied to the subject team.

In conclusion, subject leaders need to keep at the forefront of their minds that their work in accountability has both a professional and moral dimension. An ability to handle bureaucracy and keep up to date with paper work is clearly important but of far greater significance is their ability to engage teachers, pupils and parents in the accounting process in ways which demonstrate trust and belief in their versions of the truth. The way may then be open for them to work towards their version of *intelligent* accountability.

BIBLIOGRAPHY

Becher, T., Eraut, M., Barton, J., Canning, T. and Knight, J. (1979) 'Accountability in the middle years of schooling: an analysis of policy options', final report of the East Sussex LEA/University of Sussex Research Project, Brighton: University of Sussex.

Boyd, W. (1997) 'Environmental pressures and competing paradigms in educational management', *ESRC Seminar Series Paper*, Leicester, June.

Bush, T. (1999) 'The vanishing boundaries: the importance of effective external relations', in J. Lumby and N. Foskett (eds) *Managing External Relations in Schools and Colleges*, London: Paul Chapman.

Fleming, P. and Amesbury, M. (2001) *The Art of Middle Management in Primary Schools*, London: David Fulton Publishers.

Gray, J. (2000) *Causing Concern but Improving: A Review of Schools' Experience*, London: DfEE.

Halstead, M. (1994) 'Accountability and values', in D. Scott (ed.) *Accountability and Control in Educational Settings*, London: Cassell.

Harris, A. (2002) 'Effective leadership in schools facing challenging contexts', *School Leadership and Management*, 22, 1: 15–26.

Maclure, S. (1994) 'Act of faith amid the heart of battle', *The Times Educational Supplement*, 6 May.

O'Neill, O. (2002) 'A question of trust', Reith Lecture Two, BBC Radio 4, 23 April.

Scott, D. (1999) 'Accountability in education systems', in J. Lumby and N. Foskett (eds) *Managing External Relations in Schools and Colleges*, London: Paul Chapman.

TTA (1998) *National Standards for Subject Leaders*, London: Teacher Training Agency.

Waring, S. (1999) 'Finding your way: sensing the external environment', in J. Lumby and N. Foskett (eds) *Managing External Relations in Schools and Colleges*, London: Paul Chapman.

FURTHER READING

Glatter, R. (2002) 'Governance, autonomy and accountability in education', in T. Bush and L. Bell (eds) *The Principles of Educational Management*, London: Paul Chapman.

Lumby, J. and Foskett, N. (eds) (1999) *Managing External Relations in Schools and Colleges*, London: Paul Chapman.

Scott, D. (ed.) (1994) *Accountability and Control in Educational Settings*, London: Cassell.

Leading Effective Teaching and Learning

2.1 Leading Effective Teaching and Learning

Ian Terrell and Ed Powell

INTRODUCTION

OBJECTIVES

By the end of this Unit you should:

- Be able to clarify and develop the role of subject leader in managing teaching and learning;
- Understand the characteristics of an effective department for teaching and learning;
- Realise the importance of developing collaborative monitoring and evaluation for improvement;
- Be aware of the main issues in collaborative planning of learning and assessment;
- Be able to ensure that appropriate models of learning are developed.

In the last 30 years there has been considerable interest in 'effective schooling'. Until quite recently much of this has been focused upon the effective management of schools at a whole school level. Very recently interest has been shown in 'effective teaching and learning strategies' through the work of Creemers (1994), Cullingford (1995), Joyce et al. (1997) and Muijs and Reynolds (2001).

However, the leap from interest in the whole school to interest in classroom level effectiveness has missed a whole level, particularly in secondary schools, of what happens in a department or subject area. This seems illogical. Pupils are frequently taught different subjects in departmental or curriculum areas by different teachers. The curriculum is organised and delivered by a curriculum team, not the whole school or an individual teacher alone.

As Head of Department you are responsible for leading teaching and learning and ensuring that both are carried out effectively in your subject area of the curriculum. This might be made easier if there were some clear and universally accepted definition of effective teaching and learning. Unfortunately, there is not, although a starting point will be the Ofsted definition. There are too many different aims, purposes and goals, too many individual needs and contexts, too many learning styles, too many subjects and topics. Leask and Terrell (1997) suggest that building consensus on what effective teaching and learning looks like in your subject area is a good first step to improvement.

Three notions underpin this Unit:

- Improving practice may be supported by relevant published empirical work
- Theoretical models help to analyse and predict effective practice
- Teachers need to critically evaluate, apply and develop empirical and theoretical ideas in their own contexts.

A core assumption, therefore, is that collaborative critical reflective practice is central to building effective teaching and learning that continuously improves and maximises the learning of all pupils.

THE SUBJECT CO-ORDINATOR'S ROLE IN TEACHING AND LEARNING

Leadership, according to Whitaker (1993: 73), 'is behaviour that enables and assists others to achieve planned goals' and nothing could be truer of the subject co-ordinator who needs to work with teachers in the department to improve pupils' learning experiences. Brown and Rutherford (1996), using Murphy's 1992 analysis of leadership roles, have developed a classification of roles:

Head of Department as Servant Leader
Leading from the centre of a network of interpersonal relationships and working with people. Using their professional expertise and professional wisdom to guide, inspire and empower members of the department. To build consensus, collaboration and clarify values.

Head of Department as Organisational Architect
The Head of Department's role is in creating the architecture of the department that facilitates effectiveness and continuous improvement. Such architecture involves collaboration, involvement and participation of teachers, critical reflection, enquiry, development planning and evaluation, holding of meetings, and ensuring progress.

Head of Department as Social Architect
The Head of Department creates the culture and tone of interrelationships between members of the department. Promoting success and achievement. Establishing space for good communication and dialogue.

Head of Department as Moral Educator
The Head of Department is explicit about values and beliefs about teaching and learning. They emphasise the learning ability of all children. They are knowledgeable and clear about what constitutes worthwhile learning.

Head of Department as Leading Professional

The Head of Department is up to date and a more than competent teacher. They are a promoter and practitioner of critical reflection on practice.

(Brown and Rutherford, 1996)

If this model is applied specifically to leadership of teaching and learning, key areas of the role are revealed in structuring opportunities for teaching and learning to develop and in inspiring and motivating staff.

CHARACTERISTICS OF EFFECTIVE DEPARTMENTS FOR TEACHING AND LEARNING

Effective subject leaders will wish to build effective departments. Research has shown a number of characteristics of effective departments and these are now the basis for DfES and Ofsted advice.

Research by Sammons *et al.* (1996, 1997) has shown that a number of factors are associated with high performing departments. These include:

- High expectations and a belief in the capabilities of children
- Academic emphasis and the high priority of assessment and homework
- Shared vision, goals and commitment
- Clear leadership including team building and teamwork and involving staff
- Effective relationship with SMT
- Consistency of policies and practice within the subject and across the whole school
- Quality teaching including clarity of goals and planning challenging work
- A student centred approach where enjoyment, interest and achievement are stressed
- Parental support and involvement.

The DfEE National Standards (1994) provided a useful checklist for subject leaders. These concentrated upon:

- Auditing the curriculum to ensure learning for all pupils
- Establishing curriculum planning
- Developing effective teaching and learning strategies with staff
- Using assessment to establish targets for improvement with teachers and pupils
- Improving teaching and learning through monitoring and development
- Ensuring cross-curricular themes of numeracy, literacy and citizenship are developed
- Developing partnerships with parents and the community.

(From the National Standards for Subject Leaders, TTA, 1998)

In addition to the leadership learning function outlined by Rutherford and Brown and focusing on the inspiration and relationships within the department there are some key tasks to achieve as subject leader to ensure that learning is effective for all pupils. We have identified four key areas in the simplified model in Figure 2.1. These are:

- A. Collaborative monitoring and evaluation for improvement
- B. Collaborative planning of learning and assessment
- C. Ensuring teacher knowledge and skills are applied
- D. Ensuring appropriate models of learning in a repertoire for specific learning outcomes.

Collaborative monitoring and evaluation for improvement

The subject leader may ask what the quality of teaching and learning is in the department, in order to provide a starting point for planning to improve. However, working with the subject team as a whole has been shown to be more effective in leading to improvement.

Hopkins distinguishes between:

- Evaluation of improvement
- Evaluation for improvement
- Evaluation as improvement.

Hopkins calls this approach 'Evaluation as Improvement', where the department continuously enquires into what is going on and what might be improved (Hopkins,

Figure 2.1 The components of leading effective teaching and learning

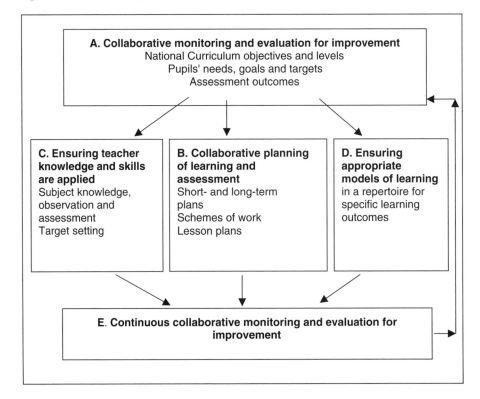

1989). In this form evaluation and monitoring are a way of working together for the purpose of improvement. The process involves working together to collect information, observing lessons, analysing assessments and discussing strategies for improvement.

Subject leaders' standards produced by the TTA in 2002 suggest that subject leaders should ensure:

- Curriculum coverage, continuity and progression in the subject for all pupils, including those of high ability and those with special educational or linguistic needs;
- Teachers are clear about the teaching of objectives in lessons, understand the sequence of teaching and learning in the subject, and communicate the information to pupils;
- Guidance is provided on the choice of appropriate teaching and learning methods to meet the needs of the subject and of different pupils;
- Effective development of pupils' literacy, numeracy and information technology skills through the subject;
- Teachers of the subject are aware of its contribution to pupils' understanding of the duties and opportunities, responsibilities and rights of citizens;
- Teachers of the subject know how to recognise and deal with racial stereotyping;
- Effective development of pupils' individual and collaborative study skills necessary for them to become increasingly independent when out of school.

This list provides a useful checklist. At the heart of leadership of teaching and learning is using approaches to evaluation based upon finding out about 'Where we are now' so that we can plan to improve.

The standards, however, have a tone of the individual subject leader taking on these responsibilities, rather than the collaborative team. However, in reading the standards a number of self-evaluation questions are suggested, including:

- How do you ensure curriculum coverage, continuity and progression for all pupils?
- How is coverage, continuity and progression ensured for:
    - Gifted and talented pupils?
    - Special Educational Needs pupils?
- What evidence of this is found in lesson plans and schemes of work?
- How is information about pupils translated into plans and learning activities?
- What use is made of SEN information and Individual Education Plans (IEPs)?
- How do you ensure that teachers are clear about the teaching objectives and sequences in your subject?
- How do you ensure that pupils are clear about the teaching objectives and sequences in your subject?
- How do you ensure that all parents are clear about the teaching objectives and sequences in your subject?
- How do you assess the appropriateness of teaching and learning methods?
- What evidence is there that your subject develops pupils' literacy and numeracy and information technology skills?
- What is the policy for assessment, recording and reporting achievement to pupils?

- How is this information conveyed to parents?
- How is assessment information translated into targets for pupils?
- What kind of targets are set for pupils in your subject and how is this achieved?
- How do you set expectations for students and staff that are challenging and realistic?
- How do you evaluate the teaching of your subject?
- What evidence do you use?
- How do you establish goals for improvement?
- How is the contribution of your subject evaluated in terms of developing citizenship?
- What information do parents receive concerning:
  - The curriculum?
  - Pupil attainment?
  - Progress?
  - Targets?
- How do you currently develop links with business and the local community in your subject area?
- How do these links develop pupils' wider understanding of your subject?

These questions might be worked on collaboratively as the basis of subject area discussions in evaluating the work of the department for the purpose of improvement. Evidence and data collected from pupils' work and from classroom observation are at the heart of these discussions.

Clearly one aim, as a subject leader, will be for the department to answer these questions in relation to an Ofsted inspection. Two additional questions might be posed:

- Where is the evidence that supports your answers and proves that what you say happens does?
- Can your answers to these questions form your department policy for teaching and learning and their monitoring?

EVALUATING THE CURRICULUM TO ENSURE LEARNING FOR ALL PUPILS

A key area of collaborative evaluation for improvement is auditing the curriculum to ensure provision for all pupils so that development may take place. Sources of data might include:

- Benchmark data such as 'The Autumn Package' (available online: http://www.standards.dfes.gov.uk/performance) and Key Stage assessments. It is data produced jointly with Ofsted and QCA and contains National Summary Results, Value Added Information and Benchmark Information. This allows schools to:
  - understand what progress they are making
  - compare the progress made by individual pupils with progress made by other pupils with similar prior attainment
  - compare their performance with similar schools.

- The plans for the curriculum (schemes of work and lesson plans)
- Assessment data for all pupils, grouped according to ability and gender
- An analysis of curriculum materials
- Assessment and target setting data
- Observation of lessons.

Such analysis needs to take place within departmental discussions. As a result of such discussions the department might make some general statements, for example:

- The planned programme has not focused enough on developing analytical skills in years 8 and 9 to ensure progression to GCSE studies.
- Highly able pupils make good progress in Key Stage 3 but less so in Key Stage 4.
- Support for the linguistic development of less able children is excellent but less so for moderate and highly able children.

Areas of strength can be celebrated and areas of weakness need to be prioritised for future development.

Pupil pursuit

Some teachers have tracked a pupil for a day to see what an individual child experiences.

VIGNETTE

Pupil pursuit
Teachers at one school followed a group of less able and poorly motivated children around the school for one day. The main focus was to identify teacher behaviours that motivated and demotivated this group of pupils. The teachers were able to identify key interactions that demotivated students. Recommendations for teachers in dealing with this group were made, including:

- Using more encouragement and praise
- Avoiding pupil and teacher behaviours that led to demotivation
- Developing strategies that motivate.

ANALYSIS OF ASSESSMENT BY GENDER OR ABILITY

The National Curriculum testing and assessment regime provides much data on what can be assessed of pupil learning. The implicit theory of progression is that students will make progress through the curriculum at predictable rates.

The basic theoretical model for progression is shown in Figure 2.2. Essentially progress will be shown by learners at predictable rates. Key variables affecting this will be characteristics of the learner and the differential effects of different approaches

Figure 2.2 Basic progression model (issues affecting student progress)

Year	7	8	9	10	
level	4	5	6	7	
level	3	4	5	6	
level	2	3	4	5	

Pupils' effects:
Gender
Ability
Motivation
Maturation

Progress better than 'expected'

Basic progress model

Progress as expected

Teacher's effects

Progress worse than expected

to teaching. Implied in the theory is that teachers can act to maximise their effect on all pupils if they can identify groups that are underperforming. Indeed, we would suggest that if this holds to be true then teachers might be able to act to do better than 'normal progression' predicts.

There is much here to debate and contest concerning this notion. For instance:

- Progression may not be incremental
- Assessment is not an accurate measure
- Testing is neither accurate nor complete for many subjects e.g. KS2 in Maths and English, which must be used as surrogate measures in other subjects
- There are variations in assessment techniques and curriculum that affect progression.

Some research shows that teachers frequently believe that the pupil characteristics have an overwhelmingly powerful effect. It should be noted that Sammons *et al.* (1996) found that effective departments believed that they could make a difference and planned actions that could achieve this goal.

This information is only valuable if teachers and pupils turn it into plans for action. For the latter, targets need to be negotiated which are motivational and specific enough to work upon. Merely saying 'must work harder' would not be enough without saying precisely the kind of qualities that need to be developed and how they might be achieved (see below).

For the teachers in the department assessment data is useful to track the progression of individuals and groups of pupils. The key questions are whether progress for individuals is as you would expect, better than you would expect or worse.

Baselines may be identified using a variety of sources, including:

- Cognitive ability tests (CATS), Yellis
- Key Stage Tests and teacher assessments
- Equivalent Subject assessments.

The results of such analysis might lead the department to conclude, for instance:

- More able students make good progress or better
- Less able students make the progress that is expected of them or worse
- The progress of girls is better than expected and greater than boys'.

Table 2.1 Tracking assessment

Name	Ability band	Gender	KS2 Standard Assessment Tests English	History assessment (May)	History assessment (June)
Brown, J.	Top	M	5	7	6
Blue, B.	Top	F	5	7	7
Green, T.	Middle	M	3	4	5
Black, E.	Middle	M	3	4	4

These are useful generalisations for the department to agree upon. However, they will be of no use unless the department can suggest some causation and some strategies to make a difference.

Records of tracking assessment need to be kept as in Table 2.1. These might clearly indicate who is, and is not reaching the expectations based upon past best performance. However, the department must be clear about a number of assumptions made by this model:

- Assumption One: This is not rocket science with absolute certainties predicted.
- Assumption Two: Progress being 'as expected' is not good enough if you genuinely believe that teachers can make a difference and pupils can learn.
- Assumption Three: Changing syllabus, course and groupings will achieve so much, making teaching and learning more effective can achieve even more.

Sammons *et al.* (1996, 1997) emphasised the quality of planning in effective departments and such findings are supported by Ofsted inspection.

PURPOSE OF PLANS

How important are your curriculum plans, schemes of work and lesson plans to you and your department? What purpose do plans serve? Are they seen as an unnecessary administrative burden? Do staff feel that they get in the way of good teaching?

Good plans are a prerequisite for a good Ofsted inspection, because they are a good source of evidence of effectiveness.

Some of the purposes of plans might be that they could ensure that:

- The National Curriculum is covered
- All learning goals for the subject, for individual learners and for the development of literacy, numeracy, information technology skills and for independent and collaborative learning are covered
- Learning can take place for pupils of all abilities
- Teachers are clear about curriculum objectives
- Long-term curriculum goals are translated into medium- and short-term lesson plans
- Activities can meet the curriculum goals
- Learning activities and styles are varied
- Resources are organised and available at appropriate times
- Review and improvement can take place systematically
- The department can work collaboratively.

The purpose of plans is not to constrain teaching. Teachers should be encouraged to adapt the plan if they feel it is more appropriate to follow a different course of action for a short while. They should be encouraged to use their professional judgement, for example, where:

- the class or individuals have not grasped an idea sufficiently
- an opportunity comes up that provides learning, interest and motivation.

Bloom's taxonomy of educational objectives is a key theoretical construction that is applied by every teacher in the planning of lessons and in ensuring pace and progression (Bloom, 1964).

Essentially Bloom categorises objectives as:

- Knowledge
- Understanding
- Synthesis
- Analysis
- Evaluation.

Skills and attitudes are also categories of objectives identified by Bloom's taxonomy.

Most teachers would recognise these categories as similar to examination syllabuses. However, in our own research we have found that some teachers are not aware of the balance in the syllabus between these objectives. Knowledge and understanding for example is commonly 30 per cent of many Key Stage 4 assessment criteria. This suggests that ample time should be given to teaching and learning methods that promote knowledge (recall) and understanding as well as ample time for methods that result in analytical and evaluative skills.

THE FORMAT OF PLANS

Long term plans or schemes of work can be found in many formats, although the landscape grid on A4 paper is quite common and easy to read. A long term plan or scheme of work may include the following:

- Unit title
- Key ideas and concepts
- Key skills and abilities
- Cross-curricular skills (literacy, numeracy and IT)
- Key words and language
- Attitudes
- Learning activities
- Independent learning activities (e.g. 'homework')
- Assessment activities
- Resources
- Time.

Short term plans or lesson plans can be developed from these. It is now widespread practice to have these for each lesson and to hand them to any Ofsted inspector at the beginning of the lesson. However, their importance is beyond that. With a plan both teacher and pupils can be clear about developing activities that achieve specific learning outcomes.

PLANNING TEACHING AND LEARNING ACTIVITIES

Turning plans into advance organisers and study guides for pupils and parents

A criterion of effectiveness used by Ofsted is that pupils understand what they are doing and why, and the learning objectives of lessons. The term 'advance organiser' has been widely adopted by Ausubel (1976) and others. Clearly, students who have such information can be more prepared to work independently of the teacher. Furthermore we could argue that the interested parent could also target and support the learning of pupils more effectively if they had such information.

DEVELOPING MODELS AND A REPERTOIRE OF TEACHING AND LEARNING STYLES

Three notions have dominated the literature on teaching and learning (Joyce *et al.*, 1997; Muijs and Reynolds, 2001; Smith, 1996). They are:

1 Using a wide and varied repertoire of teaching approaches to meet a variety of learning styles.
2 Using a 'model of learning' to achieve the specific desired learning outcomes, e.g. mnemonics for recall, role-play for understanding, empathy and social skills.

Figure 2.3 Suggested content for a study guide

Topic title
Assessment tasks
Independent learning tasks or homework
Timescales
Course content
Learning activities
Key objectives
List of terminology used
Assessment criteria at different levels
Examples of good quality work
Sources of additional information (texts, websites, museums, exhibitions)
Self assessment exercise
Individual targets for the unit of work
Individual pupil learning contract

Source: Derived from 'Raising Achievement at GCSE' by Terrell, Rowe and Terrell, 1996, Lancaster: Framework Press.

3   Emphasising teaching learners meta-cognitive strategies i.e. helping them to know 'how' to learn effectively in order to develop awareness and control of their thinking and learning.

Joyce *et al.* (1997) have classified different approaches to learning and teaching under the heading of 'models'. Models with similar goals are grouped in the following 'families':

- Information processing – including inductive thinking, concept attainment, advance organisers and mnemonics.
- Social – including co-operative group learning, role-play and group investigations.
- Personal – including non-directive teaching.
- Behavioural – including Direct Teaching, Mastery Learning and Simulation.

The importance of the models is that each emphasises different learning outcomes. In our work with teachers we do not regard the models as final conceptualisations. Rather, we regard them as interesting ideas to be developed and evaluated by practitioners.

REFERENCES

Ausubel, D. and Robinson, F.G. (1971) *School Learning*, London: Holt Rinehart and Winston.

Bloom, B.S., Krathwohl, D.R. and Masia, B.B. (1964) *Taxonomy of Educational Objectives*, London: Longman.

Brown, M. and Rutherford, D. (1996) 'Servant, architect, moralist, professional', *Management in Education*, 10, 1: 3–4.

Creemers, B. (1994) *The Effective Classroom*, London: Cassell.

Cullingford, C. (1995) *The Effective Teaching*, London: Cassell.

DfEE (1994) *The National Standards*, London: DFEE.

Hopkins, D. (1989) *Evaluation for School Development*, Buckingham: Open University Press.

Joyce, B., Calhoun, E. and Hopkins, D. (1997) *Models of Learning: Tools for Teaching*, Buckingham: Open University Press.

Leask, M. and Terrell, I. (1997) *Development Planning and School Improvement for Middle Managers*, London: Kogan Page.

Muijs, D. and Reynolds, D. (2001) *Effective Teaching: Evidence and Practice*, London: Paul Chapman Publishing.

Sammons, P., Thomas, S. and Mortimore, P. (1996) *Assessing School Effectiveness*, London: Ofsted.

Sammons, P., Thomas, S. and Mortimore, P. (1997) *Forging Links: Effective Schools and Effective Departments*, London: Paul Chapman.

Smith, A. (1996) *Accelerated Learning in the Classroom*, London: Network Educational Press.

TTA (1998) *The National Standards*, London: TTA.

TTA (2002) *Subject Leader Standards*, London: TTA.

Whitaker, P. (1993) *Managing Change in Schools*, Milton Keynes: Open University Press.

FURTHER READING

Novak, J.D. (1990) 'Concept maps and Venn diagrams: two metacognitive tools for science and mathematics education', *Instructional Science*, 19: 29–52.

Novak, J.D. and Gowin, D.B. (1984) *Learning How to Learn*, New York and Cambridge, UK: Cambridge University Press.

WEBSITES

http://cmap.coginst.uwf.edu/info/

http://www.graphic.org/concept.html

http://www.fed.cuhk.edu.hk/~johnson/misconceptions/concept_map/concept_maps.html

http://www.acceleratedlearningnetwork.com/multiple.htm

2.2 Models of Teaching and Learning

Ed Powell and Ian Terrell

INTRODUCTION

OBJECTIVES

By the end of this Unit you should:

- Have a clear understanding of the role of subject leader in leading teaching and learning;
- Be able to outline the characteristics of an effective department for teaching and learning;
- Understand the importance of ensuring teacher knowledge and skills are applied;
- Be able to build collaborative planning of learning and assessment;
- Be able to ensure that appropriate models of learning are developed.

> Thinking about the roles that make up teaching can make you dizzy. Just for starters, these roles include helping students grow in understanding, knowledge, self-awareness, moral development and the ability to relate to others ... To the best of our ability, we modulate across roles according to individual and group needs as we select and create learning experiences for all our students. Creating these learning experiences requires a large repertoire of teaching strategies.
>
> (Joyce *et al.*, 1997: 11)

Innovative and diverse responses to the needs of individual learners are key features of the White Paper, 'Schools: Achieving Success' (September 2001). Advances in neuroscience, learning styles, and current demands to raise standards impact on strategic approaches to learning and teaching. Managing change to ensure quality learning and teaching at the classroom level presents challenges for teachers and learners.

> Subject leaders provide guidance on the choice of appropriate teaching and learning methods to meet the needs of the subject and of different pupils.
>
> (TTA, 1998)

This Unit aims to provide subject leaders with examples of imaginative and creative learning and teaching methods used by secondary school teachers to raise standards and achievement. Practice evidence, underpinning theory and research findings are combined to support the case for the effectiveness of each method in achieving learning gains. Specific methods are used to enable learners to achieve intended learning outcomes that are not restricted to a subject-specific agenda. Hopkins *et al.* believe that

> the most important long-term outcome of instruction may be the students' increased capabilities to learn more easily and effectively in the future because of the knowledge and skill they have acquired, and because they have mastered learning processes. How teaching is conducted has a large impact on students' abilities to educate themselves.
>
> (Hopkins *et al.*, 2000: 32)

The self-education model is continuous with learning as a social process. Through such learning episodes transferable knowledge, understanding, values, democratic working practices and skills are acquired and developed. Recent research by Beresford (1998) concludes that there is still a mismatch between teaching methods and how learners prefer to learn. Furthermore, the evidence points to learners wanting more opportunities for social learning activities. According to Tileston (2000: 13) 'life is not a spectator sport; it is an exercise in active involvement, and education should reflect that active involvement'. The following methods promote the active engagement of learners in learning.

Joyce *et al.* (1997) refer to 'models of learning' which are in fact 'tools for teaching'. Models are grouped into families and the following scenarios are examples of the application of some of these models by practitioners in secondary schools.

Figure 2.4 Information processing

Information processing
↓

Model (examples)	Purpose
↓	↓
Inductive thinking	→ Development of classification skills Hypothesis building and testing, and how to build conceptual understanding of content area
Mnemonics	Increase ability to acquire information, conceptual systems and metacognitive control of information processing capability

VIGNETTE

Inductive thinking

Subject leader: Paul Peacock

GCSE Electronics – Product Analysis Enquiry: what have tin openers got to do with it?

Purpose
To facilitate a process by which learners:

- Improve their knowledge and understanding of the concept of product analysis
- Assume more responsibility for their own learning through experiential activities.

The model

> The inductive model causes students to collect information and examine it closely, to organize it into concepts and to learn to manipulate those concepts. Used regularly, this strategy increases students' abilities to form concepts efficiently and increases the range of perspectives from which they can view information.
>
> (Joyce *et al.*, 1997: 39)

Phases of the model

1   Collection and presentation of the data that are relevant to a topic or problem
2   Examining and enumerating the data into categories whose members have common attributes
3   Classifying the data and developing labels for categories so that they can be manipulated symbolically
4   Converting the categories into hypotheses or skills.

(Joyce *et al.*, 1997: 39)

Every inductive experience should be designed to help students learn to:

•   Collect and organize information
•   Form categories and hypotheses
•   Develop skills and use knowledge.

The process: model-in-action
Pupils were asked to bring various examples of tin openers from home to the lesson. Initially, we pooled all the openers on a large table and began observing and examining them. The pupils were amazed by the number of different types of tin openers. Not all were recent, modern designs. Many were old and were on loan from grandparents.

Next steps
Pupils were asked to think of categories or ways of grouping the openers. They rearranged the openers into groups. Suggested titles for each group were recorded on the whiteboard as pupils brainstormed names for different categories. Some tin openers could be put in more than one category.

The pupils were very involved in the work and it was pleasing to see arguments being put forward as the debate about criteria for categorization and association developed. Eventually, it was agreed that the pupils could not realistically decide upon criteria being met for two of the suggested categories, namely ease of use and effectiveness. They arrived at this decision as a result of acknowledging their limited experience in determining which tin openers were ergonomically sound and which were not.

Following my intervention, the group decided to produce a product analysis questionnaire. All pupils brought completed questionnaires to the next lesson. Results were tallied on the whiteboard. Pupils set about classifying the data obtained. It was agreed that tin openers could be placed in more than one category. The group was very enthusiastic and discussions were encouraging. The various categories were shared and recorded on the whiteboard. Pupils were asked to look carefully at the results and their subsequent classifications. They were asked to write down brief descriptive statements for the various tin openers, which incorporated their survey results and their classifications. They were forming hypotheses.

Impact of the process on pupils' learning

Pupils were learning the concept of product analysis. They were developing an understanding of the fundamental parts that come together to form the analysis of any given product. Pupils were learning how to collect and organize information. This also included a valuable introduction to questionnaire design. Additional, significant learning outcomes included categorization, formulating hypotheses, developing key skills and using new knowledge.

Value of the process

This was a very worthwhile exercise for both the pupils and me. It will definitely be developed further and repeated with other examination groups. The inductive process generated high levels of pupil interest; ideas were exchanged and pupils demonstrated improved understanding of product analysis. Pupils' responses to my probing questioning indicated a depth of understanding. This learning and teaching strategy is worth further development.

Implications for the teacher

The teacher is a facilitator of the process. In this facilitative role, I focused on the pace of the lesson and provided guidance as required and directed the group towards desired markers as their enthusiastic analysis unfolded. I was able to challenge the more able pupils by asking them extension questions to encourage product design development. The facilitative approach allowed me valuable pupil observation time. During this time, I made mental notes of possible modifications and improvements to the inductive learning method.

Impact of the process on the teacher

I learned a great deal from the exercise. I was able to observe pupils' responses to the activity and obtain a feel for the interest and enthusiasm generated. The hands-on approach with real life objects being examined was instrumental in creating pupil motivation for the exercise. The variety of different products and the fact that pupils had brought some of the exhibits contributed to the high levels of interest and participation.

I realized that the emphasis of the inductive process is on discovery learning and pupils responded positively to this approach. I did not have to provide all the answers.

What next?

This prototype product analysis exercise has shown it is worthy of further development. A simple handout explaining the stages of the lesson would be beneficial and the pupils would then have a useful document for their extension task when they have to carry out a product analysis for their own coursework. Building up an extensive collection of different artifacts would be an extremely useful resource. Extension tasks could involve the pupils compiling and printing their own group questionnaires. This lesson involved the use of tin openers because of their simplistic design and ease of availability. Future developments could involve other simple products. These products could be more relevant to the particular examination subject. For example, a torch would have direct relevance to electronic product analysis. A second, pupil-designed, questionnaire could then be used to collect new data referring to the pupils' categorization of the product. This could then help test out their hypotheses. The mixed ability pupil groupings can be used to advantage and I have witnessed how successful the more able pupils are in assisting the less able pupils.

LEARNING FROM REFLECTING ON THE MODEL-IN-ACTION: AN OBSERVER'S VIEW

This vignette suggests that the inductive thinking process allows learners to assume greater responsibility for their learning. Learners learn from each other through co-operative enquiry, which is characterized by a forward movement in the learning process. Engaging in the inductive process enables learners to formulate concepts and 'the application of concepts/generalizations. It [the inductive model] nurtures attention to language and the meaning of words, and attention to the nature of knowledge' (Joyce *et al.*, 1997: 42).

While understanding, acquisition and transferability of knowledge are seen in this vignette to be important, the desirable learning outcomes go beyond a subject-specific agenda. Rogers argued that

> the only [person] who is educated is the [person] who has learned how to learn ... that only the process of *seeking* knowledge gives a basis for security. Changingness, a reliance on *process* rather than upon static knowledge, is the only thing that makes any sense as a goal for education in the modern world.
> (Rogers, 1967: 1)

Bruner (1960: 6) asserted 'that learning properly under optimum conditions leads one to "learn how to learn"'. The notion of learners mastering how to learn is not, therefore, a recent development. The other agenda is concerned with providing learners with opportunities to assume more control over their learning, which is a characteristic of an empowering process. Teachers become facilitators with, among other things, the ensuing benefits of non-participative observation of pupils' learning as articulated by this subject leader.

Table 2.2 Sample scheme of work

	Lesson	Lesson plan	Knowledge and skills	Homework	Resources
Week 3	1	Discuss in more detail the Design and Make assignment (charities assignment) and the planning section 'Brainstorming' Obj – start planning brainstorming sheet	Brainstorming (3a) Attribute analysis (3a) Observational drawing (3a)	Work on brainstorming for D & M assignment	Examples of work produced by previous group Textbooks
	2	Continue with brainstorming. Give pupils examples of other products to prepare brainstorming. Obj – complete examples	Brainstorming (3a) Observational drawing (3a) Investigative drawing (3a)		Examples of work produced textbooks
	3	Continue with brainstorming Emphasise the need for good quality presentation (e.g. linework/use of colour) Obj – complete final brainstorming sheet	Brainstorming (3a) Observational drawing (3a) Investigative drawing (3a)		Examples of work produced textbooks
Week 4	1	Research logo design work on design ideas sheet for charity logo (use master sheets). Also work on evaluation.	Sketch 2 dimensional form (A2c) Freehand drawing Evaluation – How far they meet need (7a) Does it indicate charity (6c)	Research logo designs (6c)	Textbooks Magazines
	2	Continue with work related to charity logo design. Emphasis placed on good quality presentation Obj – pupils will set own targets	Two dimensional form (2c) Evaluation – How far it meets the need (7a) Does it indicate the charity effectively (6c)		Examples of previous work. Magazines and books
	3	Continue with logo designs relating to logos. Emphasis on logo designs and their evaluation Obj – logos constructed with Ev	Two dimensional form (A2c) Evaluation – How it meets the need (7a) Does it indicate the charity effectively (6c)		Examples of previous work, magazines and textbooks
Week 5	1	The first half of the lesson will be devoted to shading techniques in relation to logo design. Towards the end of the lesson introduce pupils to research techniques.	Thinking (3e) Observing (3e) Using books and magazines (3e) Ergonomics (3e) Questionnaire (3e)	(1) Research books and magazines. (2) Construct questionnaire	Examples of various research techniques. Chalkboard

	2	A complete logo. Work on research for packaging. Construct a questionnaire to find out the opinions of members of the public. Obj – questionnaire construction; continue with research for packaging.	Thinking (3e) Observing (3e) Using books and magazines (3e) Ergonomics (3c)		Examples of various research techniques Chalkboard
	3	Continue with research for packaging Obj – completed questionnaire	Thinking (3e) Observing (3e) Using books and magazines (3e) Ergonomics (3c)		Examples of various research techniques Chalkboard
Week 6	1	(1) In preparation for presenting Design ideas of packaging etc. Introduce the pupils to nets/developing Remind pupils about one/two perspective	2 point perspective 1.5 2-dimensional representation (p.5) one shading point, colouring and other tech (p14)	Produce examples of perspective Drawing freehand	Drawings on chalkboard Worksheets
	2	© Shading using three tones (1) continue with perspective Drawing (pictorial) Obj – complete two examples during the lesson	2 point perspective (P15) 2-dimensional representation (P15) Use of shading colouring and other techniques to emphasise (P14)		Drawings on chalkboard Worksheets
	3	Continue with perspective drawing. Also remind the pupils how to dimension a drawing according to BSI Obj – complete example	Same as the above Also, understanding key drawing conventions (f)		Drawings on Chalkboard Worksheets

VIGNETTE

Mnemonics

Subject leader: Frances Holloway

Year 7 French – The Alphabet: from rhythm and blues to links and laughter

Purpose

- To experiment with a set of visual mnemonics materials in order to facilitate the teaching of the French alphabet to a Year 7 class
- To compare the effectiveness of this method with my former approach which uses rhythm and a chart showing approximate pronunciation of the sound each letter makes.

The model

As a model of learning, mnemonics assists students to master large amounts of information to gain conscious control of their learning processes …

(Joyce *et al.*, 1997: 74)

Phases of the model

This is an abridged version of the phases of the model. For the fuller version refer to Joyce *et al.* (1997: 80–2).

1   Attending to the material: focus on what needs to be remembered
2   Developing connections: use memory techniques
3   Expanding sensory images: associate with more than one sense/ generate humorous associations and exaggerations
4   Practising recall.

The process: model-in-action

- In French, explain that there is a difference between the two versions of the alphabet
- Blu-tack the 26 visuals to the board, grouped as in the US GI chant that I normally use to give rhythm to the topic
- Present the sounds, drill them using the chant, gradually increasing in speed and volume
- Practise setting one half of the room chanting against the other and then marching round the room
- Follow up, the next day, by seeing how much of the alphabet they had learned in just one session and compare this with my previous experience.

Materials
Twenty-six A4 coloured visuals which give the following prompts:

a = someone at the dentist – say 'aah'

b = seaside (bay)

c = someone shouting (say)

d = sun and moon (day)

e = someone hesitating (err)

f = weightlifter making an effort (eff)

g = bird behind bars – jail (jay)

h = cigarette (ash)

i = someone taking it easy (ee)

j = horse – a gee gee (gee)

k = a car (ka)

l = bells (ell)

m= Seth from Emmerdale (emm)

n = envelopes (enn)

o = someone looking surprised (oh!)

p = wad of money (pay)

q = people queuing (kew)

r = hot air balloon (air)

s = broken handcuffs – escape (ess)

t = a table (tay)

u = pointing finger (you)

v = a loo – you need one to be vacant (vay)

w= two loos (double vay)

x = two mice (eeks)

y = bird of prey/egret (eegrec)

z = zzz in bed (zed)

Next steps
The pupils were very interested in the visuals and focused intently on them. They tried to puzzle out the sound from the picture clue before I gave it to them and reacted particularly well to the humorous aspects, especially v and w! They referred constantly to the visuals during the lesson, particularly, as I would have expected, for the letters that sound very different in French.

Impact of the process on pupils' learning
In the next lesson on the following day, we tried together to recite the alphabet in French with no prompts. It had been learned well, with hesitancy over letters whose sounds are confusing: the virtual inversion, for example, of g and j between the two languages. Interestingly, letters which usually give most problems (e, v, w and y) did not cause difficulty this time. Also, the letter r usually takes a long time to learn as 'air' in French, but caused no problems at all with its new hot air balloon prompt.

Apart from the French alphabet, they were also learning to use memory prompts to store and recall information.

Value of the process
The speed with which this group learned the alphabet in French was impressive. This is always a popular topic, but I felt that the new visual mnemonics gave a further dimension of enjoyment.

Implications for the teacher
I presented the visuals as described above. I was concerned that there would be confusion over whether the letters stood for the

French word for the picture – would they think, for example, that the French word for seaside begins with a 'b', since I had used a seaside picture to trigger the sound 'bay'. I was apprehensive because, often, when pupils first meet the alphabet, they get muddled about 'a is for apple' turning out to be 'p comme pomme' in French. However, they had no difficulty with the explanation (in French) that these stood for the sound of the letter only. I drilled the sounds carefully, highlighting the link between the sound and the picture. Then I eased into the blocks and rhythms of the chant and encouraged participation and competition between different groups. As pupils were marching about, chanting independently, still with the visual mnemonics on the board for support, I monitored their pronunciation for accuracy.

Impact of the process on the teacher

I had expected the visual mnemonics would be a strong tool to use in this context and this proved to be the case. I learned about the ease and fluency with which students acquired mastery of the more complex sounds in comparison with my previous method. Significantly, the more apparently complicated the link between the mnemonic and the sound, the more easily the link was retained and recalled. Humour is a strong motivator in retaining and recalling the link. Many students could remember most of the visuals – certainly more than half the set of 26 – the next day with no further exposure to them. They made the connections to the sounds easily.

What next?

As the next stage in using these materials, I shall have them laminated and use them as a frieze in my classroom so that they are a permanent reference point. I shall also explain them to other classes who have already been taught the alphabet and dispose of the old 'phonetic' chart. My reason for this is that since the students know that the visuals are prompts to help them recall the correct information rather than an accurate pronunciation guide, they should be able to produce more authentic pronunciation. Those who use the 'old' chart, which cannot be wholly accurate because it is not written in the true phonetic alphabet, rely too much on the 'words' they see written for the sounds. Consequently, their pronunciation is often more approximate than it need be. The mnemonic system enables pupils to be prompted to recall accurate pronunciation, which they have stored, rather than read an approximate pronunciation and not necessarily bother to recall anything. I shall need to create a German companion set!

LEARNING FROM REFLECTING ON THE MODEL-IN-ACTION: AN OBSERVER'S VIEW

This vignette provides supporting evidence for the benefits of using visual and auditory methods in achieving subject-specific learning objectives. Learners were acquiring and recalling pronunciations in an environment characterized by certain advantageous conditions: the teacher used a rigorous and insightful approach in her design of visual materials; a non-threatening learning ethos was reflected in the light-heartedness and enjoyment experienced by learners and the teacher. In this setting, the mnemonics approach was instrumental in accelerating learning gains.

The teacher is an encourager and advocate of the mnemonic process but the learners are responsible for their learning. Using memory aids in French provides the learners with an opportunity to value their application in other subject areas.

In this case, practitioner reflection on action results in knowledge creation about the effectiveness of the model in comparison with her previous approach. The reflective process led the teacher to clarify her thinking on the application and development of the mnemonics process.

Storing and recalling information effectively in the context of a predominantly content-based, assessment-led National Curriculum has demonstrable attractions for learners and teachers. Mnemonics could provide one means to that end.

ENSURING EFFECTIVE TEACHER KNOWLEDGE AND SKILLS ARE APPLIED

Teachers have and continuously develop their practical knowledge of teaching and apply skills to work with students and their subject. The subject leader's role is to ensure that this knowledge and skill is applied to create effective teaching in the subject area. It goes without saying that this is a continuous process.

Part of the leadership role is ensuring that continuous staff development may take place. This means making access available to subject teachers' materials such as:

*   Research into the best practice
*   Writing about best practice, especially by practitioners
*   The Ofsted Handbook for Inspection
*   Subject association materials.

Figure 2.6 outlines Ofsted 'Criteria for Effective Learning' (Ofsted, 1994). Although this has been superseded by later handbooks this version gives a better guide to some of the things that are important in learning.

Creemers (1994) in a review of published research identifies the kinds of classroom level variables that have been found to have a positive effect on learning. He classifies these as having strong, moderate or plausible supportive evidence. Creemers' work suggests that there are things that the department can do to maximise learning through the curriculum organisation (moderate evidence), including:

*   Feedback
*   Immediate exercise
*   Ordering goals

Figure 2.5 Worksheet review

Worksheet review
Neil Gluckman Smith
Brays Grove School

As part of an action research project, Neil reviewed the use of worksheets through collecting information from students and staff.
   He found that students **could** receive many worksheets across different subject areas in any one week in school. In an average week Year 10 students received more worksheets than those in Year 8. These worksheets included a wide variety of styles and formats.

He was able to conclude that effective teachers:

- *use a variety of worksheet styles that ask students to do different things*
- *use a variety of styles that develop different learning skills*
- *use worksheets to develop independent learning*
- *think carefully about what types of tasks and questions to set students for worksheet learning*
- *plan for progression and ensure that worksheets include extension tasks*
- *review commercially published materials to see if they meet the criteria of well designed/produced worksheets.*

- Prior knowledge
- Clear goal setting
- Emphasis on basic skills
- High expectations.

   Learning can also be maximised through grouping procedures (strong evidence) and through developing certain teaching behaviours (strong evidence), including:

- Evaluation
- Questioning
- Advance organisers
- Homework, and
- Management of an orderly atmosphere.

   Practitioners would not perhaps argue too much with this empirical evidence, although there may be much room for critical analysis. Creemers persistently uses the term instruction, and it is not clear whether he takes into account alternative teaching and learning styles. There can be many dangers of using data from across different educational systems. Furthermore we are not always sure how 'effective' is defined or measured in his study.

Figure 2.6 Criteria for effective learning

Progress made

- in knowledge
- in understanding
- in skills
- in skills of reading, writing, speaking and listening
- in skills of number
- in skills of information technology.

Learning skills

- Observation
- Information seeking
- Looking for patterns
- Looking for deeper understanding
- Communicating information and ideas in various ways including speaking, writing and graphically
- Posing questions
- Solving problems
- Applying what has been learned to unfamiliar situations
- Evaluating work that has been done.

Attitudes to learning

- Motivation
- Interest
- Ability to concentrate
- Co-operation
- Working productively.

Fortunately, there is some, although not complete correlation with Ofsted criteria for effective teaching (see Figure 2.7).

These criteria are the best-detailed exposition of what Ofsted inspectors are looking for. As such they might be usefully turned into an observation checklist for use in a subject area.

SUBJECT KNOWLEDGE: KEEPING UP TO DATE

A teacher's lack of subject knowledge may not be a common occurrence but it may be a problem to a Head of Department. This may be particularly so where:

- Staff are teaching a subject for which they are not trained
- The curriculum has changed
- The subject knowledge base has changed.

Figure 2.7 Effective teaching

- Teachers have clear objectives for their lessons
- Pupils are aware of these objectives
- Teachers have a secure command of the subject
- Lessons have suitable content
- Activities are well chosen to promote that content
- Teaching methods:
    - engage all pupils
    - motivate all pupils
    - challenge all pupils
    - enable all pupils to progress at a suitable pace and to be aware of their achievements.

Source: Adapted from Ofsted, 1994.

The subject leader might consider the following tasks:

- How would you identify a lack of subject knowledge in your department?
- How could you correct a lack of subject knowledge in your department?
- What resources are available to update teacher subject knowledge?
- Identify the likely 'hotspots' where you may find lack of subject knowledge.
- List the ways that you would: a) identify, and b) deal with a lack of subject knowledge by a teacher in your department.

CONTINUOUS COLLABORATIVE EVALUATION FOR IMPROVEMENT

Effective teaching and learning is built through evaluating teacher knowledge and skills and pupil performance. Where this is done collaboratively this can be shown to be more effective. Yet the process is a continuous one. An example of how this works is shown in the vignette below where a department focused upon 'Using assessment to establish targets for improvement with teachers and pupils'.

VIGNETTE

Target setting in the Humanities at St John's School, Epping

Niamh Devlin

Niamh and the humanities department at St John's School, Epping decided to investigate the practice of target setting in the school with a view to identifying what practice was most effective in improving learning in the humanities.

   She investigated through collecting student and teacher views and through analysing the targets that were set. Her main findings were:

- All the students interviewed believed being set a target was a useful and valuable aid to learning.
- The majority of students questioned felt that targets often encouraged better work and behaviour and helped them to understand what aspects of their work were important.
- The most frequent type of target set by the teacher was to do with descriptions/explanations.
- Of this type of target – most set were to do with accuracy and paying more attention to detail.
- For the majority of students, the most commonly set target related to improving the quality of their answers. The second most commonly set target was to do with improving spelling.
- Targets were most commonly communicated to students in their topic assessments or in their notebooks.
- Students felt that the best place for a target to be communicated was in their notebooks or in their profile sheets.
- The vast majority of students questioned felt that verbal communication from the teacher was the worst way to communicate a target, as was being set a target in their planner.

She then produced the following suggestions entitled:

What teachers can do

- ensure orally given targets are also written down
- clarify and develop a student-friendly language for targets
- ensure that targets motivate less able students
- develop methods for monitoring targets across a topic and use this to reward students.

REFERENCES

Beresford, J. (1998) 'Matching teaching to learning', *The Curriculum Journal*, 10, 3: 321–44.

Bruner, J.S. (1960) *The Process of Education*, Cambridge, MA: Harvard University Press.

Creemers, B.P.M. (1995) *The Effective Classroom*, London: Cassell.

DfES (2001) *Schools Achieving Success*, Consultation on Education White Paper, London: DfES.

Gluckman Smith, N. (2000) 'Worksheet review', Brays Grove School. Unpublished. West Essex Action Research Report.

Hopkins, D., Harris, A., Singleton, C. and Watts, R. (2000) *Creating the Conditions for Teaching and Learning: A Handbook of Staff Development Activities*, London: David Fulton.

Joyce, B., Calhoun, E. and Hopkins, D. (1997) *Models of Learning: Tools for Teaching*, Buckingham: Open University Press.

Ofsted (1994) *Handbook for the Inspection of Schools*, London: HMSO.

Rogers, C. (1967) in Thorpe, M., Edwards, R. and Hanson, A. (eds) (1993) *Culture and Processes of Adult Learning: A Reader*, London: Routledge.

TTA (1998) *National Standards for Subject Leaders*, London: HMSO.

Tileston, D.W. (2000) *10 Best Teaching Practices*, Thousand Oaks, CA: Corwin Press.

FURTHER READING

Joyce, B., Calhoun, E. and Hopkins, D. (1997) *Models of Learning: Tools for Teaching*, Buckingham: Open University Press.

Joyce, B., Calhoun, E. and Hopkins, D. (1999) *The New Structure of School Improvement*, Buckingham: Open University Press.

2.3 Using Information and Communications Technology in Learning

Ian Terrell and Stephen Powell

INTRODUCTION

> ### OBJECTIVES
>
> By the end of this Unit you should:
>
> - Have a greater understanding of the growing importance of ICT in managing teaching and learning;
> - Understand some of the broad theoretical approaches to teaching and learning and their relationship to the use of ICT;
> - Be able to identify some of the opportunities for the use of ICT in the curriculum.

There can be no doubt that over the next few years there will be increasing use of information and communication technology in learning both within the school, the community, and the family. In the school, the department and middle level leader will be at the forefront of this work and will face the challenge of making sense for students and integrating the knowledge gained outside of the classroom with that which is being taught within.

The scene is set with increasing access for teachers through government computer schemes, ongoing training initiatives, a commitment to broadband access and with that the development of an interactive-rich curriculum online. All this with a background of increasing home use of computers by students for overt learning and learning through recreation including games. The direction set by the DfES is manifested in messages from key players such as the BBC, Channel 4, BT, Granada Learning and other educational publishers, mobile phone companies and so on and that is that we are at the start of a dramatic transformation of the use of ICT in education. Such change is potentially awesome for the head of department and will require a planned and strategic approach if they are to grasp the opportunities offered by these impending changes. The 'traditional' classroom work cannot compete with the engaging materials and activities that are increasingly available and accessible to learners. You may wish to explore the International Conference on E-learning looking at this further (at http://www.bbc.co.uk/wales/ice/stevenson-pres.shtml/).

Millwood asks,

> As business, education and wider society have rushed to embrace that most sophisticated of tools, the general purpose computer, it is necessary to pose the question how will teaching and learning be affected by new modes of communication, new tools for expression and new ways for the representation of knowledge?
>
> (Millwood, in Gamble and Easingwood, 2000: 67)

Clearly, there are and will continue to be some excellent subject specific software programmes available for departments. However, subject leaders would be wise to evaluate what is effective learning using ICT. To answer this question some understanding of what constitutes learning is required, as well as a clear view of what learning is for.

One perspective is that learning is about passing examinations, memorising information, developing skills, and learning examination techniques. This view should not be dismissed lightly as student, parents and the school may with good reason believe this is important. However, learning may also be construed as a continuous process of constructing understanding, developing the human personality – tolerance, compassion, etc. – and learning how to learn. These have been categorised by Caley (2002) and might be equally important. Joyce *et al.* (1997) particularly favour the development of these 'meta-cognitive' abilities and John West-Burnham (2002) emphasises the development of the 'whole person' within the context of society and family.

Of significant benefit also are the motivational effects that the good use of ICT can have on some students through its ability to unleash creativity and level the playing field for those students who find difficulty with the traditional approaches to learning and communication for whatever reason.

Table 2.3 is a simplified representation of theoretical approaches to learning. It could be argued that a behaviourist approach offers a model with less teacher involvement and more reliance on computer technology to enable student learning. This model is attractive in that it promises to release teacher time for other activities and provide individualised learning opportunities tailored to the student's needs allowing them to progress at their own pace. Constructivists would argue that the learning achieved is largely, and at best, second rate in that it does little for developing understanding and transferable skills required for students' growth as learners and members of society. It is, perhaps, from a social constructivist perspective that ICT has most to offer if applied with thought and planning.

Table 2.3 Broad theoretical approaches to learning
Source: DfES (2000)

Behaviourist learning	Stimulus-response
	Programmed learning
	Software packages using Question and Answer
Cognitive constructivist learning	Constructing understanding
	Questioning
	Enquiry
	Exploration
	Manipulation
	Website materials; virtual learning environments – simulations, personal reflective journals
Social constructivist learning	Group discussion – dialogue and debate
	Networking
	E-mail
	Community software

ICT OPPORTUNITIES

The subject leader should be aware of the possibilities of using information and communication technologies to enhance learning in their area of the curriculum. While having regard to the programmes of study in their discipline, reference to those for ICT itself make a useful starting point to consider the range of opportunities. Depending on the model of ICT delivery and assessment in the school, students may also use their ICT work across the curriculum to evidence achievement in ICT itself as well as in the subject concerned. Use of these technologies is not done in isolation, there is always a context, and the subject leader can arrange for this to be drawn from their own schemes of work.

The National Curriculum (DfES, 2000) identifies four strands in the requirements for ICT:

- Finding things out
- Developing ideas and making things happen
- Exchanging and sharing ideas
- Reviewing, modifying and evaluating work as it happens.

In mapping these strands into a scheme of work, the subject leader should be cogniscent of the range of technologies that students may use. While ICT is predominantly seen as the use of computers, software and associated peripheral hardware, students today will be familiar with a wider range of devices for capturing, communicating and sharing information.

In relation to the use of ICT in education, we might ask how the learning relates to these purposes and processes outlined in Table 2.4.

Table 2.4 Generic suggestions for the incorporation of ICT into a subject's schemes of work

Finding things out	Use of CD-ROMs, DVDs and Internet as resources; Use of digital cameras, video, audio and other input devices such as sensors to capture information for later analysis and presentation.
Developing ideas and making things happen	Use of software for drafting ideas, tailoring them for specific audiences; Use of software for collaborative tasks such as shared writing; Editing text, audio, images and video to meet the needs of different audiences and different contexts.
Exchanging and sharing ideas	Presenting work for different audiences; Use of specialist hardware such as whiteboards and data projectors; Use of e-mail for exchanging ideas and collaboration at a distance; Use of community learning software; Producing final copies of work in printed form, on CD-ROM or the web.
Reviewing, modifying and evaluating work as it happens	Evaluating the veracity of information, evaluating authenticity of sources, comparing data and information from one source with that from another; Using templates and online databases for individual and group evaluations; Comparing the use of different hardware and/or software for a similar task.

ACCESSING CONTENT OR UNDERSTANDING THE PROCESS OF LEARNING

There is no doubt that information is out there on the Internet. A brief play with the Google search engine revealed in 0.21 seconds 432,000 web pages concerned with the author T.S. Eliot. It took a stunning 0.07 seconds to find 967,000 web page references to Browning the poet; 0.04 seconds to find 127,000 references to landforms. Information about art, architecture and music is also freely available on the Internet, in fact the whole range of human endeavour and interest is represented somewhere on the Internet. Clearly not all this material is relevant to the Year 7 curriculum and neither is all of this information valid or reliable. Rather than having too little informa-tion one problem is the sheer amount now available – all users of the Internet suffer at one time or another with information overload.

But it is not the vast amount of content or information that offers most in terms of enhancing learning and teaching in schools. It is the process of learning that enables deeper and profound learning through the use of ICT as a tool for learning, which is important, through:

- sharing ideas – presenting findings and ideas
- engaging with fellow students and teachers in online conversations – collaborative learning over distance and time
- critically evaluating resources
- synthesising different sources of information
- manipulating and interrogating data sets – analysis
- locating real time information about events – bringing the real world into the classroom.

The integration of ICT into higher level programmes of study and schemes of work is essential if ICT is to be embedded in the practice of teaching and learning. Case study evidence suggests that even with this embedded and integrated approach, the extra commitment that is still required in most schools to access ICT means that its use is often the first thing to give when the everyday pressures on teachers mount – the sharp edges of innovation are blunted and we are left with the lumpen and conservative core!

IDENTIFYING OPPORTUNITIES FOR THE USE OF ICT: A CASE STUDY

How to integrate ICT? The following process was used by the humanities department (geography, history, and religious education) in one comprehensive school to identify and integrate ICT opportunities. The aim was to identify a coherent set of opportunities for learners to use ICT across the faculty from Years 7 to 13.

The process was inclusive of the whole faculty and was given priority in time allocated for training and development. The initial meeting devised the programme explained below and asserted the expectation that everyone had a responsibility to contribute to the collective aim of implementing a rolling plan to further develop the use of ICT across the department. The stages included:

1 Articulation of school's pedagogical approach and how this should be applied to the use of ICT within the humanities department. This included: focus on group work; emphasis on development of learning skills; encouraging pupils' self-direction as learners – the ability to plan and action their own enquiries; opportunity to access as wide a range of differentiated learning opportunities as possible.

2 An enquiry phase to identify what other departments within the school and humanities departments from other schools are doing.

3 Review current provision – an audit of the use and effectiveness of ICT throughout the department.

4 Seminars to share findings from activities 2 and 3 and link them to activity 1.

5 A mapping exercise to identify ICT opportunities within schemes of work for department courses across subjects and Years taught.

6 Rolling programme of activity development with teachers working in pairs (mixture of subject specialists) to develop lessons.

7 Cascade model of implementation with identified opportunities for paired teaching to enable spread of expertise and support with lessons, activities developed.

8   Internal review process of effectiveness of lessons led by team developing particular lessons/activities.

9   Whole college annual review with teachers from other faculties assessing learning and teaching including the use of ICT.

USING MULTIMEDIA – DIGITAL VIDEO AND SLIDE SHOWS: A CASE STUDY

Presenting and communicating ideas, and indeed in doing so analysing and exploring them, is key to the learning process.

Why not turn learners into reporters, say,

- Investigating and producing a video report
- Creating a slide show using PowerPoint or QuickTime
- Producing a radio 'analysis' programme?

One example of using creative media is the BETT 2002 Creative Media Project at Colbayns School, Essex found at http://improbability.ultralab.net/bett-2002.

The following is an extract taken from the website that explains the project:

> Four students from Colbayns High School, Clacton, Essex pioneered the way in Internet broadcasting at the BETT show (British Education and Training Technology) at Olympia, London. Students broadcast live video footage produced daily by visiting schools and art groups. The eight-hour daily broadcast entertained visitors at the first-floor stand and also in the food court downstairs with work created hourly by children filming and editing at the show and live cameras showing the visiting school and community groups at work. The software used for the broadcasting, 'LiveChannel', is newly developed in Israel by ChannelStorm (http://www.channelstorm.com/) and is tipped to revolutionise and democratise the way students broadcast moving video image. Ultralab (http://www.ultralab.net/), the leading learning technology research centre, based at APU in Chelmsford, responsible for organising the broadcasting event for the show, is extremely proud of the achievements of the Colbayns pupils as was Phil Langshaw, Head of Creative Arts & Media at Colbayns school. After a short training session at Ultralab, no more than one hour, the four pupils were technically competent broadcasters and having started, they can confront all the issues facing professional broadcasters – a challenge they savoured. This software has much potential, including the opportunity for schools to quickly and easily set up their own broadcasting TV stations using the Internet to reach a worldwide audience. Richard Millwood, reader and Apple Distinguished Educator at Ultralab, said 'The main purpose will be to act as a focus for TV and radio broadcasting on the net which requires a different, quick thinking, decision making, "on-the-fly" mentality compared to the more considered composition with iMovie. Also it will provide a series of deadlines for broadcasting events which we intend will stimulate creativity for iMovie compositions, not to say the ability to cut between two live cameras, an audio input and a titling overlay to add life to the whole shebang!'

SOURCES OF INFORMATION INCLUDING LESSON PLANS AND ACTIVITIES ABOUT THE USES OF ICT

Further sources of free information including content, activities and opportunities to talk to colleagues concerning the use of ICT in learning can be obtained at a number of websites (see Table 2.5).

COLLABORATIVE DISCUSSION

The Head of Department thinking through the ICT and learning strategy might consider how learning could be based upon collaborative discussion. That is learners may engage in discussion with each other or with selected adults.

Collaborative discussion using ICT makes possible a number of learning strategies. For example, learners might be supported in discussing their work with artists, museum curators, or parents with specialist expertise such as law, health or business. Alternatively, eyewitnesses might be carefully questioned on topics such as changing geography, recent historical events or local issues such as the building of a new bypass.

Table 2.5 Sources of information: ICT in learning

TeacherNet	www.teachernet.gov.uk	Site with further links (not all ICT)
Teachers Evaluating Educational Multimedia	http://www.teem.org.uk/	Practising teachers' evaluations of multimedia, CD-ROMS and websites
BBC	www.bbc.co.uk/learning	Interactive resources, links to educational programmes, and many more resources
Learn.co.uk	www.learn.co.uk	Site provided by the *Guardian* offers online lessons and other materials (not all ICT)
Interactive Education	http://www.interactive education.ac.uk/	Research project website; you may want to contact the people involved and search for further information
Think.com	www.think.com	Free online community software for schools
The Teacher's library	www.teacherslibrary. org.uk	A teacher's library of resources
BETT 2002 Creative Media Project at Colbayns School. EssexSchoolzone	http://improbability. ultralab.net/bett-2002	An example of using creative multimedia
BECTA	http://www.becta.org.uk/ teachers/index.cfm	DfES funded agency responsible for use and development of ICT in education to raise standards, and improve skills

Communication can be through using e-mail, however, there is also software available to enable both synchronous and asynchronous discussion. Some schools have used Think.com from ORACLE to establish communities of learners (see www.think.com). Others have used Blackboard (http://products.blackboard.com/), First Class or other products.

DEVELOPING ICT WITH THE DEPARTMENT

The first task of the subject leader is to find ways of ensuring access to ICT equipment. In using that term we might include everything from computers (laptops and desktops) to digital cameras, and video. We might also include other uses of new technology such as the mobile phone and so on.

Access for teachers has been shown to be a major step forward, allowing the development of skills in using ICT. A second step is creating opportunities for students to access equipment, whether this is a school ICT room or department based. Many, including IDG (see www.apple.com.uk) have promoted the use of wireless laptops based on a mobile trolley as being a flexible option.

Yet, access is not the only or even the main problem. How to develop learning using new technologies is the major and central problem. The development of ICT in learning is an excellent focus for an action enquiry programme for the department.

BIBLIOGRAPHY

Caley, G. (2002) 'Fostering effective work-related learning', Chartered Institute of Personnel and Development/Education and Science Research Council (CIPD/ESRC) Seminar, February 2002, Edinburgh.

DfES (2000) *National Curriculum for ICT*, accessed at http://www.nc.uk.net/servlets/Subjects? Subject=ICT on 14 January 2003.

DfES (2002) *The National Curriculum*, London: HMSO.

Gamble, N. and Easingwood, N. (2000) *ICT and Literacy*, London: Continuum.

Joyce, B., Calhoun, E. and Hopkins, D. (1997) *Models of Learning: Tools for Teaching*, Buckingham: Open University Press.

West-Burnham, J. (2002) *Education, Leadership and the Community*, available at http://www.cybertext. net.au/tct2002/keynote/west-burnham.htm

FURTHER READING

Gamble, N. and Easingwood, N. (2000) *ICT and Literacy*, London: Continuum.

WEBSITES

Apple at www.apple.com.uk

Blackboard at http://products.blackboard.com/

ChannelStorm at http://www.channelstorm.com/

Creative media project at http://improbability.ultralab.net/bett-2002

DfES National Curriculum for ICT at http://www.nc.uk.net/servlets/Subjects?Subject=ICT

International Conference on E-learning at http://www.bbc.co.uk/wales/ice/stevenson-pres.shtml/

Think.com at www.think.com

Ultralab at http://www.ultralab.net/

Leading and Managing Staff

3.1 Leading, Managing and Developing People: The Learning Organisation from Learning Departments

Ian Terrell and Kathryn Terrell

INTRODUCTION

> ## OBJECTIVES
>
> By the end of this Unit you should:
>
> - Develop collaborative monitoring and evaluation for improvement;
> - Build a learning department through collaborative critical evaluation;
> - Develop the skills of staff;
> - Engage in performance management.

The last 20 years has seen much writing concerning leadership and the management of school improvement. In 1984, Hargreaves published his *Improving Secondary Schools* report for the Inner London Education Auhtority (ILEA). In 1989, the DES, as then, published its guidance on 'School Development Planning'. Central to this work since the 1990s has been the notion of 'the learning organisation' following the work of writers such as Senge (1993), Joyce *et al.* (1997, 1999); Hopkins *et al.* (1994, 2001); Hadfield *et al.* (2002).

More recently the notion of 'distributed leadership' (Hadfield *et al.*, 2002) or 'leadership from the middle' (Leask and Terrell, 1997) has emphasised the role of the subject leader and the department in contributing to the whole school culture of improvement. Unit 3.1 looks at the building blocks for creating a learning organisation from learning departments.

Day (2000) has found agreement amongst Headteachers that successful leadership depends on skills and being:

- Values-led
- People-centred
- Achievement-orientated
- Inwards- and outwards-looking.

Collarbone (2002) has outlined the ingredients of leadership:

- Vision
- Personal values
- Trust
- Open communication
- Empowerment and self-determination
- Teamwork and involvement
- Transformational style.

These characteristics might be used as tools for self-assessment and analysing your own personal performance as leader of a subject.

The DfES standards for subject leaders include statements concerned with creating effective working relationships, developing the skills and performance of people, and leading the subject team (DfES, 2001).

Figure 3.1 DfES standards for subject leaders

- Help achieve constructive relationships with pupils.
- Establish clear expectations and constructive working relationships among staff, including through team-working and mutual support; devolving responsibilities and delegating tasks; appropriate evaluating of practice; and developing an acceptance of accountability.
- Appraise staff as required by the school policy on performance management and use the process to develop the personal and professional effectiveness of the teacher.
- Lead professional development through example and support, and co-ordinate the provision of high quality professional development by methods such as coaching, drawing on other sources of expertise as necessary, for example higher education, LEAs and subject associations.
- Ensure that trainee and Newly Qualified Teachers are appropriately trained, monitored, supported and assessed in relation to standards for the award of Qualified Teacher Status, the career entry profiles and standards for induction.

Source: DfES, 2001

CREATING LEARNING DEPARTMENTS

The task of the middle manager then is to establish the culture of continuous improvement based upon the notion of a learning organisation. Some of the characteristics of a learning department might be:

- Shared values and beliefs
- A focus on learning and learners
- Moral purpose
- Sharing
- Collaboration
- Co-operation
- Enquiry
- Reflection
- Evaluation
- Criticality
- Involvement
- Engagement in the department
- Leadership from different people on different tasks
- Good interpersonal relationships
- Positive humour
- Vision
- A sense of direction
- A sense of achievement
- Having clear departmental policies and procedures (e.g. on the motivation and management of pupil behaviour, or marking and assessment)
- Having policies that are developed from school policies and the school improvement plan.

These ideas are not new. The work of Likert (1967), McGregor (1960) and others outlined many of these characteristics under the title of 'effective teamwork' over 40 years ago. So this is part of a long tradition of management and educational writing. Subject leaders may wish to reflect upon the work of these authors in pursuit of better practice through self-reflection.

The culture of the learning department is dominated by a relaxed atmosphere. There is a high level of discussion about learning and learners. The department has a common aim and a focus to their improvement strategies. New ideas are listened to positively and discussed. Decisions are made by consensus building although there may have to be a degree of compromise and trialling of new ideas. Yet constructive analytical criticism is valued. The team constantly reviews their progress and strives for improvement.

If these ideas have been around for so long how is it that we may need to strive for learning departments? Why is it often difficult to achieve? The subject leader may wish to reflect on this. There are more analytical tools to be found in the literature and research on organisations, teams and leadership that may help. Handy, for example, suggests the idea of stages of team development, called 'Forming', 'Norming', 'Storming' and 'Performing' (Handy, 1986). Perhaps the team is locked in one of these stages. Knowing where the team is helps to move them on.

Belbin's work (Belbin, 1994) suggests that there is a need for a balance of team roles and uses an inventory to assess the balance between:

- Implementers
- Co-ordinators
- Shapers
- Innovators
- Resource investigators
- Monitor evaluators
- Team workers
- Completer finishers.

However useful the analysis is it is difficult to apply Belbin's work with a team where, for example, everyone is naturally an 'innovator' and nobody is a 'completer finisher'. Nevertheless, the model is useful in analysing what roles the team needs and what might need to be worked at to improve team performance.

Perhaps not discussed enough in relation to middle management is the considerable amount of work undertaken by teachers in the department in their own classroom. Thus, the team of teachers spends the vast majority of their time working as individuals in their own classrooms (perhaps 21 hours per week). Whereas, working as a member of the team is either in small amounts of directed time, such as in team meetings, or is implicit and indirect (see Figure 3.2). The key for middle managers is to help staff to manage both of these roles effectively to improve pupil achievement and to raise standards.

Leask and Terrell (1997), borrowing the work of Fleishman and Harris (1972), Blake and Mouton (1985), Hersey and Blanchard (1982) and Thomas (1976), describe the tensions of leadership. They group two basic tensions: on the one hand concern for task, focusing on challenging, directing and assertive leadership behaviour, and on the other hand 'concern for people through supporting and co-operative behaviour' (Leask and Terrell, 1997: 53). Again this model may be a useful tool for subject leaders to analyse team characteristics.

In a similar model, Cockman *et al.* (1992) remind us that in our concern for action plans and tasks to be achieved we often forget about the process issues. These include our interpersonal relationships, mutual respect, warmth, and so on. Brundrett (1999)

Figure 3.2 Teachers as individuals and as part of a team

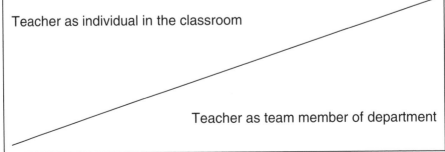

Teacher as individual in the classroom

Teacher as team member of department

reviewed work by Morris and Murgatroyd (1986) and 'noted that management training should be based on communication skills, social skills, group processes and human relations' (Brundrett, 1999: 7).

Further they call for training for Headship to be based upon:

- Self insight and awareness on the part of the individual
- Team building and relationships
- Counselling
- Family therapy techniques

Interpersonal relationships are the key factor in leadership and management at all levels, but especially at middle management. This area of work takes most time and energy. Facilitating individuals or groups of staff requires skill and professionalism, not least because so much takes place in time-pressured scenarios such as between lessons, at breaks or when pupils are around. Issues which you may need to work on with the team include performance and under-performance, disaffection, over-enthusiasm, inexperience, stress, overwork and so on.

REFERENCES

Belbin, M. (1994) *Team Roles at Work*, San Diego, CA: Pfeiffer.

Blake, R.R. and Mouton, J.S. (1985) *The Managerial Grid*, Houston, TX: Gulf Publishing Co.

Brundrett, M. (1999) *Principles of School Leadership*, Dereham: Peter Francis Publishers.

Collarbone, P. (2002) *Reflections on Headship*, available at http://www.ncsl.org.uk/index.cfm?pageid=ev_auth_collarbone

Cockman, P., Evans, B. and Reynolds, P. (1992) *Client Centred Consultancy*, Maidenhead: McGraw-Hill.

Day, C. (2000) *Developing Teachers*, London: Falmer Press.

DfES (2001) *Professional Standards for Subject Leaders*, London: HMSO.

Fleishman, E.A. and Harris, E.F. (1972) 'Patterns of leadership behaviour related to employee behaviour', *Personnel Psychology*, 15: 43–56.

Hadfield, M., Chapman, C., Curryer, I. and Barrett, P. (2002) *Building Capacity: Developing Your School*, Nottingham: NCSL.

Handy, C. (1986) *Understanding Organisations*, London: Penguin.

Hargreaves, D. (1984) *Improving Secondary Schools*, London: Inner London Education Authority.

Hersey, P. and Blanchard, K. (1982) *Management of Organsational Behaviour*, Englewood Cliffs, NJ: Prentice Hall.

Hopkins, D. (2001) *School Improvement for Real*, London: RoutledgeFalmer.

Hopkins, D., Ainscow, M. and West, M. (1994) *School Improvement in an Era of Change*, London: Cassell.

Joyce, B., Calhoun, E., and Hopkins, D. (1997) *Models of Learning: Tools for Teaching*, Buckingham: Open University Press.

Joyce, B., Calhoun, E., and Hopkins, D. (1999) *The New Structure of School Improvement*, Buckingham: Open University Press.

Leask, M. and Terrell, I. (1997) *Development Planning and School Improvement for Middle Managers*, London: Kogan Page.

Likert, R. (1967) *The Human Organisation*, New York: McGraw-Hill.

McGregor, D. (1960) *The Human Side of Enterprise*, New York: McGraw-Hill

Morris, G. and Murgatroyd, S. (1986) 'Management for diverse futures: the task of school management in an uncertain future', *School Organisation*, 6, 2: 46–63.

Thomas, K.W. (1976) 'Conflict and conflict management', in M. Dunnette (ed.) *Handbook of Industrial Management Psychology*, Skokie, IL: Rand McNally.

Senge, P.M. (1993) *The Fifth Discipline: The Art and Practice of the Learning Organisation*, London: Century Business.

FURTHER READING

Bush, T. and Middlewood, D. (eds) (1997) *Managing People in Education*, London: Paul Chapman Publishing.

Williams, J. (2002) *Professional Leadership in Schools: Effective Middle Management and Subject Leadership*, London: Kogan Page.

3.2 Putting the 'Each' Back into Teaching

Ian Terrell and Kathryn Terrell

INTRODUCTION

OBJECTIVES

By the end of this Unit you should:

- Understand the importance of operating a 'no blame' culture in departments;
- Realise the importance of giving people the opportunity to lead;
- Be aware of the importance of praising colleagues for their work;
- Understand the key role of the subject leader or middle manager in creating the vision for a department.

On the way to becoming school leaders, we would argue, some of us have lost sight of the people we lead and manage, particularly the teachers. We have focused on league tables, benchmarking, target setting, inspection, monitoring and so on. Have we become too mesmerised by management speak to notice the people that we work with and their needs? Is it the 'performance indicator', or 'performance management' or the person who is performing that is important? We have placed the profession under the dictates of 'school reform'. We 'monitor' and 'observe' those serving time.

Day has suggested that,

> Much of the existing literature on what makes successful leadership is anecdotal, borrowed from the world of business or based upon self reports or impenetrable theory.

(Day, 2000: 5)

Hence, perhaps, a cause of the current teacher shortage. We have 50 per cent of teachers leaving the profession within 10 years. Perhaps, too, we have lost the sense of conviction that we teachers were doing children some good. Have we not created our own crises? Let us move to a more humane form of leadership and management that looks after the individual and nurtures the group.

Teachers are a very special and selected breed. They choose to spend their working days with young people, some of whom are known, even by their parents, to be difficult at times but, often unknowingly, are able to reward their teachers with success and delight. Leaders should not block the equation that teachers gain motivation, enjoyment and pleasure from working with young people who reward them through gaining success in learning defined in their own terms.

Teachers are required to have the very best academic results at A level or equivalent, including currently English and Maths GCSE at GCSE level C or above. They more often than not have a degree and a teaching qualification that meets the requirements of the DfEE standards. Since September 1999, they have a further year of 'induction' and assessment to continue in the profession. In addition, they have to undertake further professional development on at least five days of the year in addition to attending in-service training on new initiatives such as Curriculum 2000.

If they get through all of that, they have a demanding day interacting with young people, other staff, parents and others, often (and particularly in the primary sector) with very little 'non-contact' time. A number of teachers also choose to undertake part time study, for a master's degree, for example. This takes place in their own time, at evenings and weekends and has to be fitted around the demands of lesson planning, teaching and marking.

Let us not patronise these teachers. They are able, intellectually and practically. They are frequently selected as high achievers and work at a high intellectual level. They are motivated to become teachers and the best have a sense of purpose and vocation. So then, how should we lead and manage such teachers in a new age?

LESSONS FROM GEESE

We first came across the notion of Lessons from Geese on the Internet site http://henderson.ces.state.nc.us/newsarticles/4-H/99-09-07ho.shtml. There is also an excellent Understanding British Industry video using the same theme. The idea is so powerful that we felt the need to include it here.

Lessons from Geese

Fact 1

As each goose flaps its wings, it creates an uplift for the birds that follow. By flying in a 'V' formation, the whole flock adds 71% greater flying range than if each bird were flying alone.

Lesson: People who share a common direction and sense of community can get where they are going quicker and easier on the thrust of another.

Fact 2

When a goose falls out of formation, it suddenly feels the drag and resistance of flying alone. It quickly moves back into formation to take advantage of the lifting power of the bird immediately in front of it.

Lesson: If we have as much sense as a goose, we stay in formation with those headed where we want to go. We are willing to accept their help and give our help to others.

Fact 3

When the lead goose tires, it rotates back into the formation and another goose flies to the point position.

Lesson: It pays to take turns doing the hard tasks and sharing leadership. As with geese, people are interdependent on each other's skills, capabilities, and unique arrangements of gifts, talents, or resources.

Fact 4

The geese flying in formation honk to encourage those up front to keep up their speed.

Lesson: We need to make sure our honking is encouraging. In groups where there is encouragement, the production is much greater. The power of encouragement to stay by one's heart or core values and encourage the heart and core of others is the quality of honking we seek.

Fact 5

When a goose gets sick, wounded, or shot down, two geese drop out of formation and follow it down to help and protect it. They stay with it until it dies or is able to fly again. Then they launch out with another formation or catch up with the flock.

Lesson: If we have as much sense as a goose, we will stand by each other in difficult times as well as when we are strong.

(Abridged from http://henderson.ces.state.nc.us/
newsarticles/4-H/99-09-07ho.shtml
By: Helen Owen, Extension Agent, 4-H, 7 September 1999)

We would wish to add some of own translations of the goose theory in terms of modern school leadership.

Fact 1

It is important for a leader to provide clear vision and direction. It is even more important to ensure that all members of the school community share that vision and know what is expected of them in the drive to realise it.

A good leader constantly seeks to ensure that all know what is expected of them. This is true of all leadership at all levels in the school.

Fact 2

People are not superhuman. There will be times when people perform better than at others. There is no problem in asking for clarity and additional support. We should not operate a blame culture, which makes people ashamed to seek help and advice. Good leaders provide systems of support for all members of staff through well-structured line management systems, and mentoring and buddy systems.

Fact 3

A good leader recognises the strengths and skills of all members of the department and school community and plays to those. This is vital when allocating tasks to departmental members or allocating teachers to groups. And knowing in advance when teachers are likely to need support.

Staff who do not appear to be performing well in one role of responsibility may not be suited to that particular role. We should not seek to blame, write them off immediately and seek to begin capability procedures. It may be that they can perform to a high standard in a different capacity within the school. For example, a good head of department will not necessarily make a good head of year.

It is also important to allow people the opportunity to take a lead in areas where they have the superior knowledge and skill. A Headteacher is not the fount of all knowledge. They do not know everything about everything nor should they be expected to. The person responsible for whole school assessment should be the expert in that field and lead the staff forward. The person responsible for PSHE should lead on that and so on. Poor leaders fear to relinquish the lead position.

Fact 4

Praise and encouragement, always seeking to promote the positive, helps people to feel a sense of achievement. A good leader ensures that individual progress in terms of teacher performance and welfare is regularly checked upon. There are several ways including the line management and mentoring systems mentioned earlier. Half hour, fortnightly meetings with heads of department and heads of year can help; also letting staff know when you will be available for people to drop in; following up on information received from other people; and checking out clues picked up from people's body language. Nothing is worse than allowing people to dwell on something and build it all out of proportion when it may be a misunderstanding. Check it out!

Fact 5

In the current climate we are far too keen to seek to apportion blame and to claim that it's not our fault. Knowing who to blame is not much of an insight into how to make things better. If someone is not performing it is up to the manager to find out why before taking action. Some teachers get very stressed out and it has become taboo to admit to suffering from stress. However, early intervention can prevent long term damage to the teacher and therefore helps the school. We should seek to problem solve together for the benefit of the whole school community.

Fact 6

As a leader and manager you have a key role in developing and building the common direction. This is partly building a joint vision but also a sense of community. Community spirit and being part of a common venture are key. This involves building an attachment and identity with the team efforts. Communicating regularly is vital to this. Stoll and Fink (1996) developed the notion of 'invitational leadership' involving communicating to people that they are valued, trusted and responsible.

EMPOWERMENT: SHARING LEADERSHIP

The notion of leading others to take leadership roles is an interesting concept, clearly only attained by some.

Illustration

Tim was proud that so many staff had gained experience in the school and moved on to promotion in other schools. To him this was testament to the quality of the school as a learning environment and all the staff knew that it was a testimony to him enabling them to gain experience leading projects and initiatives in the school.

Negative illustration

'Thank you for your memo suggesting and volunteering for the above project. Please be assured that the matter has been discussed at a Senior Management meeting and a project team has been formed to progress the work.'

Empowering staff to believe that they can take on leadership roles and make a difference is not easy and some Heads of Department find it hard to accept that they could play a fundamental role in raising achievement.

Empowering staff is also about creating positive opportunities for people to develop. Staff may feel balked by leaders who do not wish for their leadership territory to be invaded.

Creating opportunities is an active step. Consider the two different messages concerning dangerous cliffs. Which one do you think keeps the public safe and away from danger?

> Danger: Keep Away
> Falling Cliffs

> Walk this way for the very best safe view

COMMUNICATION, RAPPORT AND SUCCESS

Have you spoken to every member of staff you lead today, this week, this month? What did you say? How did it come across?

Illustration

Simon was an affable sort of Headteacher. His staff said that sometimes they did not really understand him. He would say hello and be friendly sometimes but other times he would be in school early in the morning busy going about his business and he would not even acknowledge that you too had turned up early.

Humans need to achieve and teachers need to achieve perhaps much more than others do.

Illustration

One manager asked every member of staff to review the successes that each person working for him had achieved. 'What were the things that led to this success?' he would enquire. Asked why he never concerned himself with the failures he replied that very little could be learned from the failures, only the success taught us much about what we needed to repeat.

BIBLIOGRAPHY

Belbin, M. (1994) *Team Roles At Work*, San Diego, CA: Pfeiffer.

Brundrett, M. (1999) *Principles of School Leadership*, Dereham: Peter Francis Publishers.

Cockman, P., Evans, B. and Reynolds, P. (1992) *Client Centred Consultancy*, Maidenhead: McGraw-Hill.

Collarbone, P. (2002) *Reflections on Headship*, available at http://www.ncsl.org.uk/index.cfm?pageid=ev_auth_collarbone.

Day, C. (2000) *Developing Teachers*, London: Falmer Press.

DfES (2001) *Professional Standards for Subject Leaders*, London: HMSO.

Hadfield, M., Chapman, C., Curryer, I. and Barrett, P. (2000) *Building Capacity. Developing Your School*, Nottingham: NCSL.

Hall, D. (1997) 'Professional development portfolios', in L. Kydd, M. Crawford and C. Riches (eds) *Professional Development and Educational Management*, Buckingham: Open University Press.

Handy, C. (1986) *Understanding Organisations*, London: Penguin.

Hopkins, D., Ainscow, M. and West, M. (1994) *School Improvement in an Era of Change*, London: Cassell.

Leask, M. and Terrell, I. (1997) *Development Planning and School Improvement for Middle Managers*, London: Kogan Page.

Open University (1981) *P533 The Curriculum in Action: Practical Classroom Evaluation*, Milton Keynes: Open University Press.

Owen, H. (1999) *Lessons from Geese*, available at http://henderson.ces.state.nc.us/newsarticles/4-H/99-09-07ho.shtml.

Senge, P. (1990) *The Fifth Discipline*, London: Century Business.

Stoll, L. and Fink, D. (1996) *Changing our Schools*, Buckingham: Open University Press.

FURTHER READING

Cockman, P., Evans, B. and Reynolds, P. (1992) *Client Centred Consultancy*, Maidenhead: McGraw-Hill.

Leask, M. and Terrell, I. (1997) *Development Planning and School Improvement for Middle Managers*, London: Kogan Page.

3.3 The Staff Development Role

Ian Terrell and Kathryn Terrell

INTRODUCTION

OBJECTIVES

By the end of this Unit you should:

- Adopt a number of roles supporting the development of staff in the subject area;
- Be aware of the main issues connected with coaching, mentoring and acting as a consultant;
- Understand the relevance of a professional development portfolio;
- Have a clear understanding of the role of practitioner research projects in developing a department.

A major role of the subject leader is in the leadership of staff development in the subject. However, it has long been understood that curriculum development, professional development and personal development are intertwined aspects of this role.

The development of thinking skills activities in History, for example, requires some changes in curriculum and teaching methods. It also involves changes in the way people see themselves as teachers. It may affect the teacher's self-perception and the way they might see themselves as a teacher, the kind of teacher they want to be. One would hope that the experience of change is one of growth and that the teacher gains confidence and motivation.

The staff development role takes place in both formal and informal environments and activities may include:

- Leading department and subject discussions
- Introducing new ideas and approaches to teaching

- Supporting staff developing effective teaching in the subject
- Mentoring staff
- Acting as a leading consultant
- Observing classrooms and discussing those observations
- Coaching staff in specific techniques
- Development planning with the department
- Establishing practitioner research and development
- Leading in-service activities
- Being involved in 'performance management'.

COACHING, MENTORING AND ACTING AS A CONSULTANT

Coaching, mentoring and acting as an internal consultant to staff are different roles. Coaching tends to be more like acting as say an athletics trainer does and being concerned with perfecting agreed techniques or skills. The coach observes and provides techniques to improve performance, frequently giving feedback on progress.

Mentoring tends to be more advisory and acting in a counselling role. It explores feeling and problems more. Negotiating agreed solutions to problems is a central part of mentoring.

Consultancy can span both coaching and mentoring (Leask and Terrell, 1997).

Whatever role you may wish to adopt, the improvement cycle is important and involves:

a. Gathering information
b. Planning a solution
c. Implementing a plan
d. Evaluating the results.

Gathering information: where are we now?

The initial stage of development is about investigation and collecting data. This might be through discussion with teachers, observing lessons or analysing pupil work. Catalytic internal consultants ask the question 'tell me what happens when …?'.

Planning a solution: what do we need to do?

Coming to a collaborative decision about who needs to do what is a problem solving activity.

Implementing a plan

Further support is needed at the implementation stage. Classroom life may, surprisingly enough, be more difficult as people try to use new techniques which they are unfamiliar with. This is known as the 'performance dip'.

Evaluating the results

Evaluating the results is but the start of a new process of development. It is a system of checking where the department has got to and what needs to be done next.

Leask and Terrell (1997) following Cockman *et al.* (1992) recommend a variety of approaches as an internal consultant including balancing being 'prescriptive' with being 'catalytic'. This involves using statements such as 'You need to' and 'You have to', as well as a more exploratory approach such as 'Have you tried …?', 'What happens if …?', 'What are your options …?'. These approaches deal with emotions with questions like, 'How does it feel when…?', as well as confronting what people say and do.

KEEPING A PROFESSIONAL DEVELOPMENT PORTFOLIO

In these days of 'Performance Management', threshold payments and an emphasis on professional development, there should be few teachers who do not keep some form of record of their professional development. Field (2002) has suggested a formal port-folio. Guidance is available from the DfES (2001) and from many LEAs who, often in collaboration with HEIs, have developed effective practice with teachers (Hall, 1997).

The portfolio helps you to connect your own development and the development of the department with the school improvement plan. As such it is worth your while creating and using one and promoting their use in your department. Field argues that this might form the basis for articulating their starting point or where they feel they are now. They can plan, record and review both their long-term and their short-term development activities.

The portfolio is a place to keep evidence of learning and development, in the form of lesson observation records, pupil assessments, and evidence of the impact of professional development activities.

Your contacts with HEIs and LEAs could explore using the portfolio to gain credit for academic award. In any case the achievements of people within the department should be celebrated formally.

ESTABLISHING A PRACTITIONER RESEARCH AND DEVELOPMENT PROJECT

The middle manager can be proactive in developing practitioner research and development projects. Support for such work can often be found in local HEIs or from an LEA support team. One example, is the West Essex Action Research (WEAR) project. Details of this are outlined below by way of illustration of what needs to be managed by the subject leader.

Figure 3.3 shows the stages and activities associated with such projects. The model includes articulating and developing the desired model of learning, collecting baseline data and evidence of improvement in learning.

The first West Essex Action Research (WEAR) project was established in 1997 to develop practitioner collaborative research and development of teaching and learning in local secondary schools. We are currently in the third 'delivery' phase of WEAR

Figure 3.3 Practitioner research and development project

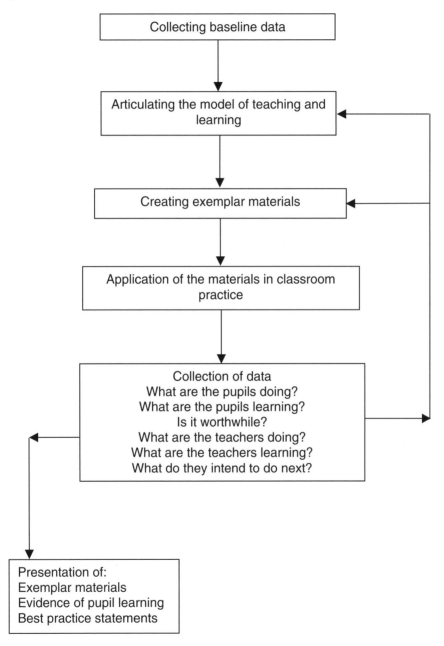

projects and we have also developed experience through other projects of a similar nature. Examples of Phase 3 WEAR projects include:

- Developing thinking skills in Year 8 Geography to raise pupil attainment
- Cognitive acceleration in science
- Co-operative group learning
- Developing effective teaching and learning strategies for the development of literacy across the curriculum
- Improving communication in KS3 History.

The evaluation of the WEAR projects at the end of the second phase established the following:

- Teachers can undertake practitioner research that has an impact on the learning of pupils, their practice and that of their colleagues in their school.
- Impact of the research projects on the teaching and learning of pupils is maximised where:
    - Teachers are working on school or department agenda
    - The focus of the project is on teaching and learning activities
    - Teachers are provided with time to undertake the research and development activities
    - Teachers are linked to departments or working groups in the school
    - There is a clear dissemination strategy within the school
    - There is a structured programme of support for the research
    - There is active support and supervision from senior managers.
- The impact of the projects to develop collaboration across institutions is strengthened where:
    - Senior staff meet to plan, implement and review the project
    - Teachers are working on a common focus across the schools.
- Impact is diminished when:
    - Teachers don't have time
    - Teachers withdraw from the programme because of a variety of reasons
    - The role of the teacher concerned is not commensurate with effecting change.

Since this was written we have gone on to consider a further collection of points about how we manage our projects and some of our conclusions are outlined below, under ten overlapping key areas.

1. Getting established

The characteristics of such projects, in our experience, include being constrained by the time and energy teachers are willing and able to put into them. Projects are undertaken by practitioners and their first priority is to teach, not to research. Effective research demands a rigorous and systematic approach on the part of the teacher researcher. Consequently, the subject leader should consider both how to motivate staff and to garner the time to undertake such important work.

Funding, to support staff, to consult with HEIs, or to pay for extra release time may be available from inside the school, from LEAs or from other external sources such as the Best Practice Teacher Research Scholarships (see http://www.canteach.gov.uk/community/research/grant/ for details).

Deciding upon the scale of research activities can also be problematic but is also crucial. We wish to be clear to participants how much time is required. The tendency we have found is to attempt higher quality and larger scale research than the time schools are able to commit allows for. Clearly more may be achieved with a 600-hour project than with a 100-hour project. Projects have to be practical, resource bounded, and efficient. We have needed to learn that these compromises mean that what we reveal is not always flawless.

2. Showing projects have had an impact upon practice

We have found that a key to effective management of projects is to collect sound evidence of improvement. This includes evidence of:

- improved pupil learning
- improved teaching practice by the teachers involved in the research
- ideas being disseminated across the school (and beyond) particularly in the form of policies and changes to practice.

Our experience shows that planning the data collection for this needs to be done at the start of the project, rather than the end. Planning to collect evidence that pupil learning has been improved is a particular challenge that has required a lot of thought. We advise teachers to:

- collect data on the performance of children before intervening in the learning process with a new approach to teaching
- collect data from comparable groups (from previous years or different classes)
- collect data on the performance of children using a different approach to teaching.

Data collected from the WEAR 2 Projects (see http://wear.ultralab.net/Index.html) showed that the research led to improvements in practice associated with the topic areas, for example in:

- Pair work in Modern Foreign Language (MFL)
- Target setting for pupils
- The design of worksheet materials
- Strategies for teaching examination skills in science
- The structuring of non-fiction reading tasks.

Greater understanding of the teaching process was also evident in such statements as:

> What we found was that we were putting them into exams without actually teaching them examination skills.

And

> I am more aware of the targets and we do actually value them. There is a whole policy now in school on target setting. It's more at the forefront now.

3.   Developing a clear philosophy and purpose

In reviewing our work to date, we have established several principles which we believe to be key factors in structuring successful research across a network of schools. These are:

- School based and focused projects
- Participant led and collaborative enquiry
- Flexible, enquiry based learning
- Implementation and development by supported school based groups
- Underpinning by analysis of the principles of learning
- Challenging discussion and reflection
- Sharing with professionals within and outside of the schools
- Distributed leadership of change and improvement
- A focus on supporting implementation
- Sticking with it over a long period
- Celebrating the success and achievements of teachers.

Where such projects are focused upon the department, we have found implementation is maximised. In addition where they are part of a whole school initiative, further success in implementation is suggested.

4.   The set-up and selection of projects process

The key to a successful Best Practice Research Project appears, from the outset, to be located in the negotiating phase between schools, individual teachers, departments and the project team and, in our case, across different schools in the consortia. This 'contracting' (Cockman et al., 1992) is important so that everyone knows what is intended, what is expected of them, how it might affect their work and what resources would be available and so on. Effective partnership is characterised by the practice of explicit contracting throughout the project process.

Contracting, in our experience, needs revisiting regularly, partly to remind all participants of what was once agreed, but also, because understanding what it means to be in a 'Best Practice Research Project' is rarely clear until you are in the middle of one. Hence, our approach has been for 'firm structure with flexibility' as we attempt to negotiate our way through projects.

At the same time as this technical detail is being explained and negotiated a second concept of 'entry' has to be worked upon (Cockman et al., 1992). New schools in particular are, and ought to be, suspicious of those bearing the gifts of school improvement. Clearly at this early stage all parties have to be convinced of the likelihood of the success of the project.

Negotiating a focus also can be more difficult than one would first imagine. We have examples where teachers begin with an important and interesting topic such as independent learning, collaborative group work or analytical skills. A first task is to explore what is meant by such terms and what the key components might be. Gaining consensus, based upon different experiences of practice, is one stage.

Another we have used to some effect is, at this point, to look at research, particularly best practice research and literature to explore what we regard as the conceptual model. We have noted that at this stage, in particular, the demand of implementation can interfere with the demand to research. So, for instance, the demand for every teacher to implement the literacy strategy of the school takes over from an investigation into what teachers do that makes them effective. We note that it is easy to lose sight of a genuine researchable question.

Selection of staff participants

Negotiating participation is not easy. One desire is to identify and collaborate with the 'shapers and movers' in schools. These are those people in school who are in a position to make things happen. A sub category or further characteristic would be those staff who have a track record of *completion*. Some schools may want to include some staff to *bring them on* in their experience. Others are selected because it may *move them on*. Experienced researchers are useful to have, although rarely has it been used as a criterion for involvement. We have found clear benefits in terms of implementing strategies where teams of staff are involved in a department or school working group, rather than individuals working alone.

In our more recent work we have developed the notion of exclusivity. Anyone can join us in our collaborative projects, but we only want to work with those committed enough to see them through to completion. This has helped us in making sure that projects are completed.

5. Developing starting point questions

We are finding that there is a clear phase at the beginning associated with developing 'starting point' questions. Schools have a variety of issues to deal with.

Suggestions like 'the effectiveness of the literacy strategy' are big issues, involving too many aspects. We ask teachers to concentrate on what effective teachers do that makes them maximise the learning of pupils. Hence, for us, good questions are:

- What are the effective ways of organising collaborative group work?
- How does a teacher develop thinking skills?
- What does a teacher do to develop analytical skills?
- How can teachers get children to work more independently?

Defining concepts

We have found that time needs to be spent in *defining key concepts* for each project in order to determine the key contributory factors. For instance, when investigating how teachers can effectively develop independent learning we may ask:

- How do we define independent learning?
- How many different types of independent learning are there?

- What does the student do when they are working independently?
- What key factors allow the student to work independently?
- What factors might hinder the student working independently?

Exploring these sort of questions has helped teachers to focus their reflection and data collection on developing their own conceptual model of teaching. Significantly, teachers report that this moves their thinking on and, therefore, the centrality of effective questioning should not be underestimated. If you know the question, you are halfway to the answer.

6. Managing it

There is a clear timeline for the project. Our own timeline includes whole group sessions, working with individuals and cross-school groups. The whole group sessions focus upon:

- Presentation of exemplar projects and invitations to participate
- Negotiation of school focused projects within collaborative consortia
- Planning projects for whole school development
- Data collection and analysis
- Planning and practising for dissemination
- Dissemination to an external audience.

7. Supporting the methodology

The subject leader will need to support the project methodology either themselves or by working with senior manager, HEI or LEA partners.

Achieving high quality research and development is not easy but is not impossible for teachers. Hopkins *et al.* (1994) take the view that teachers have the skills to undertake research into teaching and learning. Our experience supports this view. However, we have found that teachers often lack the confidence in their ability and are frequently unhappy with their perception of lack of rigour with time constrained, context bound practitioner research.

Support has consisted of using materials, such as research workbooks, to record planning and negotiations, exemplar materials of data collection tools and dissemination reports. The latter have been found most beneficial to staff for a number of reasons. These benefits include keeping staff on task and focused as well as enthusiastic and re-motivated. Workshop sessions have also facilitated problem solving and provided technical advice.

We have found that support needs to involve both senior managers inside the school and members of the project team from an HEI or LEA. This appears to be associated with something to do with credibility and external expertise but it is also about account-ability to an 'outside' audience. Not least in this process has been the end point dissemination conference, which has loomed large in the minds of teachers partici-pating in the project.

Support materials for teachers have focused upon:

- Systematic planning of a research project
- Developing a conceptual model or framework for teaching
- Developing exemplar materials
- Collecting baseline data
- Frameworks for creating dissemination materials.

8.   Using frameworks

We use a number of different planning frameworks in developing the projects. Figure 3.3 shows one such framework at the planning stage and we also use an adaptation of the TTA framework for writing brief research dissemination reports.

A further framework we have found useful is derived from the one in the Open University *Curriculum in Action* pack (Open University, 1981) which they call 'The Six Questions'. We have adapted the wording of these for collaborative groups of teachers to use, as follows:

- What are the pupils doing?
- What are the pupils learning?
- Is it worthwhile?
- What is the teacher doing?
- What is the teacher learning?
- What should the teacher do next?

We have found that teachers find it difficult to articulate what effective teachers do. Partly this appears to be because staff are unwilling to identify effective and ineffective practice in that judgmental sense, particularly when working with colleagues. However, it also involves their uncertainty in determining what is effective in the classroom and what can be generalised to all classrooms. We have tried to concentrate on creating 'Best Practice Statements'. This we conceptualise as guidance statements for colleagues attempting to teach in the same way. An example would be 'When using inductive thinking activities with young children use no more than ten sets of data'. Such data are derived from the experiences of the participants.

9.   Ensuring completion and evaluation

Much of the work of the school based project manager is concerned with ensuring completion and dissemination within the school. Two main factors have been identified as key to success and they are *finding time* and finding the balance between *pressure and support*. In the former, we have found that creating time for teachers to get together to complete specific tasks to do with the research is important, particularly in department or school groups.

Tracking progress and discussing the achievement of the timeline is important. Often renegotiating what might be achievable is required.

10. Overcoming external constraints

A last management issue relates to overcoming external constraints. These are the factors outside of the project that tend to adversely affect the successful completion of the project.

External constraints we have faced are:

- Ofsted Inspection of schools
- Promotion of key staff
- Illness of key staff
- General pressure of work on teachers
- Alternative local or national initiatives
- Pressure of work due to staff shortages.

These constraints can be overwhelming and insoluble. Our best advice is that the strategies above, and in particular careful planning and contracting at the start, mitigate the worst effects.

BIBLIOGRAPHY

Belbin, M. (1994) *Team Roles At Work*, San Diego, CA: Pfeiffer.

Brundrett, M. (1999) *Principles of School Leadership*, Dereham: Peter Francis Publishers.

Cockman, P., Evans, B. and Reynolds, P. (1992) *Client Centred Consultancy*, Maidenhead: McGraw-Hill.

DfES (2001) *Guidance on Professional Development Portfolios*, London: DfES.

Field, K. (2002) *Portfolio for Professional Development*, London: Optimus Publishing.

Frost, D., Durrant, J., Head, M. and Holden, G. (2000) *Teacher-Led School Improvement*, London: RoutledgeFalmer.

Hall, D. (1997) 'Professional development portfolios', in L. Kydd, M. Crawford and C. Riches (eds) *Professional Development and Educational Management*, Buckingham: Open University Press.

Hopkins, D., Ainscow, M. and West, M. (1994) *School Improvement in an Era of Change*, London: Cassell.

Leask, M. and Terrell, I. (1997) *Development Planning and School Improvement for Middle Managers*, London: Kogan Page.

Open University (1981) *P533 The Curriculum in Action: Practical Classroom Evaluation*, Milton Keynes: Open University Press.

FURTHER READING

Field, K. (2002) *Portfolio for Professional Development*, London: Optimus Publishing.

Frost, D., Durrant, J., Head, M. and Holden, G. (2000) *Teacher-Led School Improvement*, London: RoutledgeFalmer.

WEBSITES

http://www.belbin.info/

http://www.teamtechnology.co.uk/myers-briggs-type-indicator-home.html

http://www.ncsl.org.uk/index.cfm?pageid=managing-docs-perform

3.4 Performance Management for Middle Managers

Kathryn Terrell

OBJECTIVES

By the end of this Unit you should:

- Have developed an understanding of approaches to performance management as a subject leader;
- Be aware of the stages in the performance management cycle;
- Be more confident in carrying out classroom assessments.

It became a statutory requirement for all maintained schools in England and Wales in September 2000 to review their existing arrangements for the monitoring and appraisal of staff and to agree a new performance management policy. Every school had to have a performance management policy, agreed by the governing body, by 31 December 2000.

> We want to improve school performance by developing the effectiveness of teachers, both as individuals and teams. The evidence is that standards rise when schools and individual teachers are clear about what they expect pupils to achieve. That is why performance management is important.
>
> (DfES, 2000: 3)

Schools have always managed performance, and often effectively. However, these requirements were enforced to make the systems more formalised, to replace the, shall we say, ineffective, poorly thought of and failing teacher appraisal schemes of the 1980s and 1990s and to promote further the notion of performance related pay, a thing that has been and still is met with very mixed feelings and, most commonly, rejection on the part of the teaching unions.

DfE circular 0051/2000 Performance Management in Schools – Performance Management Framework states:

> Performance management demonstrates schools' commitment to develop all teachers effectively to ensure job satisfaction, high levels of expertise and progression of staff in their chosen profession.

But what is performance management? There does not appear to be a standard definition. Hartle *et al.* offer us the following to think about:

> A process that links teachers, support staff and their respective roles to the success of pupils and the school.

> A process for establishing a shared understanding of what has to be achieved and how, and managing staff in such a way that it will be achieved.

> A process for ensuring that staff are doing the right things in the most effective way to the best of their ability.

> (Hartle *et al.*, 2001: 3)

Most schools have developed a performance management policy using available models and following wide consultation with staff in the school. We are aware of a number of schools in which middle managers played a key role in helping to develop such policies. We believe that schools who followed this route adopted a sensible approach as middle managers, referred to by the DfE as 'team leaders', have a crucial part to play in this process.

The DfES guidelines were keen to emphasise some important issues. The performance management cycle is ongoing – planning, monitoring and reviewing. It is intended to bring together the teacher's priorities, the needs of the pupils and the teacher's professional and personal development priorities with the school improvement plan therefore becoming an integral part of the school's culture.

In our experience it is very important to have a clear line management 'tree'. Nothing is worse than teachers who are working in more than one department having several people responsible for managing their overall performance. Team leaders need to ensure that teachers have clear job descriptions.

The role of the team leader is to agree the focus for the teacher's work at the start of the performance management cycle. They have to ensure that each teacher understands what their objectives are and that they are related to the school improvement plan. They need to ensure that teachers are in a position to achieve them. They need to ensure that all teachers understand how and when these objectives are likely to be reviewed. This includes the issue of evidence. What will they be looking for to show that an objective has been achieved? This requires them to have knowledge and understanding of such benchmarking information as the school's performance and assessment (PANDA) report, other school performance data and prior attainment of pupils.

An effective manager pays constant attention to progress throughout the year. This requires a great deal of time and commitment from the team leader. They have to ensure that they themselves fully understand the school's policy and then pass that on to staff. They have to encourage and support staff in meeting their objectives. They have to monitor staff performance, including observing lessons.

The team leader then has to review the performance of the teacher. The intention is that the teacher and the team leader can reflect upon the teacher's performance in a structured way. The team leader needs to take into account the position of the teacher within the school, e.g. are they an NQT or an Advanced Skills Teacher (AST). They are then required to make a professional judgement about their performance. This is doubly crucial, as there may well be money involved.

'The outcomes of the performance review will be used to inform pay decisions, for example for awarding double performance increments for outstanding performance up to the performance threshold ...' (DfEE, 2000). This puts a great deal of pressure on team leaders.

In addition, performance threshold assessment is intended to work alongside performance management. It is worthwhile referring to threshold assessments at this point because some of the same principles apply.

> The School Teachers Pay and Conditions Document places a duty on teachers who manage staff to assist, on request, the head or the assessor to carry out threshold assessments of the teachers they manage ... such a manager could be a head of department.
>
> (Threshold Guidance, 2002: 19)

Application to cross the threshold is voluntary. However, the majority of teachers in our experience will apply to do so. They have to be at point M6 on the teachers' pay scale as of September 2002 to have any funding allocated backdated to that point or M5 at that time to have funding allocated from September 2003. Judgements are made on eight standards:

- Knowledge and understanding
- Teaching and assessment (three standards – planning lessons, classroom management and monitoring progress)
- Pupil progress
- Wider professional effectiveness (two standards – personal development and school development)
- Professional characteristics.

All standards have to have been met for a teacher to cross the threshold. Currently, £2,000 is paid if they do, plus an opportunity to move along the upper pay scale in two years time. Although there has been some lack of clarity this year, in our experience, schools have used their performance management policies in order to make judgements about progression onto upper pay scale 2.

This means that as a middle manager you have to deal with a number of issues that may not be comfortable because of formality replacing informality and because the decision to increase the pay of certain staff is partly in your hands. This is, needless to say, a very emotive issue.

So what will help you to manage this?

A number of things referred to in other chapters will help. For example, know the strengths and weaknesses of your staff, and have clear departmental policies and procedures. However, the following action point checklist might help.

Action point

Checklist

- Do you have a copy of your school's current performance management policy? – if not get one
- Do you understand how it operates? – if not ask your line manager to go through it with you
- Do staff in your department have one? – do they understand it?
- Have you received training in holding a performance management interview? – What experience have you had in classroom observation?
- Do all the staff in your department have clear job descriptions? – if not review and revise
- In making a professional judgement what is your evidence base?

Source: DFEE, 1998

The stages of the performance management cycle are:

- planning
- monitoring progress
- reviewing.

The planning phase requires a record to be kept of four objectives covering pupils' progress and professional practice. Objectives would normally cover such things as:

- Lesson preparation
- Subject knowledge
- Teaching methods
- Communication and motivation
- Discipline
- Marking and assessment
- Use of homework
- Classroom organisation
- Implementation of school policies
- Additional responsibilities.

Classroom observation and the collection of other evidence is required in the monitoring progress phase. This might involve a number of other exercises such as:

- Scrutiny of pupil work
- Collecting information from students
- Analysis of lesson plans and documentation.

Performance management can be unobtrusive in a learning department with positive relationships and a culture of enquiry and development, since much of the information and process is a normal part of improvement. Balancing the formal requirement, the professional entitlement and the informal process of team achievement is a major problem for the middle manager.

REFERENCES

Hartle, F., Baker, C. and Everall, K. (2001) *Getting the Best Out of Performance Management in Your School*, London: Kogan Page.

DfEE (1998) *Teachers: Meeting the Challenge of Change*, London: HMSO.

DfES (2000) *Model Performance Management Policy*, London: DfES.

DfES (2000) 'Performance Management in Schools – Performance Management Framework', Circular 0051/2000.

WEBSITES

NCSL at http://www.ncsl.org.uk/index.cfm?pageid=managing-docs-perform

The Strategic Direction and Development of a Department: Leadership, Planning, Performance and the Use of ICT

4.1 Leadership for Middle Managers

Rob Bollington

INTRODUCTION

> ### OBJECTIVES
>
> By the end of this Unit you should:
>
> - Have gained a greater understanding of the nature of leadership and management;
> - Be aware of some of the strategies available to middle managers to increase their effectiveness.

The amount and pace of change since the 1988 Education Reform Act have had a dramatic impact on all aspects of education in the United Kingdom, including on the role of middle managers. The trend has been to see middle managers less in terms of managing resources for a subject and more in terms of having a key role in leading people and raising standards. An emphasis on the need for effective management has been replaced by calls for better leadership and it has become customary to talk about the need for effective leadership at all levels. One argument for this is that 'sustaining improvement requires the leadership capability of the many rather than the few and that improvements in learning are more likely to be achieved when leadership is instructionally focused and located closest to the classroom' (Harris and Muijs, 2002a). In effect, leadership at all levels, including by middle managers, has come to be seen as critical to a school's success. Middle managers, whether referred to by a job title such as head of department or a generic label such as subject leader, are increasingly expected to foster the leadership of others in their team.

Two examples of what has been written recently illustrate the increasing expectations of middle managers. The Teacher Training Agency (TTA) describe the core purpose of the role as: 'to provide professional leadership and management for a subject to secure high quality teaching, effective use of resources and improved standards of learning and achievement for all pupils' (1998: 4). The more recent DfES guidance for subject leaders at Key Stage 3 refers to 'three core roles: judging standards; evaluating teaching and learning; and leading sustainable improvement' (2002: 1).

These roles require middle managers, or to use the name of the National College for School Leadership's (NCSL) programme, those 'leading from the middle', to combine subject and curriculum expertise with well developed interpersonal and leadership skills. Middle managers need to be able to organise and plan, make effective use of performance data and complement their own teaching ability with the capacity to evaluate the teaching of others. Above all they need to be able to challenge colleagues, pupils and senior managers to improve what is achieved in their area in line with a clear vision of how that area might be. Getting the balance between challenging and supporting staff, enabling others to develop and take a leadership role, keeping people motivated and getting the job done has become more complex.

DEFINITIONS OF LEADERSHIP AND MANAGEMENT

Often management is seen as concerned with operational matters and with implementing policies and procedures. On the other hand, leadership is often seen as concerned with providing direction and a sense of purpose. Bennis, for example, argues:

> The manager administers; the leader innovates.
> The manager is a copy; the leader is an original.
> The manager maintains; the leader develops.
> The manager focuses on systems and structure; the leader focuses on people.
> The manager relies on control; the leader inspires trust.
> The manager has a short-range view; the leader has a long-range perspective.
> The manager asks how and when; the leader asks what and why.
> The manager has his eye always on the bottom line; the leader has his eye on the horizon.
> The manager imitates; the leader originates.
> The manager accepts the status quo; the leader challenges it.
> The manager is the classic good soldier; the leader is his own person.
> The manager does things right; the leader does the right thing.
>
> (Bennis, 1989: 45)

A similar attempt to differentiate between leadership and management is provided by West-Burnham (Figure 4.1).

In practice, an effective middle manager needs to be able to combine management and leadership. In fact, day to day management tasks can be transformed if seen as a means of providing leadership. The way a middle manager deals with routine tasks conveys his or her values and sets the tone for the team involved. Indeed it can be argued that the role

> is about being able to see the future and wider picture but also deal with the present and the nuts and bolts of day-to-day organization. Of course, an obsession with the nuts and bolts is not healthy and may indicate that a team

Figure 4.1 Leading or managing?

Leading is concerned with:	Managing is concerned with:
Vision	Implementation
Strategic issues	Operational issues
Transformation	Transaction
Ends	Means
People	Systems
Doing the right things	Doing things right

Source: West-Burnham, 1997: 117.

leader has got his or her priorities wrong. However, a middle manager who can help colleagues do a good job by having efficient systems for day-to-day organization in place will gain much respect.

(Fleming, 2000: 117–18)

At this point, however, it is as well to bear in mind that 'the problem with many organisations, and especially the ones that are failing, is that they tend to be over managed and under led' (Bennis and Nanus, 1985: 21). Raising standards, school improvement and handling change all depend on people at all levels in a school providing effective leadership.

Action point

Reflect on your own work over the past week. What did you do that could be seen as providing leadership? What did you do that falls into the category of management? How could you have been more effective in using the management tasks you carried out to provide leadership?

APPROACHES TO LEADERSHIP AND MANAGEMENT

People tend to be more comfortable working for one middle manager than for another even when what is being asked for is the same. The major cause is often how the person puts across what is required and comes down to a matter of leadership and management style and how someone sees his or her role. Style is perhaps best defined as how a person's typical way or manner of doing things is perceived by others. In many cases, this typical style is seen in sharpest focus when things go wrong or the middle manager is under pressure.

Theories of leadership and management often distinguish between

- participative, democratic, laissez-faire and authoritarian approaches, and between
- concern for people and relationships and concern for tasks or results.

Concerns over the last twenty years or so with handling change and securing improvement have led to both calls for more participative approaches and an emphasis on the value of developing a vision.

The various theories provide a starting point for personal reflection. They are perhaps best seen as lenses through which to view our own approaches and experience. In this section, a discussion of leadership is organised under three separate but overlapping headings: contingency approaches, transformational approaches and participative approaches, before a review of leadership characteristics.

Contingency models

Contingency theories of leadership focus on the links between the behaviour of the leader and the context they operate in. An early example, which provides insight into management and leadership style, is Blake and Mouton's grid (1964). The grid is based on the idea that leaders vary along a nine-point scale in both their concern for people and their concern for getting the job done (see Figure 4.2). The ideas presented provide middle managers with a useful set of insights, given the often conflicting pressures of keeping the team happy while pressing for higher standards and improvement.

Each of the two axes of the grid is a nine-point scale. The various typical management and leadership styles indicated vary in their emphasis on maintaining relationships and achieving results. Table 4.1 describes some of the key styles and looks at how these relate to middle management.

This model has been very influential. It highlights the need to balance a concern for efficiency and getting the job done with satisfying staff needs and maintaining morale. On the face of it the 9.9 style appears to be the ideal and has often been advocated because it is associated with participation, involvement, trust and mutual support and respect. Clearly for middle managers when the focus is on evaluating

Figure 4.2 People or production?

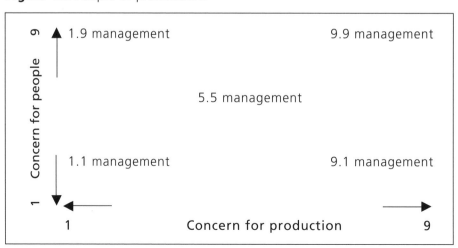

Source: Blake and Moulton (1964).

Table 4.1 Management and leadership styles

1.1 'Impoverished management'	Low concern for results Low concern for relationships	This style describes a situation where a middle manager has withdrawn and become passive. Events are allowed to take place without planning or anticipation.
1.9 'Country club management'	Low concern for results High concern for relationships	This style refers to a situation in which a middle manager is concerned with keeping the department happy and avoiding conflict, rather than with results.
5.5 'Middle of the road management'	Moderate concern for results and relationships	This style is where a middle manager works on the basis of a compromise between achieving results and maintaining good relationships. The risk is that insufficient attention is paid to both.
9.1 'Task oriented management'	High concern for results Low concern for relationships	This style describes where a middle manager puts results before people. The emphasis is on the tasks not the people.
9.9 'Team management'	High concern for results High concern for relationships	This style is where a middle manager places a strong emphasis on achieving results through a concern for the welfare of staff, high morale and effective teamwork.

teachers' effectiveness and on raising standards, there is a danger in focusing on results at the expense of relationships. The ideas presented here are a reminder of the need to think about the balance, especially over time.

Taking the view that different situations require different styles of leadership and management, Hersey and Blanchard (1988) developed their model of 'situational leadership'. In this model, the appropriate style is said to vary according to factors such as the competence, capability and commitment of the team or individual members of staff. Where a middle manager is dealing with someone lacking in competence or tackling an area in which they feel uncertain, then a directive style of leadership is appropriate. On the other hand, as confidence, commitment and competence increase, a middle manager needs to move from directing to coaching to supporting to delegating. In practice, we know when we have adopted the wrong style from the reactions we get.

People vary in terms of the speed and degree to which they are able to progress through the four stages (see Table 4.2). In judging an appropriate style, a middle manager needs to give weight to both the competence and commitment of the team or individual. In other words, just because someone is well motivated and committed does not mean they are capable of doing a job.

This model provides a useful basis for analysing leadership and is a helpful starting point in raising self-awareness about how effectively a middle manager is performing. The model can raise the question for an individual middle manager as to whether there are situations in which he or she could usefully vary their style. It can be a useful means of analysing the best approach to take in situations involving giving feedback on performance such as performance management or mentoring. For example, in the context of performance management, the choice is sometimes between bringing up an issue and encouraging the member of staff to talk in the hope that they will bring it up. Listening to where the member of staff is coming from is the key. Phrases such as, 'I'd really like some ideas on this', indicate the need for more direction, whereas comments like, 'I want to try out some ideas I'd like to tell you about', show the need for a more hands-off approach. The clear message, however, is that 'there are four leadership styles: Directing, Coaching, Supporting and Delegating. BUT … THERE IS NO ONE BEST LEADERSHIP STYLE' (Blanchard *et al.*, 1994: 46).

Transformational leadership

In some discussions of leadership, there has been a shift from a concern with style to a focus on the role of a leader's vision. The idea developed is that a leader's effectiveness relates to their ability to create a shared vision among those around him or her. This perspective can be seen in the concepts of transactional and transformational leadership (Burns, 1978).

Transformational leadership refers to an approach to leadership which places an emphasis on engaging people in a shared vision for the organisation. On the other hand, transactional leadership refers to an approach where leaders offer some kind of reward or incentive in return for the achievement of goals. In other words it is about an exchange of one thing for another. In many ways, the distinction is similar to that drawn earlier between leadership and management.

Table 4.2 Styles of situational leadership

Style 1: Directing style	When members of staff take on an unfamiliar task or lack confidence, they tend to need direction, structure and feedback. They can become difficult or anxious if direction and feedback are not provided. A middle manager needs to spend time clarifying expectations and providing guidance on how to carry out the task. Monitoring is essential.
Style 2: Coaching style	As members of staff gain confidence and competence, they reach the second stage in the model and need to be sold on an idea, supported with feedback and provided with fresh ideas and coaching. They need both direction and support. Again the middle manager needs to be active and attentive.
Style 3: Supporting Style	The third stage is the 'supporting' stage. Members of staff at this stage are more confident in their ability to decide on what tasks need to be done and to plan ahead. On the other hand, they also need to participate in decision-making with the leader of the team. At this stage, they need praise and to be listened to. They benefit from a facilitative style of leadership. Many middle managers appear to find this style and style 2 the most natural ones.
Style 4: Delegating style	At the fourth stage, delegation, the middle manager sets out the broad parameters for the task, knowing that people are now able to get on with their work without close supervision or constant feedback. People's experience means they need little direction and their commitment means they need little support. Often middle managers find this a difficult style to adopt, worrying that the task will not be done in the way they would do it. Also, unless this style is properly judged, there is the risk that delegation can be seen as dumping.

The concept of transformational leadership has been further developed by Leithwood *et al.* (1999) who describe eight dimensions of transformational leadership: 'building school vision; establishing school goals; providing intellectual stimulation; offering individualised support; modelling best practices and important organizational values; demonstrating high performance expectations; creating a productive school culture; and developing structures to foster participation in school decisions' (Leithwood *et al.*, 1999: 9). The interest here is in developing an approach to leadership that can create dynamic learning communities that are able to change and improve.

Southworth, writing about primary headteachers (1998: 43–55) provides a useful discussion of the place of transactional and transformational leadership in schools seeing the two approaches as 'complementary and supplementary'. For him 'transactional leadership primarily focuses on the maintenance functions of a school. Transformational leadership is concerned with a school's development needs and goals.

It is leadership that contributes to school improvement.' He argues that transformational leadership is about:

- 'empowerment;
- team leadership;
- development;
- learning;
- vision' (Southworth, 1998: 48).

These ideas have relevance to other levels of leadership and to other settings. For middle managers, the issues are to do with influence and the way their roles and the role of the headteacher in developing the school's vision relate. Nevertheless, the capacity of a subject leader, coordinator or head of department to bring together their team behind a shared vision of how they would like the subject to develop is critical. Empowerment, team leadership, development, learning and vision are just as appropriate at departmental or subject level as they are at whole school level. Typically transformational leadership depends on the leader taking the initiative. It 'aspires, more generally, to increase members' efforts on behalf of the organization, as well as to develop more skilled practice' (Leithwood *et al.*, 1999: 20).

Action point

To help clarify your vision as a middle manager, think about how you would like things to be in three years time. What would you like to see? What would you like to hear people say? How would things feel different from how they are now?

Participative leadership

Underlying much of the discussion of leadership is the issue of how far a leader shares leadership with his or her team. There has been a good deal of recent interest in the idea of dispersed or distributed leadership. Harris and Muijs, for example, make the case strongly for dispersed leadership:

> In the USA, Canada and Australia the notion of 'dispersed, 'distributed' or 'teacher leadership' is particularly well developed and grounded in research evidence. This model of leadership implies a redistribution of power and a re-alignment of authority within the organisation. It means creating the conditions in which people work together and learn together, where they construct and refine meaning leading to a shared purpose or set of goals. Evidence would suggest that where such conditions are in place, leadership is a much stronger internal driver for school improvement and change (Hopkins, 2001). In practice, this means giving authority to teachers and empowering them to lead. Taking this perspective, leadership is a fluid and emergent rather than a fixed phenomenon. It implies a different power

relationship within the school where the distinctions between followers and leaders tend to blur. It also opens up the possibility for all teachers to become leaders at various times and suggests that leadership is a shared and collective endeavour that can engage the many rather than the few.

(Harris and Muijs, 2002b: 2)

Clearly, this line of thinking is challenging to a school where there is a strong emphasis on hierarchy. Nevertheless, having the confidence to encourage others to lead and to promote a collegial approach can do much to secure motivation and release the collective energies and talents of a team. The underlying assumptions are that those closest to the action are best placed to make decisions and that full involvement will lead to greater commitment. This approach is a long way from a traditional authoritarian model of leadership in which the team are dependent on the headteacher or team leader initiating and directing matters. A middle manager committed to this approach will be looking continually to encourage and foster leadership by members of his or her team.

Action point

How far do you encourage leadership by others in your team? Think of examples. What else could you do to encourage others to take on a leadership role? Are there any pitfalls in this approach?

Leadership characteristics

Style, behaviour, skills and attributes are closely linked and all help to determine a middle manager's success. A number of attempts have been made to identify the key ingredients that go into making an effective middle manager. The Teacher Training Agency's *National Standards for Subject Leaders* lists the following skills:

a. Leadership skills, attributes and professional competence – the ability to lead and manage people to work towards common goals ...
b. Decision-making skills – the ability to solve problems and make decisions ...
c. Communication skills – the ability to make points clearly and understand the views of others ...
d. Self-management – the ability to plan time effectively and to organise oneself well ...

and attributes:

i. personal impact and presence;
ii. adaptability to changing circumstances and new ideas;
iii. energy, vigour and perseverance;
iv. self-confidence;
v. enthusiasm;
vi. intellectual ability;

vii. reliability and integrity;

viii. commitment.

(TTA, 1998: 7–8)

Such a list is useful when reflecting on our own performance. It also provides a basis for professional development planning. Another approach to identifying the characteristics of effective leadership comes from the National Education Assessment Centre (NEAC). The characteristics identified are:

Administrative competencies

1. *Problem analysis.* Ability to seek out relevant data and analyse information to determine the important elements of a situation.
2. *Judgement.* Ability to reach logical conclusions and make high quality decisions based on available information: to set priorities; to show caution where necessary.
3. *Organisational ability and decisiveness.* Ability to plan and schedule effectively; to delegate appropriately; to recognise when a decision is required and to act upon it.

Interpersonal competencies

1. *Leadership.* Ability to motivate others and involve them in the accomplishment of tasks: to secure general acceptance of ideas. Willingness to engage in pro-active behaviour.
2. *Sensitivity.* Ability to perceive needs, concerns and problems from differing viewpoints and to act accordingly; to value the contribution of others.
3. *Stress tolerance.* Ability to perform under pressure.

Communicative competencies

1. *Oral communication.* Ability to make clear oral presentation of facts or ideas.
2. *Written communication.* Ability to express ideas clearly in writing; to write appropriately for different audiences.

Personal breadth competencies

1. *Interests and motivation.* Desire to participate and to achieve in activities both on and off the job. Evidence that work is important to personal satisfaction. Evidence of continuing action to improve personal capability. Ability to be self-evaluating.

2.   *Educational values.* Possession and demonstration of a well-reasoned educational philosophy.

(Oliver, 1993 in Cleland, 1999: 96–7)

Again, such a list is helpful as the basis of personal feedback, individual reflection and professional development. Such a list can be used as the basis of a professional discussion or in performance management.

An alternative summary is provided by Sadler (1997). This comes from outside the world of education and provides a complementary perspective. Sadler argues that 'leader behaviours which are generally cited as contributing to effectiveness include:

- developing and articulating a vision;
- listening;
- empowering;
- role modelling;
- problem solving;
- walking the job;
- demonstrating confidence;
- representing and protecting the group' (Sadler, 1997: 151).

It is worth stressing that the NEAC competencies, the TTA skills and attributes and Sadler's effective leader behaviours are applicable to people in a range of management and leadership positions. In other words, the ingredients of successful leadership tend to be similar regardless of position. The main variable is the arena in which they need to be deployed.

All the characteristics listed imply the need for active and visible leadership. They also need to be seen in the context of the need for a middle manager, indeed for any manager, to manage in different directions. In effect, a middle manager needs to manage him or herself, the team he or she leads, relationships with colleagues and relationships with senior staff as well as relationships with parents, pupils, governors and the wider community. When Sadler refers to 'representing and protecting the group', he signals not only the need for a middle manager to show loyalty to his or her staff but also the need to ensure that the place of the team's work in the school as a whole is properly considered. It is worth remembering, however, that different beliefs about how a leader should operate will point to the need for some behaviours rather than others. For example, if you are committed to a participative approach, then skills of interpersonal communication will be a priority. It is also important not to fall into the trap of thinking that everyone has to lead in the same way.

Action point

Take either the TTA list of skills and attributes, the NEAC competencies or Sadler's list of effective leader behaviours. Use the list as the basis of personal reflection. For each characteristic, think of examples in what you have done that provide evidence of your strengths or weaknesses. How can you build on this? You may find it helpful to discuss your thoughts with a colleague.

LEADING THE TEAM

If leadership at all levels is the weft of an effective school, then good teamwork is the warp. The shift from seeing middle managers as mainly responsible for resources to mainly responsible for leading and developing people places the spotlight on their role in both individual and team development. Key characteristics of an effective team appear to be:

- clear shared goals
- a focus on what matters
- a sense of team identity
- good communication
- mutual trust
- a willingness to work through and utilise professional differences
- high expectations of what can be achieved
- clear procedures and ground rules
- members whose skills and experience complement each other
- encouragement of everyone to contribute and make an appropriate input
- an ability to seek out and use information as the basis of making decisions
- the flexibility to work in a variety of ways and to share leadership
- encouragement of individual development of team members
- an ability to seek appropriate external support and resources
- a willingness to reflect on and evaluate the effectiveness of the team.

Action point

How far do these criteria for an effective team match your own experience? How well is your own team operating in each of these areas? Try to identify one or more aspects where your team could be improved. What can you do to improve the way your team works?

In practice, teams have a life of their own and typically go through stages in their development. Often these stages are referred to as forming, storming, norming and performing (Tuckman, 1965). Changes of personnel or circumstances can totally transform the effectiveness of a team. The role of the team leader is to move the team forward, recognising when changes are needed and creating conditions in which the team and those in it can develop and perform to the best of their abilities. At the forming stage the task is to provide plenty of opportunities for the team to come together and to clarify what is needed and to encourage communication. As the team finds its feet and people begin to assert themselves (storming) such communication will help differences be worked through and agreed aims and procedures be established. Sweeping differences under the carpet or pretending they do not exist will not allow the team to develop effectively. Once norms and procedures are in place, however, and the team is performing well, the task is to maintain and reinforce procedures in a positive way. At some point, though, particularly in the case of a well established team in danger of becoming complacent, the task is to make changes when to all appearances things are going well. Leaving the changes until problems appear can mean leaving things too late.

Adair (1987: 203) captures three areas of focus for team leadership:

- Achieving the task;
- Developing the individual;
- Building and maintaining the team.

Adair comments that,

> the three circles overlap ... If you have a good group, for example, you are more likely to achieve the task. If the individuals concerned are fully involved and motivated, then they are going to give much more to the task and much more to the group.
>
> (Adair, 1987: 62)

The model draws attention to the need for a team leader to balance the competing needs of the team as a whole, the tasks to be completed and the requirements of individual team members. For middle managers, this model provides a useful tool for evaluating the balance that is being achieved and thinking about where intervention is most needed.

LEADERSHIP, STANDARDS AND EVALUATING PERFORMANCE

Expectations of middle managers have increased in relation to their role in raising standards of pupil performance and in evaluating the work of other staff. Monitoring, evaluation and review are now essential aspects of the role. Whether it is a case of interpreting and using pupil performance data, evaluating a lesson or setting targets, the role of a middle manager depends on deploying analytical and interpersonal skills.

> A starting point for this is the DfES cycle of school improvement.
>
> *How well are we doing and how do we compare with similar schools?*
>
> Improvement planning begins with an audit designed to establish secure judgements about standards of pupils' achievement, the current quality of teaching and the appropriateness of the curriculum.
>
> *What more should we aim to achieve this year and what must we do to make it happen?*
>
> Improvement targets are established against the audit and strategies developed to achieve the targets set.
>
> *Taking action and checking that it happens.*
>
> The improvement strategy is put into action and progress is monitored. Judgements about standards are made to identify whether they have been raised.
>
> (DfES, 2002: 2)

In order to ensure that this approach is followed, the following areas for attention for subject leaders are put forward:

Judging standards
- Analyse and interpret data on pupils' attainment in the subject.
- Review with teachers their assessments of progress for classes, identified groups and individuals.
- Sample pupils' work.
- Discuss work, progress and attitudes with sample groups of pupils …

Evaluating teaching and learning
- Evaluate … schemes of work to ensure that they focus on effective teaching and learning.
- Observe teaching and feed back to colleagues.
- Review teachers' planning …

Leading sustainable improvement
- Lead the department in discussion about priorities for the subject …
- Agree targets for raising pupils' attainment … in the context of whole-school targets.
- Develop a strategy for the improvement of the subject …
- Lead the improvement of teaching quality.
- Lead the review, the construction and resourcing of the curriculum.

(DfES, 2002: 4–5)

The list of tasks is taken from the context of the national Key Stage 3 strategy but has been edited here so that it does not refer to Key Stage 3 specifically. The tasks reflect the growing emphasis in recent years on the middle manager's role in monitoring and evaluation. All of the tasks can be carried out in a variety of ways, however, involving more or less participation and collaboration. A middle manager's preferred style of leadership, assumptions and values will be reflected in how he or she responds to these expectations. Leadership has a crucial role to play.

Action point

Think about the tasks listed above and the variety of ways you could approach them. What would a participative and collaborative approach involve?

CONCLUSION

This chapter has been written against the background of increasing expectations of middle managers and from the standpoint that managers and leaders are 'made' rather than 'born'. Given the demands of the job and the need to develop the necessary skills, appropriate continuing professional development, CPD, is essential. CPD has, of course, changed significantly over recent years. There has been a shift in emphasis from reliance on courses to using a variety of approaches. A key concern has been to ensure that all CPD makes a difference. There is now a national CPD strategy predicated on the value of access to a variety of forms of high quality CPD. The National College for School Leadership (NCSL) is driving forward leadership development and research. We have reached the stage where it is possible to speak of CPD as an entitlement throughout someone's career and to define CPD as any opportunity where teachers learn.

This view moves us from seeing CPD as something external to our job to seeing the job itself as providing opportunities for learning. Hopkins *et al.* (1996: 177) note that 'successful schools encourage co-ordination by creating collaborative environments that encourage involvement, professional development, mutual support and assistance in problem solving'. The daily tasks of management and teaching provide countless opportunities for teachers and managers individually and collectively to learn and develop. Learning in one school can be shared with colleagues in other schools.

In terms of leadership and management development, there are many opportunities available from formal programmes, which typically include a research element, to school based activities, such as job shadowing, performance management, practitioner research and enquiry, and mentoring. Middle managers need to consider what steps they are taking in terms of their own professional development and what they are doing to promote the professional development of others. Harris and Muijs (2002b: 17–21) identify four dimensions involved in promoting the development of teacher leadership. These involve:

1   creating time for professional development and collaborative work
2   providing opportunities for continuing professional development to enable people to develop their role
3   equipping people with good interpersonal skills
4   motivating people to undertake a leadership role.

The challenge for a middle manager committed to the involvement and development of other staff is to take steps in these areas. The potential for improving the quality of leadership, raising morale and energising schools is enormous.

REFERENCES

Adair, J. (1987) *Effective Teambuilding*, London: Pan Books.

Bennis, W. (1989) *On Becoming a Leader*, Boston, MA: Addison and Wesley.

Bennis, W. and Nanus, B. (1985) *Leaders: The Strategies for Taking Charge*, New York: Harper and Row.

Blake, R. and Mouton, S. (1964) *The Managerial Grid*, Houston, TX: Gulf Publishing.

Blanchard, K., Zigarmi, P. and Zigarmi, D. (1994) *Leadership and The One Minute Manager*, London: HarperCollins.

Burns, J.M. (1978) *Leadership*, New York: Harper and Row.

Cleland, G. (1999) 'Early experience of middle management assessment: lessons from the NEAC scheme', *Teacher Development*, 3, 1: 95–107.

DfES (2002) *Key Stage 3 National Strategy – Securing Improvement: The Role of Subject Leaders*, London: DfES.

Fleming, P. (2000) *The Art of Middle Management in Secondary Schools*, London: David Fulton Publishers.

Harris, A. and Muijs, D. (2002a) *Teacher Leadership: Principles and Practice*, available at www.gtce.org.uk.

Harris, A. and Muijs, D. (2002b) *Teacher Leadership: A Review of Research*, available at www.gtce.org.uk.

Hersey, P. and Blanchard, K. (1988) *Management of Organisational Behaviour: Utilising Human Resources*, Englewood Cliffs, NJ: Prentice-Hall.

Hopkins, D. (1996) *Improving the Quality of Education for All*, London: David Fulton Publishers.

Hopkins, D. (2001) *School Improvement for Real*, quoted in A. Harris and D. Muijs (2002) *Teacher Leadership: A Review of Research*, London: Falmer Press. Available at www.gtce.org.uk.

Leithwood, K., Jantzi, D. and Steinbach, R. (1999) *Changing Leadership for Changing Times*, Buckingham: Open University Press.

Oliver, J. (1993) *Headstart*, Oxford: National Educational Assessment Centre, quoted in G. Cleland (1999), 'Early experience of middle management assessment: lessons from the NEAC Scheme', *Teacher Development*, 3, 1: 95–107.

Sadler, P. (1997) *Leadership*, London: Kogan Page in association with Coopers and Lybrand.

Southworth, G. (1998) *Leading Improving Primary Schools*, London: Falmer Press.

TTA (1998) *Standards for Subject Leaders*, London: TTA.

Tuckman, B.W. (1965) 'Developmental sequence in small groups', *Psychological Bulletin*, 63, 1: 133–42.

West-Burnham, J. (1997) *Managing Quality in Schools*, 2nd edn, London: Pitman Publishing.

FURTHER READING

Brundrett, M., Burton, N. and Smith, R. (2003) *Leadership in Education*, London: Sage.

Bush, T. and Bell, L. (2002) *The Principles and Practice of Educational Management*, London: Paul Chapman.

4.2 Development Planning in the Secondary School

Bob Smith

INTRODUCTION

OBJECTIVES

By the end of this Unit you should:

- Understand the development planning as both process and product;
- Be aware of the importance of auditing and consultation;
- Have a clear knowledge of how to construct and evaluate a development plan.

Over the past two decades or so, the need for schools to effectively plan their development has become increasingly important. In the 1970s public concern with the quality of education led to demands for increased accountability. This was reflected in many HMI reports which challenged schools to address weaknesses identified in the inspection process. At this time the main responsibility for monitoring and evaluating the performance of schools lay with the Local Education Authorities (LEAs) which were also responsible for the management of finance, resources, premises, staffing and pupil numbers. Some authorities, such as the Inner London Education Authority (ILEA), encouraged their schools to engage in a process of self review and produced guidelines for this purpose. The 1988 Education Reform Act required LEAs to devolve funding, resources and the responsibility for decision-making to schools, making them responsible for their own management, including planning.

In 1989, the Department for Education and Science (DES) commissioned Hargreaves and Hopkins to undertake a research project, the School Development

Plans Project, which led to all schools being issued with two booklets – *Planning for School Development: Advice for Governors, Headteachers and Teachers* (HMSO, 1989) and *Development Planning: A Practical Guide* (HMSO, 1991). The project was more fully written up in *The Empowered School: The Management and Practice of Development Planning* (Hargreaves and Hopkins, 1991).

The Education Act of 1992 brought into being the Office for Standards in Education (Ofsted) whose remit was to develop a framework for school inspection, and instigate and oversee a system of four-yearly school inspections. The Ofsted framework, *The Handbook for the Inspection of Schools* (Ofsted, 1992: 20), specified that final Ofsted reports would include, 'A judgement on the quality of the school development plan …'. More recently, the 1995 edition of the Ofsted handbook made reference to the requirement for a 'school development plan or equivalent planning document' and stated that, 'The school's aims and priorities will be drawn from the prospectus, the school development plan and from discussion' and 'the school, through its development planning, identifies relevant priorities and targets, takes the necessary action, and monitors and evaluates its progress towards them' (p.31). The most recent edition (Ofsted, 1999: 91) states that, 'Development and improvement planning should reflect the school's stated aims and objectives and promote high standards'. Thus the requirement for schools to produce a School Development Plan (or School Improvement Plan) is now effectively mandatory.

Whilst school development planning is effectively mandatory, it would be a mistake to view it simply as another bureaucratic imposition. It provides significant advantages for schools, for teachers, *and especially for heads of department and curriculum leaders*. The early research carried out by Hargreaves and Hopkins indicated that the main benefit of development planning for schools is that it

> allows the school to focus on its fundamental aims concerned with teaching and learning … Many of the current changes with which schools have to cope are being imposed from outside. Development planning is the way in which each school interprets external policy requirements so that they are integrated into its own unique life and culture.
>
> (Hargreaves and Hopkins, 1991: 7)

In other words, development planning allows schools to internalise and take ownership of the ways in which they promote improvement.

Also in the research heads and teachers themselves identified a number of specific advantages arising from development planning. Heads reported that it provides a coherent approach to planning, which covers all aspects of school management, including the curriculum, teaching, finance and resources. Teachers reported that it allows them to be more involved in the development of the school and to have some control over change rather than being controlled by it thus reducing stress. It was also seen to improve the quality of staff development and help the processes of appraisal and INSET training to be more effective. For heads, teachers and pupils, it was seen to focus on the aims of education, particularly learning and pupil achievement. It is, therefore, clear from these research findings that school development planning is essentially about whole school improvement.

DEVELOPMENT PLANNING

There are two important aspects to development planning, namely the plan itself, i.e. *the product*, and the creation of the plan, putting it into effect and evaluating it, i.e. *the process*.

The development plan – the product

The school development plan is variously described as:

> In its simplest form a SDP brings together in an overall plan, national and LEA policies and initiatives, the school's aims and values, its existing achievements and needs for development, and enables it to organise what it is already doing and what it needs to do in a more purposeful and coherent way.
>
> (Hopkins, 1991: 85)

> A development plan is easily described. Priorities are selected and planned in detail for one year and are supported by action plans or working documents for staff. The priorities for later years are sketched in outline to provide the longer term programme.
>
> (Hargreaves and Hopkins, 1991: 3)

> The starting point for monitoring and evaluating school performance.
>
> (Giles, 1997: 18)

> ... the mechanism for defining a school's aims and translating them into effective education.
>
> (Davies and Ellison, 1999: 7)

Organisational planning takes place at different levels and over different timescales. Planning which relates to the long term development of the school and is concerned with the school's core aims and its values and vision, which are often encompassed in the school's mission statement, is usually called *strategic planning*. Davies and Ellison (1999: 48) define strategic planning as, 'the systematic analysis of the school and its environment and the formulation of a set of key strategic objectives to enable the school to realise its vision, within the context of its values and its resource potential'. Strategic plans typically look forward over a period of five years.

The school development plan is described by Giles (1997: 35) as, 'the medium to short-term operational plan of the school'. It translates the long-term vision of the strategic plan into a number of shorter-term goals, providing a means of 'translating a vision into meaningful objectives for those involved on a day-to-day basis' (Middlewood and Riley, 1995: 10). It is, therefore, concerned with *tactical* rather than strategic issues and is more specific than the strategic plan. The development plan sets goals for one year at a time – 'Detailed objectives are set for one year; the objectives for later years are sketched in outline' (DES, 1991: 2).

In turn, the development plan itself needs to be turned into more detailed operational plans variously described as *action plans, programme plans or project plans*. The DES (1991) sees action plans as the 'final' plans which turn the development plan into specific targets whilst Giles (1997: 19) differentiates between these operational plans. He describes programme plans as 'interconnected projects concerned with implementing the mandatory and discretionary goals of the school', project plans as 'smaller and separate portions of programmes' (p.20) and describes action planning 'not as a type of plan but as a planning technique' (p.20).

There is no single prescription as to the content of a school development plan, which might vary between a fairly simple list of goals and an elaborate and detailed document. The types of goals identified as priorities might include prescriptions – things which the school *must* do such as the national curriculum, managing the budget, etc.; expectations – things which the school believes it *should* do such as developing a particular culture; and predilections – things the school *would like* to do.

As a minimum, the plan should contain:

- Detailed goals in order of priority for the coming year and in outline for the next two or three years, which take into account the context of the school, national and local policies and initiatives, action points arising from Ofsted reports and issues emerging from the audit (see below).
- Action plans, which include clear targets and standards, are fully costed, specify responsibilities for implementing, monitoring and evaluating progress and contain agreed, realistic task timescales.
- A clear indication of staff development and training needs, linked to the staff development policy and the appraisal process.

(After Giles, 1997: 45)

Development planning – the process

In the simplest terms, the planning process can be reduced to asking four basic questions:

- Where are we now? (Audit)
- Where do we want to go (i.e. what are our goals)? (Construction)
- How are we going to get there? (Implementation)
- How well did we do it? (Evaluation)

Since development planning is a repetitive annual process, it can be seen as a cycle in which the evaluation of one year's plan informs the formulation of the following year's plan.

The audit – where are we now?

A school audit involves taking stock of where the school is now. It examines current provision and practice systematically and self-critically, comparing what the school is trying to achieve with what it is actually achieving. The purposes of the audit are to determine the state of the school and its strengths and weaknesses and, since the school development plan involves setting a limited number of goals from the broader strategic plan, to provide a basis for selecting priorities for development.

A whole-school audit is necessary when a school embarks upon the process of development planning for the first time. It then provides a basis for development planning for several years into the future. A very useful workbook, *The Secondary Whole-School Audit* (Drakeford and Cooling, 1998), provides a comprehensive and coherent approach to whole-school planning, 'in response to Ofsted's explicit inspection criteria' although, sadly, it is based on the outdated 1995 Ofsted Framework. It might, however, provide a useful basis, together with the current Ofsted Framework, from which a school might develop its own scheme as is mentioned below.

A whole-school audit involves a great deal of time and effort, perhaps spread over a whole school year and is usually inappropriate today since most, if not all, schools already carry out development planning or some equivalent process. It is, therefore, usually more appropriate to carry out a series of smaller-scale audits, focused on specific key areas from which action plans can be formulated and implemented as part of that year's development planning activities. A planned series of these small-scale audits over successive years then provides a rolling programme, eventually providing a picture of the whole school.

When considering the key areas for audit, the first step is clearly to look back to the previous year's development plan in which the areas suggested for the current year's plan might have already been outlined. An alternative, or possibly complementary approach, is to undertake a 'SWOT' analysis of the school and its provision, i.e. an analysis of the school's *Strengths*, *Weaknesses*, the *Opportunities* available to it and any *Threats* to which it is exposed.

Another alternative is to consider the areas listed in the Ofsted *Evaluation Schedule* (Ofsted, 1999), which might usefully provide a basis for the selection of areas for audit in a single year, or indeed for a whole-school audit, thus aligning the school development planning process with the requirements of Ofsted inspections. These are:

1. What sort of school is it?
2. How high are the standards?
   2.1 The school's results and pupils' or students' achievements
   2.2 Pupils' attitudes, values and personal development
3. How well are pupils or students taught?
4. How good are the curricular and other opportunities offered to pupils or students?
5. How well does the school care for its pupils or students?
6. How well does the school work in partnership with parents?
7. How well is the school led and managed?
8. What should the school do to improve further?
9. Other special features
   School data and indicators
10. The standards of quality of teaching in areas of the curriculum, subjects and courses.

(Ofsted, 1999: 6–104)

The areas to be audited will usually be selected by the head in consultation with the governors and staff, especially *senior staff*. In some schools this will be formalised in a School Planning Team (SPT) which might, for example, comprise the head or a deputy head, *heads of department*, a governor, representatives of the teaching and non-teaching staff and a representative of parents (possibly a parent governor). The responsibility for carrying out specific audits will normally be allocated to a senior teacher or team of teachers, *often led by a head of department or curriculum leader*. The head, a senior member of the staff or the chair of the SPT will then bring together and summarise the results of the audits. Once the areas to be audited have been decided, those *middle managers* taking responsibility for the audit have to decide on a strategy or strategies. There are three general strategies available from which to choose:

1   External perspective – in which an external perspective of the area chosen for audit is provided by, for example, advisors, inspectors, consultants (sometimes from higher education) or 'critical friends'. The advantages of this strategy include:

- provides a dispassionate view and an opportunity to talk through issues with outsiders
- reduces demands on staff
- reveals strengths as well as weaknesses
- may bring in new ideas and encourage staff to question what they take for granted.

The disadvantages include:

- it may not be possible to arrange visits to suit the school's needs or the school's planning cycle
- it may have a focus different to those of the school
- it may not, on its own, lead to school development
- it may miss or neglect the school's inner strengths.

2   Using a published scheme – various published schemes are available including the Drakeford and Cooling workbook mentioned above and, for example, *Institutional Development Planning* (Parsons *et al.*, 1994). The advantages of this approach include:

- it is able to take account of the views of all staff
- it is likely to be comprehensive
- it is less time-consuming than devising a customised scheme for the school
- it helps to be objective and impartial.

The disadvantages include:

- it is not specific to the school and neglects the school's context
- values implicit within the schemes may not be apparent
- the use of questionnaires may be considered too mechanical
- it may not be appropriate for collecting the views of pupils, parents or the community
- it may be dated and not reflect the current approach to evaluation.

3   Devising your own scheme – schools or individuals devising their own schemes allows a variety of techniques to be used such as questionnaires, interviews, discussions, focus groups, observations, scrutiny of records and documents, etc. and allows the views of pupils, parents and others to be elicited. The main advantages of a school-devised scheme include:

- it generates ownership and commitment to the findings
- it focuses on what the school thinks is important
- it can be timed to fit in with the work of the school.

The disadvantages include:

- it requires staff time
- it may require skills which are not available
- key issues may be missed because they were not thought of or seemed not to be important
- the validity of the approach may be questioned by some.

(After DES, 1991: 17)

These three strategies are not exclusive. An external perspective can add to the findings determined by either of the other strategies. Also schools may use a published scheme (or, as mentioned above, the Ofsted *Evaluation Schedule*) as a basis for developing their own scheme. This approach has the advantage of tailoring a comprehensive published scheme to suit the school's own needs and to take account of the context of the school.

Constructing the plan – where do we want to go?

There are two main considerations when beginning to construct the development plan:

- the plan should be *realistic* so that the goals set are achievable with the available resources including staff time
- the plan should take account of the *context* of the school.

The school context, i.e. the main factors which affect school planning, is:

- the school's aims and mission
- national policies and initiatives such as the national curriculum, numeracy and literacy initiatives, teacher appraisal, etc.
- local policies and initiative such as links with the community, industry, etc.
- existing school initiatives such as targets set in teacher appraisal
- action points raised in an Ofsted inspection report and issues arising from the audit
- available finance and resources.

The stages in constructing the development plan are then:

1   choosing the priorities
2   producing a draft plan
3   consulting before agreeing the final plan
4   agreeing the final plan and securing and allocating finance and resources
5   writing up and publicising the plan.

Choosing the priorities

Some of the priorities for the development plan will be pre-determined, for example, statutory requirements, action points from the Ofsted inspection report, etc. The first step in choosing other priorities is consultation. The more that stakeholders are involved at the consultation stage, the more they are likely to be committed to the implementation of the plan. Consultation should not be limited to the school's teaching staff and governors. Support staff, parents and pupils may be able to provide positive contributions as might others external to the school. It is likely that the consultation process will produce a long list of largely unconnected priorities and the more widespread the consultation process, the longer the list will be.

The next crucial stage is then to determine which priorities will be tackled in the current year of the plan and which will be deferred to future years. It is very important that the plan is realistic, to avoid the risk of trying to do too much, and that it is coherent in that the priorities identified are sequenced in a way that makes implementation easier both within the current plan and between the plans for future years. In agreeing the priorities with staff, governors and other partners, four questions should be asked:

- How urgent is the priority?
- What is the scale of the priority?
- Is there a foundation already in place or is it a 'new' priority?
- Can links be made with other priorities?

Clearly, some priorities are more urgent than others and some, such as responding to government requirements or, crucially, issues identified as action points in an Ofsted report, may be unavoidable. Others may be desirable but less urgent. It is important to try not to let the urgent or unavoidable tasks squeeze out those which the school believes are desirable as there is a risk of them being squeezed out year after year and the school losing the opportunity to develop in its own way. One way of ensuring this, where the degree of urgency permits, is to divide major 'externally-driven' initiatives into a series of annual priorities thus leaving space in the plan for the school's own priorities.

In estimating the scale of priorities, it is necessary to make early judgements about the length of time required for a priority, the finance and resources it requires, the staff workload and the number of staff who might be involved. If possible, a small number of major priorities should be chosen so that there is space left for smaller, minor ones. Overall, the priorities identified in the plan must be achievable with the resources available and within the capacity of those involved.

Hargreaves and Hopkins (1991: 41) suggest an approach that can help to make decisions about the sequencing of priorities. They identify two types of priority – root innovations, and branch innovations where 'Root innovations … generate the base on which … branch innovations can be sustained' (p.43). They suggest that strong roots are provided by features such as good school management, a well-designed staff development policy, and a history of collaboration amongst staff and with the school's partners. It is likely that both types of innovation will have a place in the development plan.

It is likely that the priorities chosen for any one year will be diverse, which has the advantage of involving many (if not all) of the school's staff and partners thus increasing commitment to the plan and also spreading the workload. However, some priorities may be chosen which are closely related and these have the advantage of fostering collaboration between staff and others. The linking of priorities might also make the implementation of the plan more efficient by 'killing two birds with one stone'. *This is an area in which heads of department and curriculum leaders may have a particular role in identifying opportunities for inter-departmental and cross-curricular priorities.*

Producing a draft plan

The key element in the draft plan is, as mentioned above, to set out the detailed goals in order of priority for the coming year and in outline for the next two or three years. DES (1991) illustrates the sequencing of priorities in the development plan of a secondary school as is shown in Figure 4.3. The diagram shows that some priorities may spread over from one year to the next.

The draft plan should also include draft action plans (see below) as these will help identify the resource implications of the plan and any possible problems with co-ordination.

Figure 4.3 Sequencing of priorities in a secondary school development plan

YEAR 1			YEAR 2			YEAR 3		
Term 1	Term 2	Term 3	Term 1	Term 2	Term 3	Term 1	Term 2	Term 3
◀			NC Subjects					▶
Cross-Curric. Policy ⟶		Health Ed. Careers Ed. ⟶		Environ. Ed. Citizenship ⟶		Economic and Industrial Understanding ⟶		
Records of Achievement			⟶	Assessment and Recording				▶
Attendance⟶	PSE Programme			⟶	School-Industry Links		⟶	▶
◀			Staff Development Policy					▶

Source: After DES, 1991: 19.

Consulting before agreeing the final plan

As many of the stakeholders as possible should have the opportunity to read and comment on the plan in order to identify any difficulties and to strengthen the feeling of shared ownership of, and hence commitment to, the plan.

Agreeing the final plan and securing and allocating finance and resources

Once the consultation process is complete and any necessary changes have been made, the development plan is submitted to the governing body for final approval. The planning process is linked to the budgetary process of the school and it is important that the necessary resources are allocated to the priorities identified in the plan. For this reason, the plan might be submitted to the governors' finance sub-committee and be subject to further amendment before being submitted to the full governing body.

Writing up and publicising the plan

Once the plan has been finally approved, it should be written up and be made widely available to all stakeholders. Hargreaves and Hopkins suggest:

> a booklet of perhaps four to six pages [which] might include:
>
> - the aims of the school;
> - a review of the previous year's plan;
> - the proposed priorities and their timescale;
> - the justification of the priorities in the context of the school;
> - how the plan draws together different aspects of planning;
> - the method of reporting outcomes;
> - the resource implications.
>
> (Hargreaves and Hopkins, 1991: 48)

Implementation – How are we going to get there?

Once the development plan has been agreed, each priority will normally be allocated to a team, often led by a 'middle manager', which takes responsibility for drawing up and implementing an action plan – the operational plan or working document that describes the work to be done and, importantly, the means of measuring the success of the plan. Each priority is broken down into a number of targets which, in the action plan, are broken down into a number of specific tasks which are shared amongst the team.

Each action plan should:

- set out the priority as in the development plan
- list the targets within the priority

- list the tasks to be undertaken by each team
- identify the staff responsible for the targets and tasks with timescales or target completion dates
- set the dates for meetings to review progress
- identify the resource implications, including finance, materials and staff development needs.

Once the action plan is agreed, it is important for the teams to sustain their commitment momentum. The support of senior staff and their interest in the process will help sustain commitment. Regular team meetings will help sustain commitment *and* maintain momentum. Regular progress checks are an essential element of implementing the action plan and should be built into the process. The frequency of progress checks will depend on the action plan's timescale but they should be carried out at least once per term. Regular progress checks will also contribute to the evaluation phase of the development planning process and thus reduce workloads. It is, therefore, important that they are based on clear evidence and that they are recorded. A member of the team should be given the specific responsibility for ensuring that progress checks take place and recording them.

It is inevitable that unforeseen problems will be encountered in carrying out the action plan and, in the event of the team experiencing serious difficulties, it might be necessary, in consultation with the head or the chair of the SPT, to adopt one or more of the following tactics:

- provide extra support for the team
- re-assign responsibilities within the team
- involve other, perhaps more experienced, staff
- seek outside help
- temporarily freeze part of the action plan
- modify the timescale
- reduce the planned action to make it more manageable
- postpone a target to a later year and bring forward an alternative target.

(After Hargreaves and Hopkins, 1991: 52)

Evaluation – how well did we do it?

If the regular progress checks carried out by each team are recorded, they can form the basis of an initial evaluation of the success of the action plan. Collation of the action plan evaluations will, in turn, provide a means of assessing the extent to which each priority has been addressed and collation of these assessments will provide a basis for evaluating the success with which the development plan as a whole has been implemented.

Producing the action plan evaluations requires:

- collating the progress checks
- discussing and analysing the progress checks within the team
- writing a brief report on the extent to which the targets have been met.

Producing the final report on each priority requires:

- collating the reports on each target
- identifying implications for future work on the priority
- identifying the implications for the school as a whole.

Overall evaluation of the development planning activity at the end of each planning cycle then involves collating and analysing the reports on each of the priorities. This is usually carried out by a senior member of staff or the SPT. This evaluation is where the school establishes the success of those priorities which have been completed within the planning year and assesses the progress of any priorities whose implementation runs into the following year. The outcome of the overall evaluation is an annual report which may be submitted to the governing body but should also be disseminated to all stakeholders in some form, including pupils and parents.

The planning cycle comes full circle with the construction of the next year's development plan when the outline priorities in the current year's plan become the detailed priorities of the next year's plan subject to other factors such as:

- the outcomes of the next year's audit
- changes in national or local policies or initiatives
- the changing circumstances of the school
- the outcomes of any other evaluations such as Ofsted inspections.

CONCLUSION

Development planning is an essential part of a school's strategic planning process. It is the part of the process that converts the sometimes nebulous concepts of mission and vision into clear, tangible goals and realisable plans, and translates planning into action. It is, essentially, a practical activity. It is about delivering real change which is the essence of school improvement. In these turbulent times, schools are increasingly subject to all types of pressures for change – ever changing government policies and initiatives, Ofsted inspections, etc. Development planning allows schools to cope with these pressures in a way that enables them to take at least some control of the way that this change is managed.

It also has the potential to do much more than that. It leads the school to ask fundamental questions about its purpose and aims, especially in the audit phase of the process, from which shared aims and assumptions – key determinants of a distinctive school culture – may evolve. Furthermore, one of the key features of development planning is that it can and *should* involve the whole school. *In doing so, it provides opportunities for the greater involvement and hence development of the school's 'middle managers'.* It also facilitates greater involvement of all staff and, therefore, the democratisation of the school. At its very best, it might encourage an environment which leads to 'holistic relationships which focus on integration rather than fragmentation (and) a new form of leadership predicated on openness, collaboration and power sharing' (Bell, 2002).

BIBLIOGRAPHY

Bell, L. (2002) 'Strategic planning and school management: full of sound and fury, signifying nothing?', Inaugural Professorial Lecture, University of Leicester.

Davies, B. and Ellison, E. (1999) *Strategic Direction and Development of the School*, London: Routledge.

Department for Education and Science (1989) *Planning for School Development: Advice for Governors, Headteachers and Teachers*, London: HMSO.

Department for Education and Science (1991) *School Development Planning: A Practical Guide*, London: HMSO.

Drakeford, B. and Cooling, J. (1998) *The Secondary Whole-School Audit*, London: David Fulton.

Giles, C. (1997) *School Development Planning*, Plymouth: Northcote House.

Hargreaves, D.H. and Hopkins, D. (1991) *The Empowered School: The Management and Practice of Development Planning*, London: Cassell.

Hopkins, D. (1991) 'Changing school culture through development planning', in S. Ridell and S. Brown (eds) *School Effectiveness Research: Its Messages for School Improvement*, Edinburgh: HMSO.

Middlewood, D. and Riley, M. (1995) *Development Planning for Schools*, Leicester: University of Leicester.

Ofsted (1992) *The Handbook for the Inspection of Schools*, London: HMSO.

Ofsted (1995) *Guidance on the Inspection of Secondary Schools*, London: HMSO.

Ofsted (1999) *Handbook for Inspecting Secondary Schools*, London: HMSO.

Parsons, C., Howlett, K. and Corbett, F. (1994) *Institutional Development Planning: A Staff Development Manual for Primary and Secondary Schools and FE Colleges*, Lancaster: Framework Press.

FURTHER READING

Lumby, J. (2002) 'Vision and strategic planning', in T. Bush and L. Bell (eds) *The Principles and Practice of Educational Management*, London: Paul Chapman Publishing.

Middlewood, D. and Lumby, J. (eds) (1998) *Strategic Management in Schools and Colleges*, London: Paul Chapman Publishing.

4.3 School Leadership and ICT: Training for Integration

Tony Lawson and Chris Comber

INTRODUCTION

OBJECTIVES

By the end of this Unit you should:

- Understand how and why ICT has come to be so important in the management of schools;
- Know about the concept of the 'integrative school' where ICT is used to promote learning across the curriculum;
- Be aware of the relationship between strategic leadership and ICT.

Up until the early 1990s, the use of computers in UK schools was a relatively limited activity, often confined to particular subjects such as maths, science or technology. Since then, a steady growth in computer usage in schools led to its more widespread use in other curriculum areas, and a concomitant increase in the experience of and confidence in computing amongst teaching staff. More recently, the advent of the Internet/WWW and the widespread use of e-mail, reflected in the now common use of the acronym 'ICT' rather than simply 'IT' (the 'C' standing for 'communications'), has introduced a new dimension to educational technology, so that students no longer need to be merely 'computer literate', but also 'network literate', defined as the ability to use computers to access and create electronic resources and to communicate with others (Scrimshaw, 1997).

Meanwhile, shifts in curriculum policy which place ICT at the centre of the learning agenda have been linked together as part of the UK government's *National Grid for Learning* (NGfL) initiative, the school-focused component of which now comes under the general umbrella of the *ICT in Schools* programme. This encompasses a broad range of initiatives which have helped to equip schools, train teachers, and develop online educational resources. Within the British educational system, therefore, there has been a substantial increase in the exposure of all pupils to computers in the last decade. From a position of relative weakness, where much of the existing equipment in classrooms was described as 'incapable of running the latest software' (McKinsey & Co., 1997), the majority of schools in the UK now have modern computer suites running networked computers. Add to this the dramatic increase in home ownership of computers (DfES, 2001a; DfES, 2001b; Comber *et al.*, 2002), and we have a picture of both pupils and their teachers having much greater exposure to and experience of computer technology, and in a broader range of contexts, than was the case even five or six years ago.

INTEGRATIVE SCHOOLS

In previous work (Lawson and Comber, 1999), we have explored the personnel factors that led to the 'integrative school', that is where ICT is used to promote learning across all curriculum areas and in a seamless way. We concluded that a range of factors relating to teachers' attitudes – which included a collegial approach, a willingness to innovate, and a readiness to respond to, as well as lead, students with respect to ICT – were key components of the integrative school. An enhanced role for the ICT manager/ co-ordinator, with devolved powers typical of a distributed leadership system, was also a common feature of such schools.

One of the main characteristics of the integrative school, and to a considerable extent a prerequisite for establishing an environment where positive teacher attitudes towards ICT could thrive, was the presence of a particular type of headteacher/principal. These school leaders promoted and developed an ethos that embraced technological change and managed its implementation in educationally effective ways. This whole-hearted support for ICT as a tool for raising educational standards was signalled in various ways by leaders in schools. In particular it was exemplified by a long-term view of investment in ICT in a climate of innovation and the recognition of the efforts of those involved in promoting good practice with ICT in the school, through rewards in terms of finance, status or power. More recent evidence from the UK supports the view that a supportive and forward looking school leader is a critical component in the integration of ICT into classroom practice (NAACE, 2001).

As we have argued elsewhere, given the right conditions, ICT has the potential to be a *transformative technology* (Lawson and Comber, 2000) with the capability to shift fundamentally both the nature of the curriculum and the means of its delivery. The increasing pace at which ICT is being urged upon schools, both in the UK and elsewhere, thus constitutes a considerable challenge for schools if this potential is to be fully realised. If the integrative school is to become the norm rather than the exception, then an increasing number of school leaders will need to develop the kind of supportive leadership role with respect to ICT development described above.

However, according to a recent government report, the use of ICT by school leaders to access information or to manage data is 'currently under-developed in the majority of schools' (Earley *et al.*, 2002: 64). Effective leadership in ICT is often incidental rather than planned, with successful heads commonly those who had a personal interest in ICT and a belief in both its educational and administrative potential.

INTEGRATING ICT AND EFFECTIVE LEADERSHIP

While the characteristics of the integrative school are fairly clear, the relationship between schools that integrate ICT into their practice (whether pedagogical or adminis- trative) and those schools who are deemed to be 'effective' is less certain. Research into effective schools and the role of school leadership within them has only rarely considered the impact of ICT on effectiveness. Indeed, Rudd (2002: 1) characterises the relationship between school improvement and ICT research thus: 'reading across these two bodies of research literature one is left with the impression that these are two distinct, almost unrelated areas of educational research'. Studies into school leadership have neglected the role of ICT in driving up attainment, with some exceptions (see, for example, Bennett, 1996). Until recently (see Harrison *et al.*, 2002 and Comber *et al.*, 2002 on the ImpaCT2 research), much of the research into ICT and effectiveness has focused on issues such as motivation (see, for example, Cox, 1997) rather than achievement and underplayed the role of school leadership.

Empirical work on school leadership and effectiveness has, in the main, neglected ICT as a challenging context for exercise of leadership. For example, Sammons *et al.* (1995) identified the key characteristics of successful schools, without mentioning ICT specifically. In Neil *et al.*'s (2001) study of 'Principals in action', the log diaries of the participating principals made no mention of specific issues surrounding ICT, beyond a general concern of engaging with teaching and learning and disseminating good practice. Similarly, in a cross-cultural study of leadership, entitled 'Effective leadership in a time of change', Reeves *et al.* (1998) reported no findings directly concerned with the introduction or management of ICT in relation to effective leadership. Given that, arguably, ICT represents one of the major challenges to schools in the late twentieth and early twenty-first century, this omission from the lives and qualities of the effective school leaders is puzzling (Lawson and Comber, 2002).

In a more theoretical review of ideas on school leadership, Fidler (1997) identifies the key elements that have been put forward by various perspectives on the nature of leadership. In exploring the nature of the relationship between leadership and management, he identifies a contrast between the problem-solving and strategy- developing function of *leadership* and the planning and organisational skills of *management* as a crucial dichotomy in dealing with conditions of stability and change (op. cit. p. 26). This contrast is highly pertinent to the attempt to integrate ICT into learning and teaching, as ICT use needs both innovation and robustness of provision to be most effective in raising standards (see Comber *et al.*, 2002).

In Fidler's (1997) review of the various approaches to leadership, the absence of ICT or indeed any technological skills is noticeable in all accounts. While the general attributes of effective leaders might subsume issues about ICT, they are not specifically referred to. For example, Hughes (1985) argued that a professional organisation such as a school needed to be led by those with pedagogic and curricular high status. In the current situation where the introduction of ICT is such a high priority, the leader's knowledge and encouragement of ICT in the classroom should be exemplary and yet, no mention is made of the challenge that ICT presents to the leaders of schools.

This absence of ICT in exploring the role of management can also be seen in the work of Dimmock and Walker (2000) when they consider the impact of globalisation on schooling and school leadership. While they briefly acknowledge the importance of electronic media in the process of globalisation, they do not consider its impact on schooling itself and the new conditions that face school leaders in managing a cutting edge technology in an educational setting. Similarly, in a fascinating debate between Grace (2000, 2001) and Morrison (2001) on transformative leadership in schools, neither side gives any prominence to the potentially transformative role of ICT (see Lawson and Comber, 2000) in schooling generally. The emphasis on transformative leadership is particularly appropriate for schools facing reform and innovation (see Leithwood and Jantzi, 1999). The studies into transformative leadership (see Hallinger, 1992) have two lessons for an integration of ICT into schools. First, the direct effects of leadership on student outcomes are weak, but when mediated through other variables, of which ICT provision and use must be one, the effects can be significant (see Hallinger and Heck, 1996). Second, a form of distributed transformational leadership may be the most likely to impact upon student outcomes, so that the role of leaders other than the principal is worthy of investigation (see Fidler, 1997).

The research that does seek to examine leadership in the context of ICT tends to adopt this distributed model of leadership, often focusing on the ICT leaders in schools. For example, Anderson and Dexter (2000) argued that the analysis of 'technology leadership' is best placed to explore the inter-relationship between the numerous 'leaders' needed to integrate ICT into schools, the ability of a school to handle the complex changes that accompany the introduction of ICT into schools and the learning culture of the school. Other research has focused on the need for a school 'vision' of successful integration as represented in the policy statements prepared by school leaders (see Costello, 1997). Another approach focuses on 'teacher leaders', one of whose characteristics is their ability to model the effective use of ICT in their teaching and learning (see Riel and Becker, 2000). These teacher leaders may include or not include school leaders. Arguing from a similar perspective, Sherry and Gibson (2002) propose that innovative or integrative practice will remain an isolated phenomenon (restricted for example to an individual classroom or department) if the support of (teacher or school) leaders is absent or withheld.

One strand of the research, however, does focus directly on school leaders/principals and their role in promoting ICT integration in schools. Yee (2000) developed an ICT leadership framework from a cross-cultural study of principals, in which she identified key features of successful leadership in ICT that had many parallels with the elements of transformational leadership. These were, amongst others:

- Fair provision of ICT resources, in which access and support were equitably supplied by the school leaders;
- Having and transmitting an appropriate vision of ICT and learning (see also Chandra-Handa, 2001);

- Support for and encouragement of innovative use of ICT and risk-taking (see Jacobsen *et al.*, 2002), through direct modelling by leaders;
- Provision of development time and opportunities in ICT for staff, including leaders.

The incidental rather than systematic presence of many of the above conditions suggest that much more needs to be done to enable school leaders to plan for the effective introduction of ICT into their organisations. Despite the considerable levels of funding dedicated to encouraging teachers to explore the teaching and learning implications of ICT, relatively little has been provided by way of professional development opportunities for headteachers.

From one perspective this may not seem entirely surprising, given the relative dearth of school leadership literature which considers ICT as an important school improvement issue. However, as Rudd (2002) points out, the considerable body of research which indicates a clear link between ICT integration and the kind of leadership associated with effective schooling suggests that this is an area of need every bit as great as that of teachers. Indeed it might be argued that for teachers to fully realise their own potential, effective leadership in ICT is a prerequisite.

However, as Schiller (2000), argues, writing from experience of both UK and Australian education, the majority of school leaders are neither prepared for, nor recognise the significance of their role in the planning and management of ICT in schools. Gibson (2000: 372) agrees, noting that in the field of school leadership training 'discussions of reform have rarely focussed upon the potential impact of technology on … thinking or practice'.

There is some evidence that this issue is being recognised. MacNeil and Delafield (1998) in a large-scale study conducted in the US, examined factors which inhibit computer use in US schools, clearly identifying the principal as occupying a key role in the process of building a 'learning community'. They go on to suggest that school leaders are both ready and willing to develop their expertise in this area. What is largely missing, therefore, is the opportunity to do so. Gibson (2000) describes a doctoral programme for leadership preparation which explores this potential, a rare exception to what appears to be the general rule. While this is a welcome (and reportedly successful) initiative, it represents a substantial commitment on the part of the course participants. Examples of shorter and less intensive programmes of in-service professional development are less commonly found and, within a UK context, have hitherto been limited to occasional and local support from LEAs and professional bodies.

DEVELOPING STRATEGIC LEADERSHIP IN ICT

This gap in provision was recognised, in 2001, by the newly established National College for School Leadership (NCSL), set up to enable school leaders to acquire the 'skills, recognition, capacity and ambition' required for the development of effective and forward looking schools. Funded by the UK government, NCSL provides and supports a range of services and courses such as the National Professional Qualification for Headship (NPQH) for emergent school leaders, the Headteachers' Leadership and Management Programme (HEADLAMP) and the Leadership Programme for Serving Headteachers (LPSH).

The Strategic Leadership in ICT (SLICT) programme was launched as a series of four pilot initiatives beginning in the autumn term of 2001, with the fourth and final cohort of school leaders completing the course at the end of the summer term 2002. Each cohort was made up of between 30–40 headteachers. Each had applied to join the course (which was, for the period of the pilot initiative, offered free of charge) on a 'first come first served' basis in response to a national advertisement. The model was designed to be flexible and responsive to the differing needs of the four cohorts, which were drawn from both primary and secondary sectors, and from various geographical locations in England. The participants thus represented a broad spectrum of knowledge and experience of ICT and ICT management. What was common to all participants, however, was a desire to develop their strategic leadership of ICT within their institution.

The training model

The core objective of the programme was to encourage headteachers to examine the leadership and management implications of managing ICT in their own school, and to develop a strategic approach to ICT planning. More specifically, the course sought – in addition to developing ICT capability – to enable school leaders to develop their understanding of the use of ICT for improving school effectiveness, to enhance teaching and learning. This involved developing a whole-school approach to ICT policy and strategic planning.

One of the key issues for the course designers was to develop a model which could deliver these objectives while being appropriate to the particular context in which each school leader operated. One of the strengths of the recent government-sponsored teacher training programme (commonly referred to by schools as 'NOF' training, after the source of funding for the initiative, the New Opportunities Fund), had been that several staff at the same institution would often be working their way through the programme together. Even where training tasks required an individual response, teachers could draw upon collegial support. The relatively solitary position of a school leader, however, largely militates against this approach. Accordingly, the SLICT model incorporated a residential component: a three day event followed by a further 'consolidation' day, separated by a period of approximately twelve weeks. During this interim, course participants communicated with one another, and with course organisers, via a specially designed online environment.

The effectiveness of the SLICT approach

The effectiveness of the pilot phase of the programme was evaluated by a research team based at the School of Education, University of Leicester (Brundrett *et al.*, 2002). This involved a combination of surveys, observations of various programme activities and events and an analysis of communications within an online environment.

Model of training

This first (three day) residential element of the programme involved a broad range of activities and events which included plenary, group and individual work. Successive sessions were designed to move from the current position (as identified in the self-evaluation audit), to identifying priorities for future action and developing an action plan. A typical session involved a 'scene setting' talk from an expert in the field of ICT leadership, followed by an open discussion, succeeded by small-group workshop activities intended to encourage the participants to reflect on the topic under discussion in the context of their own institution. Separating these group sessions were visits to local schools which were regarded as exemplifying good practice in and leadership of ICT, but carefully selected to represent different areas of strength rather than each being presented as a 'super school'.

After a three month period, the group returned for a fourth 'consolidation' day. The objectives of this final day were to reflect on progress made in the interim and share good practice, to establish or further develop contacts and networks for future collaboration, to consider and discuss practical steps for short- to medium-term initiatives and to engage in the setting of a 'vision' for longer-term developments.

In order to maintain the momentum between the two residential events, communication between participants was facilitated by the online environment. This was a dedicated internet site where each cohort represented a 'community', each with its own space. Over the three month period, members of each community posted action plans, set and developed discussion topics, accessed (and added to) a bank of online resources and links, and took part in 'hotseat' debating sessions on ICT related themes.

Impact

The course was almost universally praised for its planning and organisation, while terms such as 'impressive' and 'inspirational' were used by several participants to describe their response to the programme overall. A common thread throughout each element of the course was the opportunity to hear from and share experiences and ideas with fellow professionals, regarded by the participants as a particular strength of the programme. The first residential component was especially highly valued in this regard, since the chance to spend extended time exploring the various issues raised by the course represented something of a luxury in the life of a busy headteacher. That these themes could be explored both formally during the organised sessions and (when these were completed) informally, added to the worth of this element of the programme.

One of the most positively rated aspects of the course was the visits to exemplar schools. In some senses the visits were both reassuring – in that many participants identified aspects of practice which they had already achieved or were working towards – and inspiring in that they discovered ideas or approaches which they could take back with them. Several headteachers made arrangements to maintain contact with the host schools, or developed the idea by arranging similar visits with schools back in their own area.

Relatively speaking, remote exchanges via the online environment were perceived to be less successful than face-to-face interaction. Though used with increasing frequency by successive cohorts, users did encounter some difficulties in developing and maintaining communication. While some of these were of a technical nature, it is clear that schools have yet to develop the kind of 'online culture' – the routine use of email and the internet – that is more common in higher educational and commercial settings. Along with the everyday pressures faced by the modern headteacher, such issues combined to form something of a barrier to regular participation for some. Nevertheless, despite such difficulties, the online environment was generally regarded as having considerable potential and an important component of the course.

CONCLUSIONS

There is a clear disjunction between the rhetoric of those that claim revolutionary potential for new technologies, the considerable body of research literature which indicates that realising this potential in schools is contingent on effective school leadership, and the equally substantial work on school effectiveness which hardly acknowledges these claims, let alone addresses them. We have also shown that while this issue is beginning to be recognised more widely, there have to date been only limited attempts to address it.

We have briefly described the trialling of an innovative model of professional development in the UK which has both recognised and sought to address this need. Although it is only possible so far[1] to identify the impact of the course in the short term, early indicators suggest that it has had a significant and positive effect on many of the participants, increasing knowledge and understanding of the potential of ICT for both managerial and pedagogic developments. This has manifested itself in a recognition of the need for a whole-school approach to ICT development, and a more inclusive disposition to ICT policy and planning associated with a clear acknowledgement of the necessity of supporting staff at all levels in their own professional development. We suggest that this approach to professional development in ICT leadership offers a potential model for all school leaders and other teacher leaders in ICT.

NOTE

1   At the time of writing (early 2003) the programme is into its second phase, being delivered to around 800 headteachers in England, with a view to extending the project nationwide in the near future.

REFERENCES

Anderson, R.E. and Dexter, S.L. (2000) *School Technology Leadership: Incidence and Impact*, Irvine, CA: Center for Research on Information Technology and Organizations. Available at http://www.crito.uci.edu/tlc/html/findings.html. Accessed 16 December 2002.

Bennett, C.K. (1996) 'Schools, technology and educational leadership: a framework for change', *National Association of Secondary School Principals Bulletin*, 80, 577: 57–65.

Brundrett, M., Comber, C., Sommefeldt, D., McEune, R. and Burton, N. (2002) *Strategic Leadership in ICT Programme: Interim Report* (unpublished evaluation report).

Chandra-Handa, M. (2001) *Leading Academic Change – Through Connective Leadership and Learning*, Norfolk, VA: AACE. Available online at http: //www.aace.org/dl/index.cfm.

Comber, C., Watling, R., Lawson, T., Cavendish, S., McEune, R. and Paterson, F. (2002) *ImpaCT2 Public Report Part 2: Learning at Home and School – Case Studies*, Coventry: BECTa. Available online at http: //www.becta.org.uk/research/reports/impact2/index.html.

Costello, R.W. (1997) 'The leadership role in making the technology connection', *T.H.E. Journal*, 25: 58–62.

Cox, M.J. (1997) *The Effects of Information Technology on Students' Motivation: Final Report*, Coventry: NCET.

DfES (2001a) *Using ICT to Enhance Home-school Links: An Evaluation of Current Practice in England*, Coventry: BECTa.

DfES (2001b) *Young People and ICT*, London: DfES.

Dimmock, C. and Walker, A. (2000) 'Globalisation and societal culture', *Compare*, 30, 3: 303–12.

Earley, P., Evans, J., Collarbone, P., Gold, A. and Halpin, D. (2002) *Establishing the Current State of School Leadership In England*, London: Department for Education and Skills.

Fidler, B. (1997) 'School leadership: some key ideas', *School Leadership and Management*, 17, 1: 23–37.

Gibson, I. (2000) *Information Technology and the Transformation of Leadership Preparation Programs: A Response to Calls for Reform in Educational Practice*, Norfolk, VA: AACE. Available online at http: // www.aace.org/dl/index.cfm.

Grace, G. (2000) 'Research and the challenges of contemporary school leadership: the contribution of critical scholarship', *British Journal of Educational Studies*, 48, 3: 231–47.

Grace, G. (2001) 'Contemporary school leadership: reflections on Morrison', *British Journal of Educational Studies*, 49, 4: 386–91.

Hallinger, P. (1992) 'The evolving role of American principals: from managerial to instructional to transformational leaders', *Journal of Educational Administration*, 30: 35–48.

Hallinger, P. and Heck, R.H. (1996) 'Exploring the principal's contribution to school effectiveness 1980–1995', *School Effectiveness and School Improvement*, 9: 157–91.

Harrison, C., Comber, C., Fisher, T., Haw, K., Lewin, C., Lunzer, E., McFarlane, A., Mavers, D., Scrimshaw, P., Somekh, B. and Watling, R. (2002) *ImpaCT2: The Impact of Information and Communication Technologies on Pupil Learning and Attainment*, Coventry: BECTa. Available online at http://www.becta.org.uk/research/reports/impact2/index.html.

Hughes, M. (1985) 'Leadership in professionally staffed organisations', in M. Hughes, P. Ribbins and H. Thomas (eds) *Managing Education: The System and the Institution*, London, Cassell.

Jacobsen, D.M., Clifford, P. and Friesen, S. (2002) 'Transformational leadership and professional development for digitally rich learning environments: a case study of the Galileo Educational Network', Paper presented at ED-MEDIA: World Conference on Educational Multimedia/ Hypermedia and Educational Telecommunication. Denver, Colorado, 24–29 June. Available online at http://www.aace.org/dl/index.cfm.

Lawson, T. and Comber, C. (1999) 'Superhighways technology: personnel factors leading to successful integration of ICT in schools and colleges', *Journal of Information Technology for Teacher Education*, 8, 1: 41–53.

Lawson, T. and Comber, C. (2000) 'Introducing information and communications technologies into schools: the blurring of boundaries', *British Journal of Sociology of Education*, 21, 3: 419–33.

Lawson, T. and Comber, C. (2002) 'Breaking the ICT barrier: challenges and opportunities on the way to the integrative school', Paper presented to the International Conference on Information and Communication Technologies in Education (ICTE), Badajoz, Spain, 20–23 November.

Leithwood, K. and Jantzi, D. (1999) 'Transformational school leadership effects: a replication', *School Effectiveness and School Improvement*, 10, 4: 451–79.

MacNeil, A. and Delafield, D. (1998) 'Principal leadership for successful school technology implementation', Paper presented at the Society for Information Technology and Teacher Education International Conference, Washington, 10–14 March.

McKinsey & Co. (1997) *The Future of Information Technology in UK Schools*, London: McKinsey & Co.

Morrison, K. (2001) 'Simplicity and complexity in contemporary school leadership: a response to Grace', *British Journal of Educational Studies*, 49, 4: 379–85.

NAACE (2001) *The Impact of ICT on Schooling*, Nottingham: National Association for Advisers for Computers in Education.

Neil, P., Carlisle, K., Knipe, D. and McEwen, A. (2001) 'Principals in action, an analysis of school leadership', *Research in Education*, 66: 40–53.

Reeves, J., Moos, L. and Forrest, J. (1998) 'Making sense of school leadership in the 1990s: being and becoming', *Journal of In-service Education*, 24, 2: 329–45.

Riel, M. and Becker, H. (2000) *The Beliefs, Practices and Computer Use of Teacher Leaders*, Irvine, CA: Center for Research on Information Technology and Organizations. Available online at http://www.crito.uci.edu/tlc/findings/aera. Accessed 16 December.

Rudd, P. (2002) 'School Improvement through ICT: limitations and possibilities', Paper presented to the European Conference on Educational research University of Edinburgh, 22 September. Available online at http://www.leeds.ac.uk/educol/documents/00001768.htm. Accessed 25 November.

Sammons, P., Hillman, J. and Mortimore, P. (1995) *Key Characteristics of Effective Schools: A Review of School Effectiveness Research*, London: Institute of Education.

Schiller, D. (2000) 'Facilitating the integration of computers in schools: meeting today's major leadership challenge', *Annual Computers in Education Conference Program and Abstracts*, Melbourne: ACEC. Available online at http://www.ictev.vic.edu.au/acec2000/paper_nonref/j-schiller/npaper038.htm.

Scrimshaw, P. (1997) *Preparing for the Information Age: Synoptic Report of the Education Department's Superhighways Initiative (EDSI)*, London: DfEE/NCET.

Sherry, L. and Gibson, D. (2002) 'The path to teacher leadership in educational technology', *Contemporary Issues in Technology and Teacher Education* [Online serial], 2(2). Available online at http://www.citejournal.org/vol2/iss2/general/article2.cfm. Accessed December.

Yee, D.L. (2000) 'Images of school principals' information and communications technology leadership', *Journal of Information Technology for Teacher Education*, 9, 3: 287–302.

FURTHER READING

Lawson, T. and Comber, C. (1999) 'Superhighways technology: personnel factors leading to successful integration of ICT in schools and colleges', *Journal of Information Technology for Teacher Education*, 8, 1: 41–53.

Lawson, T. and Comber, C. (2000) 'Introducing information and communications technologies into schools: the blurring of boundaries', *British Journal of Sociology of Education*, 21, 3: 419–33.

McKinsey & Co. (1997) *The Future of Information Technology in UK Schools*, London: McKinsey & Co.

NAACE (2001) *The Impact of ICT on Schooling*, Nottingham: National Association for Advisers for Computers in Education.

4.4 Using 'Value Added' Data for Raising Attainment

Lesley Saunders

INTRODUCTION: WHY 'VALUE ADDED'?

OBJECTIVES

By the end of this Unit you should:

- Have learned some practical guidelines for using value added analyses of student performance for developmental purposes;
- Understand some of the ideas of what counts as 'evidence';
- Understand the basics of measuring performance.

The introduction of the national 'value added' system in 1998 could be seen as the culmination of a decade of sustained and fairly public argument about how to measure the performance of pupils in the nation's schools in a way that sheds light on their progress as well as on standards. Measured at the school level, 'value added' is the most accurate way we have at present of calculating how well schools perform with their pupils. If only 'raw' results are used to assess a school's performance, they reveal more about the background of the pupils than about the performance of the school. 'Value added' measurement works by discounting factors tied into pupils' achievements but unrelated to institutional quality. However, this sharpened focus on more sophisticated ways of evaluating schools' performance – which may have far-reaching consequences for the education system, the schools and their pupils – means that it is crucial to get the calculation, interpretation and uses of 'value added' data right.

WHAT COUNTS AS EVIDENCE?

Leaders in schools all over the world are hungry for good evidence to use in school evaluation. The problem is, to be sure of what counts as good evidence and how you can put it all together to make sense of the complexity of your school, what it achieves and how to move it on and sustain that energy.

So in this chapter I am going to talk about performance data and particularly 'value added' analyses. This is not to say that qualitative evidence is less important, valuable or rigorous: it is a question of 'both/and', rather than of 'either/or'. We don't have to take sides: to live and breathe performance data or else hate it; to value impressionistic, subjective and experiential evidence or else to pooh-pooh it as too 'touchy-feely'. Though there are people who do. I have met heads of department who proselytize about the new database he (often a he, I must say) has spent countless precious after-school hours creating. On this, every piece of assessment information is stored about every pupil and the search is on for the single test that will generate foolproof predictions of their future performance at GCSE. Charts and tables are produced and circulated to all the other departments. Whether and how they are used is another matter...

Then there is the head of another department who folds his arms (not always a he, this time), fixes me with a hard stare and says: 'None of this [by which he means value added analyses and the like] is any use to me. After thirty years in the profession, I know what my pupils are capable of; I don't need bloody number-crunchers churning out reams of meaningless figures'. He or she adds, 'Now if you'll excuse me I've got to go and rehearse the school concert'.

I am sure both these attitudes have something to do with the sheer amount of data in schools and the public sector as a whole, and the 'high stakes' which attach to it. Reputations, jobs even, hang on percentages going always up, never down. Data does not arrive in a neutral context: people's value systems, the beliefs they hold dear about the world, the cliques or factions they align with, what they are against as much as what they are for, and, above all, the institutional power relationships in their school *immediately* mediate the meaning of any data which is generated.

But in reality *quantitative* and *qualitative* embody different ways of looking at the world which need to be continually handled and managed rather than resolved or unified. Does light consist of waves or particles? It depends on what you want to use the light for.

What may sometimes be illuminating are the discrepancies and anomalies, the things that do not fit, the puzzles and missing bits in what different kinds of evidence tell us about performance and progress. There is no such thing as totally perfect or objective data, in any case. What you choose to measure depends on prior decisions or assumptions about what is important to measure. This is the School Curriculum and Assessment Authority working party on value added, reporting to the Secretary of State in 1994:

> ... decisions about which variables to include inevitably depend on views about what is important in the real-world situation we are attempting to model ... Such decisions are therefore, almost inevitably, open to question and debate ... It therefore needs to be recognised that there is no single correct method of analysing a complex social situation ...
>
> (SCAA, 1994: 73)

The complexity of schools – and this includes the huge range of social goods the public expects schools to deliver – needs to be understood and respected. But this should not prevent us from making any statements about relative achievement and effectiveness. Educational research has given us, amongst other things, some powerful instruments for looking at pupils' performance. What matters is the use you make of the evidence, even when it is imperfect, and – crucially – whether it results in teachers talking about teaching and learning. The risk for schools is that discussions about performance data turn into a displacement activity, a political game.

UNDERSTANDING QUANTITATIVE DATA

It's important to have some basic background knowledge about quantitative data and the world of statistics because there are sometimes misunderstandings about what such data analyses can do and what they can't.

Let's be clear that the purpose of quantitative information is to *reduce the complexity* of the real world. Quantitative information deals essentially with abstractions and simplifications – that's what it's there for. The major simplifications social scientists use are the tried-and-tested ones of age, sex, ethnicity and class – the standard variables which almost always correlate with comparative differences in average outcomes.

But comparisons involving the use of statistics – such as tables of performance – mean we are dealing in probabilities, not certainties. Even the most rigorous analysis has an irreducible amount of uncertainty or error built into it. Good statistical information always makes clear how far the difference between, say, one school's results and another's could be due to sheer chance.

Furthermore, whilst statistics can usefully tell us a great deal about average and aggregate results – about trends and patterns which are not visible, so to say, to the naked eye – it has rather less to say about any particular individual. If we take regression analysis, for example – where we might be trying to look at the relationship between previous and present performance to get a view of possible future performance – we can derive many valuable insights about pupils' performance as a whole or in sub-groups. But when we get down to the level of the individual, the amount of statistical uncertainty which has to be built into the analysis is so great as to render individual 'prediction' of performance not much better than guesswork. So the activity of target-setting for individual pupils that relies solely on extrapolation from past aggregate datasets is probably unhelpful.

Effective target-setting depends upon several kinds of measure, some based on aggregate performance data across a number of different tests and others based on an assessment of each individual's aptitude and attitude. And of course a target encompasses a value judgement of some kind about improvement. It's a truism (but still true!) that if a target at the class, department or school level can be achieved without changing the way the class, department or school operates, planned improvement can't happen. To be meaningful, targets must have some strategic implications for teaching, curriculum, management and/or staff development.

But another notion to be wary of is the notion of 'success against the odds': if the terminology is well-chosen and not just a catch-phrase, we are actually saying that the probabilities, the odds, are stacked against success – no doubt because the key variables of class, sex, ethnicity and prior attainment are at work again. So we should acknowledge that the messages from schools that buck the trend are by no means sure to be transferable. Such schools may be inspiring stories in themselves, but exceptions, however inspirational, do not make a sound basis for policy.

One of the problems has been that statistics and policy have tended in opposite directions, at least so far as 'value added' analysis is concerned. Statistical analyses tell us time and again that, once the key variables are accounted for, there are not many schools which are performing above or below the norm – which is hardly newsworthy; whereas the policy drive has been rather in the direction of clearly differentiating schools from each other.

The technical term for the statistical information that reveals better or worse than average performance is 'residual'. Residuals cause commotion in staff rooms up and down the country at the beginning of the autumn term as subject leaders and heads of department peer over each other's shoulders at the pages of bar charts. But what an illuminating idea a 'residual' potentially is. In a statistical model it is what is *left over* after you have accounted for all the things you already know about and can measure. A residual represents what we *don't* know about, and can therefore only speculate over. This is the aspect (rather than the rest of the statistical model) which school leaders should put their precious effort into understanding. And of course only qualitative evidence, combined with professional judgement, can help fill in the gap.

'VALUE ADDED' IN EDUCATIONAL PRACTICE

Now we can return to look at 'value added' more closely. The large-scale statistical studies typical of school effectiveness research have given us a great deal of intelligence with which to understand comparative educational performance or 'value added' as it has come to be known. If we want to understand performance in anything other than a crude and absolute way, we must take account of the factors over which individual schools have little or no direct control. Such factors include pupils' prior attainment, sex, ethnic group, date of birth, level of special educational need and social disadvantage. These factors – whether correlated positively with performance (as in the case of prior attainment) or negatively (as in the case of social disadvantage) – turn up as empirically verifiable items in study after study, and are the cogent ones to deal with in exploring apparent differences in the performance of schools.

Researchers at the Institute of Education at London University compared a variety of 'value added' approaches and they concluded that the best approach controls for the following variables:

- pupils' prior attainments in verbal, quantitative and non-verbal ability tests
- gender
- age
- ethnicity
- mobility
- socio-economic disadvantage
  and
- previous school attended.

We know other things, too; studies of 'school effectiveness' done at the London University Institute for Education, the National Foundation for Educational Research (NFER) and elsewhere tell us that even the best schools may be effective:

- with some pupils and not others
- in some subject areas and not others
- at one time and not another
- on some outcome indicators and not others
- taking account of some variables and not others.

'Value added' analyses reveal that most schools have at least some under-achievement – pupils who have not fulfilled their academic potential. So a critical issue for raising attainment is to be able to use data to distinguish between *low* achievement and *under*-achievement. Otherwise we may not know what kinds of support and challenge will most help. How can we do this? At subject or skill level we can get quite a long way by comparing pupils' performance at a previous time with their performance at a later time, relative to national patterns. This is not full 'value added' analysis, because it takes account only of pupils' prior attainment. However, *at the individual pupil level*, this is the most salient background factor to control for. Schools can access analyses to help them examine their own pupils' individual performance, like the example in Figure 4.4 created by the statistics team at NFER.

Figure 4.4 represents pupils' performance in written mathematics at Key Stage 2 (age 11) relative to the same pupils' average performance in Key Stage 1 (age 7) in a particular primary school. Each triangle is a boy and each circle is a girl. The pattern suggests that in this school children who got below level 2 at the end of Key Stage 1 under-performed in maths at Key Stage 2. I say *under*-performed, not because their mathematics score was low in itself, but because most of the circles and triangles in the left half of the diagram fall beneath the thick black line. According to national figures, you would expect half of them to be above that line, but the diagram reveals nothing like that many. The pattern is quite different for children in this school who obtained relatively high scores. (I stress again that we are looking for patterns here, not at individuals' performance.)

Or take an equivalent analysis for a secondary school's Key Stage 4 grades relative to Key Stage 3 average levels. In Figure 4.5, one of the key things to notice is the distribution of triangles (boys) compared with circles (girls), relative to the national line.

This may already be very familiar to you from the Autumn Package, as well as from your own school or LEA datasets. And you will also be aware of the work needed to use the national data in the Package well. You might like to consider how many of your teacher colleagues are using, or are even aware of, the interactive CD-ROM for producing school/class analyses (especially if you are working in a secondary school). It is also important to think about how you can best relate the Autumn Package data to other kinds of data analyses including those produced at individual school and LEA level.

A really crucial set of data for raising achievement is that which shows individual pupil level achievement between KS2 and KS3 – how far are you and your colleagues able to calculate that information from the national patterns? The Autumn Package does indicate how the datasets might be interrogated to assist with better progress

Figure 4.4 Key Stage 2 versus Key Stage 1 mathematics, 'Anytown Primary School'

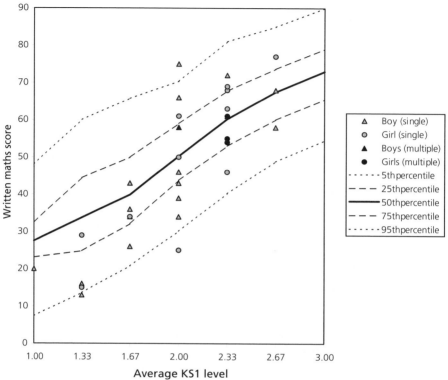

Source: National Foundation for Educational Research

monitoring, identification of under-achievement, information flow between year groups, feedback to pupils, etc. You might like to discuss with your colleagues how far you have been able to undertake the kinds of exercises it contains, and what kinds of support you and they need to get the most out of data packages like these.

There are some interesting ways of exploring low versus under-performance at the whole-school level, too. This requires 'full' 'value added' analytical techniques, which account for a range of background factors. Figure 4.6 – devised by statisticians at NFER – groups secondary schools into four contrasting categories, based on how they shape up in terms of raw scores relative to 'value added' scores. Each diamond represents a school. The vertical axis divides schools into those doing better and worse than average on raw results; whilst the horizontal axis divides schools into those doing better and worse than average on results which take account of the key independent variables or background factors – gender, ethnicity, age, disadvantage, as well as prior attainment.

Figure 4.5 Key Stage 4 (GCSE) versus Key Stage 3 mathematics, 'Newtown Comprehensive School'

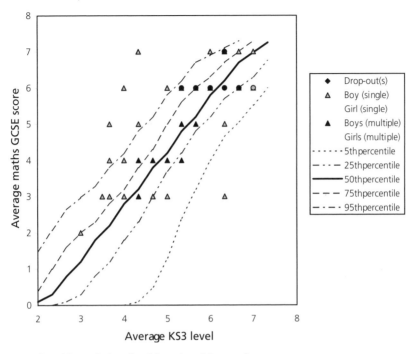

Source: National Foundation for Educational Research

Figure 4.6 Schools' 'Relative Effectiveness' (as measured by total GCSE score)

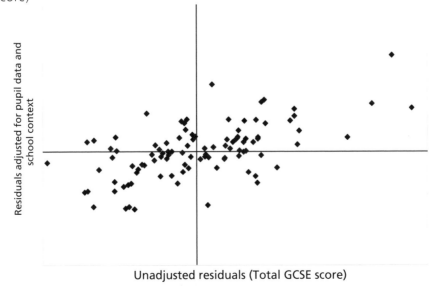

Source: National Foundation for Educational Research

USING THE DATA TO TELL A MEANINGFUL STORY

If we want to interpret the information given in Figure 4.6, then we might reasonably argue that schools in different quadrants, which we could construe as different states of development, will need different strategies of support and challenge.

Schools in the top right hand quadrant ('effective' schools) first need to know precisely what it is they are doing well, what factors have contributed to this and whether it is sustainable. Schools in the top left hand quadrant (schools whose good performance is obscured by raw performance results) probably need to do some justifiable morale-boosting, not only with governors and parents, but also with their own staff. Schools in the bottom right hand quadrant ('complacent' schools) need to take pre-emptive steps to identify under-achievement; 'value added' indicators, as opposed to raw results, provide the main incentive and instrument for doing so. Schools in the bottom left hand quadrant ('stuck', or even 'failing' schools) need much by way of support and possibly radical re-thinking: they may have become highly dysfunctional as learning institutions.

One corollary of knowing what the key variables are and the correlation they have with performance is further proof, if it were needed, that many schools cannot raise standards and achieve ambitious targets by themselves. This is especially true for schools in dire straits – the urgent need to find creative and radical ways of mobilising local communities around schooling or, better, around learning (such as through Excellence in Cities initiatives) can be readily inferred from this diagram.

Of course, to say that there are associations between institutional type and institutional outcomes provides little by way of explanation, particularly of cause and effect. It is crucial to be aware of this, because it is easy to be seduced into thinking that correlations provide reasons – or, if you are so disposed, excuses. Not at all. These analyses are based on empirical data – what can be shown, in study after study, to be the case – and so they give a sound basis for answering the question: 'Where are we starting from?' but not '*Why* are we starting from here?'

To discover *reasons*, i.e. to construct a plausible narrative, we need qualitative information. We need information about things like educational policies, resources, management and practice. Certainly. But the dead hand of past history, the half-life of previous initiatives, visions of and for the future, the interplay or conflict of personalities, the fabric and texture of personal relationships, all of these intangible or at least hard-to-measure things, are also implicated. Educationists need to do more 'joined up' thinking with complex quantitative and qualitative information; we must help each other 'tell the story' of a school's educational performance.

If this is a story told only from the top or from outside, it will have the advantage of being relatively straightforward and unambiguous. Stripped of complexity and nuance, it may lend itself, like any good fable, to having identifiable goodies and baddies. If, on the other hand, the story is written from several different perspectives, it is bound to end up more like a novel in its sheer multifariousness, provisionality and elements of surprise or shock:

> I used to think that this school cared about how well I was doing. Now I just think the only thing it cares about is how well it's doing.
>
> (Year 10 student, quoted in MacBeath *et al.*, 2000: 73)

Once upon a time, I might have assumed these were the same thing. Evidently not. So there may be no single transcendent 'truth' to be uncovered, but rather a continuing interplay of perception, transaction and interpretation. Sometimes the most instructive thing is the discrepancies, the conflicting perceptions of senior and junior teachers, or the picture given by examination results on the one hand and the tale told by pupils' experiences on the other.

From what I have observed in the many schools and local education authorities I have visited, I am convinced that the *meaning* of data, and therefore the uses to which it can be put, are intimately tied in with people's personal and hierarchical relationships with each other and the values they implicitly hold, as well as with the formal structures and objectives.

What makes all the difference is how well the processes of data gathering, analysis and interpretation are managed within the school. It is the answer to the question posed by Pete Dudley, a senior adviser in Essex who has done a great deal of work with teachers on analysing, interpreting – and acting on – pupil perception data:

> Why can pertinent, well-analysed and effectively presented school data trigger sustained improvement in one school and result in indifference, paralysis or burial in another?

> (Dudley, 1999b: 73)

Dudley says that factors associated with positive, action-oriented responses were:

- the availability of comparative data from schools felt not to be dissimilar;
- preparation for reading the data;
- prompts which focused discussion of pupil data on teaching, learning and issues which the school could influence and which developed speculation skills in teachers;
- some prior groundwork done by the discussion leader in identifying possible improvement strategies to feed into the discussion so that people did not feel 'cornered' by the data;
- the introduction of ground rules into the discussion to ensure that apparent good news or reactions to perceived external influences such as home background were sufficiently challenged;
- a climate where speculation and reflection were promoted among staff;
- a feeling that the process generating the data was valid and could be trusted.

Clearly, then, the attitudes and actions of school leaders will make all the difference to whether data is allowed to lie inert in someone's filing cabinet (or in the school secretary's pc), or is treated with cynicism and disdain, or is taken as a golden opportunity for triggering systematic discussions amongst staff about their teaching and the learning of their pupils.

Another lesson from this work is that if we do not ask students for their views, experiences and ideas, we are getting only half the picture. It is their interests which are at the heart of all this focus on data, after all, and Jean Rudduck's work in particular continues to be inspirational. I have a couple of examples to offer: when I was at the NFER, my team was asked to design a questionnaire for pupils in a secondary school which had sharp differences in GCSE results between certain departments. Year 10 pupils filled in questionnaires about their lessons, homework, anxieties and suggestions for improvement in each of the different subjects. The first thing I noticed when I looked at the results was that you do not have to go far for a plausible explanation of the differences in subject performance – the pupils' responses to the different subjects were very revealing about things like frequency and helpfulness of marking, help with problems they were having, keeping up with notes or understanding technical ideas, provision of after-school support and – particularly – whether they felt they could approach the teachers for help, and whether it seemed to matter to their teachers if they worked hard or not. The second, really encouraging thing was how prepared the subject staff were to take these responses and comments on board in their action plans – they seemed pleased to have some really concrete evidence about what they need to do next.

Good evidence can be collected in informal or unconventional ways. Some primary schools are beginning to treat what children say in 'circle time' – their hopes and anxieties and observations – as serious information to set alongside statistical data and to create a richer evidence base for school development. In more than one primary school, groups of children have been given polaroid cameras and invited to take photographs of the places in school they like and dislike being in. Then they make their photos into poster displays and talk to the rest of the class about them. One consequence of doing this is that the children and their teachers can see how 'the background' – a corner of the playground where bullies congregate, for example, or the noisy pushy corridors or the depressingly untidy science lab or the lavatories where privacy is impossible – is transformed into 'the foreground', suddenly full of meaning and feeling. And of course these meanings and feelings have consequences for how well children can work and learn in that environment. These projects have several outcomes; first, children and teachers have to accept that the same school is not actually the same for all the individuals in it. Second, it is obvious that some things need to be changed to make the environment – physical and emotional – pleasanter and more conducive to learning. The pupils are involved in suggesting and implementing the changes. Third, teachers have repeated the experiment to focus on the experiences of children new to the school who are especially restless and nervous.

I want to stress that these examples are *not* about teachers collecting evidence to explain away pupils' performance, but to understand at a deeper and more detailed level how what needs to change in the school, its teaching, its relationships, its ethos, *can be* changed. If the data does not take us back to those issues it is a mere distraction.

There are some excellent examples of whole-school projects which have got to grips with the hard-to-measure aspects in a way that is both insightful and manageable. John MacBeath's work with schools in the UK and elsewhere is exemplary, and the kinds of performance indicators he has developed include:

- Climate: school
- Relationships
- Climate: classroom
- Support for learning
- Support for teaching
- Time and resources
- Organisation/communication
- Equity

- Recognition of achievement
- Home-school links.

CONCLUSION

To sum up, I'd suggest that data can serve the aim of raising standards when:

- the purposes for collecting and analysing the data are clear and specific to the school's own situation;
- different kinds of data are used in conjunction with each other; performance data needs to be set alongside qualitative evidence on what goes on in classrooms and particularly evidence from the pupils' perspective;
- data is used to raise questions and contribute to reflective management and practice (rather than to make definitive judgements);
- discrepancies and anomalies between different pieces of information are accepted as leading to further exploration;
- data is managed in such a way as to result in conversations – between senior managers/middle managers/teachers/pupils/parents – about teaching and learning, and in changes to practice;
- (where numbers are involved) there is an understanding of the basic principles of statistics, including the fact that:
    - statistics give reliable and rigorous information about aggregate populations in the past rather than about individuals in the future;
    - statistics have an inbuilt degree of 'error', and therefore deal in probabilities rather than certainties;
- evidence is focused on what the school should now do to meet the needs of pupils as learners.

In all this talk of data, however, I try to remind myself from time to time of what Lawrence Stenhouse once wrote:

> Education as induction into knowledge is successful to the extent that it makes the behavioural outcomes of the students unpredictable.
>
> (Stenhouse: 1975: 136)

In other words, the paradox about performance data is that it essentially looks to the past, whilst learning must look to the future!

BIBLIOGRAPHY

Dudley, P. (1999a) 'Primary schools and pupil data', in G. Southworth and P. Lincoln (eds) *Supporting Improving Primary Schools: The Role of Heads and LEAs in Raising Standards*, London: Falmer Press.

Dudley, P. (1999b) 'Using data to drive up standards: statistics or psychology?', in C. Conner (ed.) *Assessment in Action in the Primary School*, London: Falmer Press.

Goldstein, H. (1997) 'Methods in school effectiveness research', *School Effectiveness and School Improvement*, 8, 4: 369–95.

Gray, J. (2000) 'How schools learn: common concerns and different responses', *Research Papers in Education*, 15, 3: i–v.

Hargreaves, D. (1996) 'Teaching as a research-based profession: possibilities and prospects', annual lecture delivered to Teacher Training Agency, April.

MacBeath, J., Boyd, B., Rand, J. and Bell, S. (1996) *Schools Speak for Themselves: Towards a Framework for Self-evaluation*, London: NUT.

MacBeath, J., Schratz, M., Meuret, D. and Jakobsen, L. (2000) *Self-evaluation in European Schools: a Story of Change*, London: RoutledgeFalmer.

Ruddock, J., Chaplain, R. and Wallace, G. (eds) (1996) *School Improvement: What Can Pupils Tell Us?* (Quality in Secondary Schools and Colleges Series), London: David Fulton.

Sammons, P. (1997) *Forging Links: Effective Schools and Effective Departments*, London: Paul Chapman.

Saunders, L. (1999) *Value Added Measurement of School Effectiveness: A Critical Review*, Slough: NFER.

School Curriculum and Assessment Authority (1994) *Value-added Performance Indicators for Schools*, London: SCAA.

Stenhouse, L. (1975) *An Introduction to Curriculum Research and Development*, London: Heinemann.

Thomas, S. and Mortimore, P. (1996) 'Comparison of value-added models for secondary-school effectiveness', *Research Papers in Education*, 11, 1: 5–33.

Wikeley, F. (1998) 'Dissemination of research as a tool for school improvement?', *School Leadership and Management*, 18, 1: 59–73.

FURTHER READING

Saunders, L. (1999) *Value Added Measurement of School Effectiveness: A Critical Review*, Slough: NFER.

Stenhouse, L. (1975) *An Introduction to Curriculum Research and Development*, London: Heinemann.

The Efficient and Effective Deployment of Staff and Resources

5.1 Financial Resource Management

Neil Burton

INTRODUCTION

OBJECTIVES

By the end of this Unit you should:

- Understand some of the technical aspects of managing finance at the departmental level;
- Be able to identify financial/political decision-making processes within the school.

At the heart of this chapter is the ultimate reality that educational activity is dependent upon the availability of financial resources. The ability of the departmental leader to make available and effectively manage financial resources will have a direct impact on the quality of learning and teaching possible. There is a responsibility to convert financial resources into an effective mix and balance of educational resources capable of delivering a curriculum in line with national and organisational objectives. It follows that subject leaders must accept these management responsibilities and be equipped with appropriate financial acumen and skills to successfully perform their duties. Clearly this will involve the handling of increased levels of bureaucracy that accompany devolved funding and bidding for additional funds within the strategic intent of the school or college.

Since the onset of devolved management responsibilities to schools within the state maintained sector, we have come to accept the notion of schools having a 'goal orientation where funding is an enabler' (Palfreyman, 1991: 26). Studies, such as the one by Levacic and Glover (1998) examine the link 'between resource input and management process variables on the one hand and educational effectiveness measures on the other' (Levacic, 2000: 16). Findings demonstrated that schools which employed rational decision-making processes to determine resource use and allocation appear, according to national measures, to be more educationally effective. The aim, therefore, is to transform the financial resources at the disposal of the school into the most effective educational resources available.

FINANCIAL AND EDUCATIONAL RESOURCES

Caldwell and Spinks (1992) list finance as only one of the seven types of resource available to schools. Financial resources refer to the cash available to obtain real resources. At various stages within the system, this money will be converted into real resources capable of delivering the required educational provision – finance, though, is the key to all other resources. In particular:

- Human resources – teachers, lecturers, support staff and, perhaps, unpaid volunteers.
- Material resources – buildings, equipment, furniture, books and teaching materials.

It is the combination and quality of human and material resources that largely determines the quality of educational provision. The other resources include:

- Leadership – power to make decisions
- Professional development – knowledge and technology
- Time.

It is money that makes possible the decision to attend staff development and money that provides teaching cover to allow the time to participate. The level to which the decision-making process (to convert financial to real resources) is devolved does vary from school to school. Some departmental leaders may have the responsibility for determining the level of staffing (both teaching and non-teaching) within their areas others may only have direct responsibilities for teaching equipment and consumables. Whatever the level of responsibility, there will be a need to demonstrate the ability to manage a budgetary process.

The teaching cycle (plan – teach – assess/evaluate – plan) is replicated in the systems for managing, over time, financial resources. This process is budgeting:

> Budgeting and costing are two different approaches to determining the necessary funds for educational activities. Budgeting focuses on the allocation of available funds; costing on the funds that are required to allow certain educational activities to take place.

> (Burton, 1999: 129)

In other words, budgeting focuses on being as effective as possible within the constraints of the resources available, whilst costing attempts to identify the resources required to achieve a desired educational outcome. Both have their place and their particular strengths in different contexts.

APPROACHES TO BUDGETING

Burton (in Anderson *et al*., 2001: 27) offers four reasons for budgeting:

- Because resources are 'scarce' – you can't do everything that you want to
- Because you are accountable for the funding that you receive
- Because you want to ensure that the things you need to do are properly resourced
- Because you want to plan ahead.

And continues:

> The budget is much more than a spreadsheet itemising income and expenditure under different section headings. It should be used as a means of expressing school or college aims and educational priorities in financial terms.
>
> (Burton, in Anderson *et al*., 2001: 27)

If employed appropriately, the budget is a key management tool, enabling decisions to be made from a position of strength. The greater understanding of monetary flows that this allows ensures that the 'curriculum should drive the budget rather than the other way round' (Levacic, 1992: 26).

To be of use to the school as an enabling factor, the budget should be an integral part of the management planning cycle, reflecting the need to control finance over both the long and short term. It should indicate how conflicting financial priorities are determined, and at what level within the organisation this consultation takes place. Above all, the system should have the flexibility to enable improvements and developments to be incorporated into plans through virement.

As Glover (2000), following the work of Levacic (1992), says, there are three distinct purposes of budgetary management:

- Control – ensuring that funding, through visible means, is directed to institutional priorities to be achieved.
- Accountability and stewardship – to ensure that funding has been demonstrably used for the intended purposes (both within the organisation and externally for bodies such as Ofsted).
- Motivation – to encourage and empower staff through the delegation of responsibility for financial decision making, which 'encourages individual initiative when it is not possible to formulate a coherent and integrated organisational response' (Caldwell and Spinks 1998: 199).

Within this overall structure there are four identifiable budgetary approaches:

- incremental budgeting;
- zero-based budgeting (also referred to as ZBB);
- priority-based budgeting (PBB) – also known as programme planning budgeting system (PPBS);
- formulaic budgeting.

Incremental – the new budget is prepared on the basis of the previous budget with marginal or 'incremental' changes to reflect the funds available.

Table 5.1 Advantages and disadvantages of incremental budgeting

Advantages	Disadvantages
Process is predictable and secure;	Past funding allocation errors will be repeated and formalised;
Limited consultation: a 'time saving' factor;	Little opportunity to respond to either internal or external change;
Avoids conflict between departments, especially if resources are allocated on the basis of general increases or reductions (Davies, 1994: 348).	Not all sources of cost rise at the same rate.

Zero-based budgeting begins with a 'blank sheet', thus requiring that all proposed expenditure is justified anew each budgetary cycle.

Table 5.2 Advantages and disadvantages of zero-based budgeting

Advantages	Disadvantages
It should avoid past discrepancies being replicated in the future;	A complete review of sources of expenditure will be a very time consuming process;
New initiatives are immediately brought into the budgetary process;	Initiatives may not receive consistent year-on-year funding;
It requires each activity of the budget centre to be evaluated and justified on educational grounds as part of the budgetary process.	Fixed costs (buildings, permanent staff) mean that many elements of the budget will be the same each year;
	The ability to produce coherent budgets will take precedence over financial needs.

Priority-based budgeting is an attempt to match educational priorities with funding.

Table 5.3 Advantages and disadvantages of priority-based budgeting

Advantages	Disadvantages
The costs associated with initiatives become an integral part of the educational debate;	Relative cost becomes an intrusive element in educational debate;
It ensures that resources are attached to school or national educational priorities.	Significant changes in priorities will lead to similar changes in budget allocations.

Formulaic budgeting attempts to rationalise the financial decision-making process on the basis of past demands on expenditure. In this way this process *can* take on board elements of all of the previous methods – it is only as good as the assumptions that underlie the formula.

Table 5.4 Advantages and disadvantages of formulaic budgeting

Advantages	Disadvantages
It is a rational and defensible process; It ensures that there is a link between need and allocation;	The equity of the system is wholly dependent upon the initial determination of the formula;
The process can be built into IT-based information management systems (e.g. spreadsheets).	The formula will need to be evaluated to ensure that it adequately reflects real need.

Action point

Consider the budget for your own department. Ask yourself what type of budgeting you currently undertake when compared to the models outlined above. Your budget and its construction will inevitably interrelate closely with the budget for other departments and for the whole school. Try to identify the way in which budget allocation takes place in your school in order to see if there is a rational model for budget allocation. This matter may well need to be discussed with a member or members of the senior management team but remember – the discussion of budget allocation can be a very sensitive issue!

APPROACHES TO COSTING

There are several ways of describing costs according to:

- perceptions – *real or actual costs and perceived or opportunity costs*
- timescale – *fixed and variable costs or initial and recurrent*
- disbursement – *total, average and marginal*
- attribution – *direct and indirect costs.*

Educational judgements about competing claims on resources (such as alternative sets of text books) without knowledge of the costs involved would lead to poor decision making. In general, 'the activity of costing is best defined in terms of its purpose or outcomes' (Burton, 1999: 129). At its best and most useful costing is:

> descriptive, telling administrators how much a given activity or process costs, and second [it] can be predictive, suggesting how resources ought to be combined in the future for cost effective use.
>
> (Hans, 1996: 93)

At a time when schools were funded by formula, costing might have seemed inappropriate and wasteful of time. As Kedney (1991: 1) notes 'if provision is up and running, the quality is judged to be at least adequate, life is generally thought to be reasonable and will stay that way, ... why bother with costing?' Increasing moves towards 'bidding' for additional funding requires that initiatives be adequately costed to ensure that sufficient resources are made available for the predicted outcome targets to be met.

Not all costs can be represented through reference to a balance sheet. In some cases it is the perception of cost that must be addressed – the cost of a new educational resource may be negligible compared to the perceived cost of change to teaching styles and existing planning. For every decision to incur costs there should be a consideration of alternative uses for that funding that might also lead to an increase in educational performance. This idea of opportunity cost is 'concerned with the "value" of the best alternative use to which the resources can be put' (Kedney and Davies, 1994: 455). More ICT furniture may be at the expense of sports equipment (assuming of course that the funds can be vired between the alternative uses). Two examples are offered by way of further explanation.

> Schools are quick to see that the opportunity cost of high fuel bills is the books they would have liked to buy, but slower to see that the traditional ways they have deployed teachers can often mask substantial opportunity costs for meeting students' learning needs in other ways.
>
> (Knight, 1993: 12)

> If it is decided to give the existing staff more non-contact time and to employ no more teachers then class sizes have to rise. There is no additional monetary cost, so no on-budget cost of increasing non-contact time. But there still is a cost: the educational benefits pupils would have experienced had they been taught in smaller classes.
>
> (Levacic, 1993: 5)

Timescale is often an important factor in the determination of costs. Costs, which are fixed in the short term (e.g. the cost of a fixed-term teacher), can be variable in the long term (whether the contract is renewed). So the period over which the costs are incurred is a crucial aspect of the calculations when comparing alternatives of equal (or differing) educational value. Lifetime costs should be the basis for consideration.

The capacity of the operation has a significant impact in terms of fixed and variable costs. Some costs are fixed over a range of activity – a teacher will probably be paid the same whether there are 15 or 30 students in the class. But the cost of materials, such as handouts, will vary according to the number of children. This leads to the issue of 'stepped costs' – at some point, when students numbers increase, there will be the need to employ an additional teacher using an additional classroom with the requisite teaching equipment. Unless these resources are already available as 'slack' in the system (i.e. currently under-utilised), there will be a considerable step up in costs incurred. At this point the additional or marginal cost of the extra student is likely to be significantly greater than the funding for that student.

The final element is to determine how closely the costs can be attributed to a particular activity of the school. Whilst the cost of a history teacher can be directly related to the teaching of history in the history department, the cost of the school secretary can only be indirectly linked to the educational activities of the students. Some resource costs can be directly linked to an educational activity; others need to be apportioned. Offering a new course at advanced level that will result in the recruitment of additional students, for example, will need to be costed in terms of the operating resources that will be required, both additional and existing, and also a share of indirect costs currently borne by existing courses.

To further appreciate cost implications on educational decision-making, it is worth considering the example of alternative 'Citizenship' schemes in Table 5.5.

Each option has its own particular advantages and disadvantages – there is not an 'ideal' solution that will suit all situations. The decision can only be made on the basis of 'local knowledge'. The first option might be best in a situation where there is confidence that the same scheme can be retained for at least five years, the likelihood of damage or loss of materials is limited and additional classes may be able to make use of the same set – and that full funding is possible from the outset! The third option offers maximum flexibility and lowest initial outlay, although the cost and time of the photocopying may be prohibitive and there are issues around student retention of the individual sheets. The second option offers a potential 'middle way' – costs are known, offering security for the life of the scheme, and larger classes would not place undue strain on the finances. In all of these cases the act of costing makes visible the impact of the decision in both finance and resource terms. When the benefit derived from each of the alternatives is not the same, a more rigorous analysis may be required.

EFFECTIVENESS AND EFFICIENCY

> Let no one deride the word 'cheaper', there is no advantage in education being more expensive than it has to be.
>
> (Knight, 1983: 15)

Table 5.5 Alternative costing

Scheme	Initial costs	Recurring costs	Marginal costs	Lifespan	Additional direct costs
Class set of individual text books	£375 (30 @ £12.50)	0	£12.50	5 years (£375)	Exercise books
Readers and individual workbooks	£225	£62.50	£2.50	5 years (£475)	None
Photocopy master	£75	0	0	3 years (£75)	Photo-copying paper and time

Educational activity is constrained by the availability of resources so if the same educational outcomes can be achieved at less cost, or more can be achieved within the resources available, then surely this is a prime objective of an educational manager.

In a more general sense there is also an issue of accountability here for the use of public funds, so:

> Policy-makers require assurances that resources are being used efficiently as well as effectively: the cost-effectiveness of educational provision has to be demonstrated.
>
> (Thomas, 1990: 46)

Part of the inspection process for schools is to demonstrate effectiveness and educational efficiency. These terms require careful definition; efficiency:

> cheapest means of accomplishing a defined objective.
>
> (Rumble, 1987: 74)

> aiming to produce the desired output in the cheapest way possible.
>
> (Thomas, 1990:58)

The key points to digest here are 'defined objective' and 'desired output'. This encompasses how as well as what – which includes elements such as a comfortable learning environment (so you can't sell off the school buildings to hire more teachers and reduce class size to improve GCSE results!). It also means that you have to be very clear about what you are asking for in terms of an educational outcome.

> Effectiveness is the fullest possible attainment of the goals and objectives of the school.
>
> (Knight, 1993: 19)

> Cost-effectiveness ... is concerned with selecting the least-cost alternative for securing the desired outcome.
>
> (Mortimore et al., 1994: 23)

Essentially efficiency and effectiveness are different ways of perceiving achievement of stated educational aims. Efficiency is about minimising the cost of meeting threshold standards of educational outcomes, whilst effectiveness attempts to maximise educational objectives within funding constraints.

At the level of course or subject leader, there are, according to Woodhall (1987: 399), five key reasons for performing a cost-effective analysis prior to decision making:

1   testing the economic feasibility of expansion plans or proposals;
2   projecting future educational costs;
3   estimating the cost of alternative actions;
4   comparing alternative means of achieving the same educational objectives;
5   improving the efficiency of resource utilisation.

The analysis performed in Table 5.5 basically relates to Woodhall's fourth point. 'Cost effectiveness', according to Mortimore et al. (1994: 22) 'is highly desirable', because 'a school that uses its resources more cost-effectively ... releases resources which can be used to promote further development'.

Once a desired educational outcome has been identified, cost-effectiveness analysis enables managers to ask the questions 'can we afford it?' and ' which way is best?' by placing alternative means of achieving this outcome in direct comparison both with each other and with the overall budget for the project. By relating the decision back to notions of opportunity and perceived cost it might also be appropriate to ask the supplementary question 'can we afford *not* to do it?' In the dynamic environment that school education exists in, remaining as you are is, in effect, a step backwards relative to other local schools. So, in terms of using cost-effective analysis as a management information tool in the budgetary process, the impact can be improved by considering the effect of not making the suggested financial commitment.

Ofsted (Office for Standards in Education) evaluates school effectiveness in terms of:

- The extent to which resources are used to maximise the achievement of the school's aims and objectives
- The extent to which the school aligns its spending priorities with its educational priorities
- The cost-effectiveness of programmes, procedures and practices
- The quality of the educational outcomes which result (Ofsted, 2000).

DECISION MAKING

The financial management of most schools now operates around the notion of 'cost centres', these being a collection of costs, arbitrarily categorised for reasons of manage-ment expediency; in education this will usually be by department, course or phase (Lucey, 1996: 111). Often 'pay' and 'non-pay' are differentiated with non-pay being devolved to subject departments or centralised costs (such as lighting and heating). The more that costs can be attributed to a source, the more rational the decision-making process can become. Activity-based costing (ABC) requires any activities performed centrally within the school to be costed so that costs can be charged to cost centres. In this way the cost to the central office of collecting money for a theatre trip can then be charged back to the English department rather than being spread across all cost centres.

Coombs and Hallak (1987: 191) claim, 'good educational cost analysts can literally be worth their weight in gold', but add the proviso that they ask the right questions and arrive at responsible answers, and provided the decision-makers understand the answers and take them seriously. Pyke further reinforces the argument that decisions need to be made on the basis of accurate information:

> For costs to be managed economically, efficiently and effectively it is necessary to have a costing system which identifies where costs arise and who was responsible for incurring them.
>
> (Pyke, 1998: 79)

Bush (2000) offers four models for financial decision making within schools:

- rational
- collegial

- political
- ambiguous

Levacic (2000: 8) describes the rational model as having 'clear aims and goals, which are pursued through formal structures and rational decision making'. Although the objectivity of this model offers strong support, there are considerable concerns as to how realistic it in fact is. Simkins claims that it 'becomes intrinsically problematic where goals are ambiguous, contested, or conflicting, or where the relationship between means and ends is unclear' (1986: 155).

Schools are intrinsically assumed to be political organisations where the decision-making processes are open to the scrutiny of different groups holding differing perceptions of 'reality'. The views of individuals will vary according to their position within the organisation – members of the maths department will tend to 'overvalue' the position of mathematics within the school, and their views of decisions will be coloured by this. This will often lead to incrementalism to preserve the 'status quo'. Particular individuals or groups might be in a position to have significant influence over the decision-making process, possibly in conflict with the rationality of the situation. The inequalities of the political influences within the school will tend to subvert the rational planning process.

Collegiality has long and often (Campbell 1985; Wallace 1988) been held up as the 'ideal' management model for education, focusing as it does on consensus decision making through formal representation of all staff on decision-making bodies, recognising and effectively employing the expertise of staff. This model would suggest that financial decisions are made on the basis of a participatory process where all staff can then have input to and ownership of the decision made. Bush (1995) and Simkins (1986) recognise the inherent drift towards political decision making with this model. In more recent times there is an acknowledgement of the often contrived nature of collegiality.

Ambiguity is a 'catch-all' model which reflects the reality of situations where the process lacks any coherent clarity, often the result of incoherent or obscured organisational goals. Management structures are fragmented and opaque masking the ability to budget on the basis of educational priorities. The bureaucratic processes will be disabling rather than enabling, often characterised by the devolution of responsibility but not power.

DEVOLVED FINANCIAL MANAGEMENT

The devolution of financial decision making from local authorities to schools has led, according to both anecdotal and more formal research evidence, to a reduction in the cost of educational provision per child (like for like). McAleese summarises this by claiming:

> Locally managed schools are certainly more efficient at using resources than central bureaucracies, not least because of the sense of scrutiny and ownership created by being directly accountable for service quality.
>
> (McAleese, 2000: 145).

It might appear from this that the next logical step is progress towards devolving a greater degree of financial decision making to departmental leaders. However, the serious concerns that impacted on the early stages of school-based financial management would be magnified. Beyond the not insignificant training needs of department heads to ensure comparability and consistency across different cost centres within schools, extending the decision-making process beyond a single member of the senior management team will inevitably require additional administrative hours to be devolved to middle managers which will have to be taken from elsewhere in the school – an opportunity cost to be resolved.

Action point

Take opportunities to become involved in financial planning wherever they present themselves. Try to understand the funding model operating in your school and its implications for efficient and effective use of resources. One of the most common areas of concern for those moving into senior management in schools is the way in which budgets are managed; any experience prior to this point will be invaluable.

CONCLUSIONS AND SUMMARY

The rationale behind effective financial management within school must be the provision of high quality education within the constraints of the available budget. The access to and organisation of information is the key to success, for both operational and strategic financial planning. Once the desired educational objectives have been identified, alternative strategies for achieving those outcomes need to be costed to ensure that the greatest possible educational benefit can be derived from the resources available. Any unnecessary expenses that are incurred will result in funding being denied for other needs. It is with the effective use of budgetary and costing tools that educational managers can maximise the educational impact of the funding at their disposal.

REFERENCES

Anderson, L., Briggs, A. and Burton, N. (2001) *Managing Finance, Resources and Stakeholders in Education*, London: Paul Chapman.

Burton, N. (1999) 'Efficient and effective staff deployment', in M. Brundrett (ed.) *Principles of School Leadership*, Dereham: Peter Francis Publishers.

Bush, T. (1995) *Theories of Educational Management*, London: Paul Chapman.

Bush, T. (2000) 'Management styles: impact on finance and resources', in M. Coleman and L. Anderson (eds) *Managing Finance and Resources in Education*, London: Paul Chapman.

Caldwell, B. and Spinks, J. (1992) *Leading the Self-Managing School*, London: Falmer Press.

Caldwell, B. and Spinks, J. (1998) *Beyond the Self-Managing School*, London: Falmer Press.

Campbell, R. (1985) *Developing the Primary School Curriculum*, London: Holt, Rinehart and Winston.

Coombs, P. and Hallak, J. (1987) *Cost Analysis in Education*, Washington, DC: The Johns Hopkins University Press.

Davies, B. (1994) 'Models of decision making in resource allocation', in T. Bush and J. West-Burnham, (eds) *The Principles of Educational Management*, London: Paul Chapman.

Glover, D. (2000) 'Financial management and strategic planning', in M. Coleman and L. Anderson, (eds) *Managing Finance and Resources in Education*, London: Paul Chapman.

Hans, J. (1996) *Cost Accounting in Higher Education – Simple Macro and Micro Costing Techniques*, Washington, DC: NACUBO.

Kedney, R. (1991) 'Costing open and flexible learning', *OLS News*, Part 30 : 1–14.

Kedney, R. and Davies, T. (1994) *Cost Reduction and Value for Money*, Coombe Lodge Report, V24: 441–524.

Knight, B. (1983) *Managing School Finance*, Oxford: Heinemann.

Knight, B. (1993) *Financial Management in Schools: The Thinking Manager's Guide*, Oxford: Heinemann.

Levacic, R. (1992) 'Local management of schools: aims, scope and impact', *Educational Management and Administration*, 20, 1: 16–29.

Levacic, R. (1993) 'Managing resources effectively', in *E326 Managing Schools: Challenge and Response*, Buckingham: Open University Press.

Levacic, R. (2000) 'Linking resources to learning outcomes', in M. Coleman and L. Anderson (eds) *Managing Finance and Resources in Education*, London: Paul Chapman.

Levacic, R. and Glover, D. (1998) 'The relationship between efficient resource management and school effectiveness: evidence from OFSTED secondary school inspections', *School Effectiveness and School Improvement*, 9, 1: 95–122.

Lucey, T. (1996) *Costing*, 5th edition, New York: DP Publications.

McAleese, K. (2000) 'Budgeting in schools', in M. Coleman and L. Anderson (eds) *Managing Finance and Resources in Education*, London: Paul Chapman.

Mortimore, P. and Mortimore, J. with Thomas, H. (1994) *Managing Associate Staff: Innovation in Primary and Secondary Schools*, London: Paul Chapman.

Ofsted (2000) *Handbook for Inspecting Schools*, London: The Stationery Office.

Palfreyman, D. (1991) 'The art of costing and the politics of pricing', *Promoting Education*, Part 2: 26–7.

Pyke, C. (1998) 'Costing and pricing in the public sector', in J. Wilson (ed.) *Financial Management for the Public Services*, Buckingham: Open University Press.

Rumble, G. (1987) 'Why distance learning can be cheaper than conventional education', *Distance Learning*, 8, 1: 72–94.

Simkins, T. (1986) 'Patronage, markets and collegiality: reflections on the allocation of finance in secondary schools', *Educational Management and Administration*, 14, 1: 17–30.

Thomas, H. (1990) *Education Costs and Performance: A Cost-Effective Analysis*, London: Cassell.

Wallace, M. (1988) 'Towards a collegial approach to curriculum management in primary and middle schools', *School Organisation*, 8, 1: 25–34.

Woodhall, M. (1987) 'Cost analysis in education', in G. Psacharopoulos (ed.) *Economics of Education: Research and Studies*, Oxford: Pergamon Press.

FURTHER READING

Levacic, R. and Glover, D. (1998) 'The relationship between efficient resource management and school effectiveness: evidence from OFSTED secondary school inspections', *School Effectiveness and School Improvement*, 9, 1: 95–122.

McAleese, K. (2000) 'Budgeting in schools', in M. Coleman and L. Anderson (eds) *Managing Finance and Resources in Education*, London: Paul Chapman.

Thomas, H. (1990) *Education Costs and Performance: A Cost-Effective Analysis*, London: Cassell.

WEBSITES

http://www.schools.audit-commission.gov.uk/

http://www.dfes.gov.uk/vfm/

5.2 Resource and Environment Management

Neil Burton

INTRODUCTION

OBJECTIVES

By the end of this Unit you should:

- Be aware of the importance of the identification of learning resources within the learning environment;
- Understand the means of managing physical resources to enhance the effectiveness of learning.

As discussed in Unit 5.1, all resources used in the educational process can be traced back to the funding that made them possible. The financial decisions that lead to the investment in learning resources in the form of equipment and the building will be addressed here. Levacic (2000: 4) stresses the 'great responsibility in the hands of school and college managers to allocate resources to the best possible effect', effectively linking educational outcomes to resource allocation. In budgetary terms, those elements relating to pay and building costs (including maintenance) are more likely to be controlled centrally, whilst the subject specific costs of equipment and materials are delegated to subject leaders.

The degree of freedom that a subject leader may experience in the management of the physical resources that they are responsible for the use of may vary considerably. Many of the resources may be pre-existing – buildings and equipment that have already been purchased for use within that department – and this will require a different approach to management than those that are obtained for the purpose of addressing specific educational priorities within the school.

RESOURCE AUDIT

As with the approach to financial management, there are two opposing directions that this problem can be approached from: starting from what you have got, or, alternatively, starting from a 'zero-base' and identifying what you need to achieve clearly stated goals. Except in the case of a new school or department, where there are no pre-existing resources, the first is the more realistic approach to adopt. However, it does need to be recognised that in adopting the second approach, it is possible to construct the vision of a department where approaches to teaching and learning are not constrained or dictated by existing resources. A comparison of both of these approaches to auditing departmental resources will clearly demonstrate the extent to which the ideal or, at least, desired learning situation has been compromised by the necessity to use what is already available.

Resources can be classified in many ways, but it is more helpful if the same terminology is used for this process and for the school and departmental budgets. Employing the terms 'fixed' and 'consumables' for designations of departmental assets is not particularly useful – both paperclips and buildings have a life span and so, in that sense, are consumables, making the period of consumption or replacement cycle an important element within the audit. Any audit should also acknowledge where resources are shared rather than exclusive to the department. The key resource will be staffing (both teaching and non-teaching), so crucial to the educational process that it will be addressed fully in Unit 5.3.

A key point to begin the auditing process from (and possibly return to) is to ask: 'Does the availability of resources determine the curriculum, or does the curriculum determine the organisation and acquisition of resources?' In reality the answer is likely to be 'yes' on both counts. Most schools cannot afford to put aside existing resources if they are found to be an inexact match to the needs of the curriculum. There will need to be a compromise through adaptation of both the resources and the curriculum. Indeed it is possible that even the purchase of new resources will need to take into account issues of compatibility with what already exists resulting in, what might be considered, less than ideal resource acquisitions. Clearly though, the purchase of new resources enables the school (or department) to move closer to acquiring the resources to support their notion of an ideal curriculum. Figure 5.1 offers an indication of the stages in the audit process.

Whichever approach is chosen there are two key questions that need to be asked in respect of the viability of the departmental manager:

- The extent to which the department can manage 'its assets' independently of the rest of the organisation;
- The degree of flexibility the departmental leader has in organising and allocating those assets.

It is important to acknowledge the extent to which the corporate entity, in terms of policies, systems and structures, has a controlling and unifying approach to the management of overall resourcing. After all, resources are primarily under the ownership of the school or college rather than the department. However one department decides to acquire and organise its educational resources will necessarily impact upon the remainder of the organisation. Students, who will almost certainly

Figure 5.1 Resource focus versus curriculum focus

Resource focus   Curriculum focus

| Identify material resources used by the department to deliver the curriculum. | Identify the desired curriculum to be delivered. |

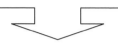 

| Identify material resources used by the department specifying those which are used wholly and those that are shared. | Identify material resources necessary to deliver the curriculum. |

 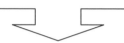

| Categorised as:
Fixed – classrooms, buildings …
Capital – items with a usable life of 5–7 years
Consumables – those which are renewable on an annual basis. | Categorised as:
Fixed – classrooms, buildings …
Capital – items with a usable life of 5–7 years
Consumables – those which are renewable on an annual basis. |

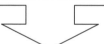 

| Compare available resources to the planned curriculum and identify overlaps and gaps. | Compare with the resources currently available to the department to deliver the existing curriculum. |

 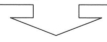

| Prepare funding allocation bid to address resource omissions, annual expenditure and an allowance for the staged renewal of capital items. | Prepare funding allocation bid to address resource omissions, annual expenditure and an allowance for the staged renewal of capital items. |

work across several departments, will be aware of any differences in the ways in which different subjects deploy resources.

If we adopt the 'resource focused' approach, it is quite likely that a proportion of the resources identified as belonging to the department will no longer be of any educational use due to developments in learning technology and the curriculum. These redundant resources need to identified and assessed. Some may have the potential to be adapted for alternative uses within the department or another department within the school. Others may need to be disposed of through sale, donation or as refuse. In each case, disposal may result in a cost to the department, the funding for which will need to be found from somewhere within the budget.

DELEGATED RESOURCE MANAGEMENT

Delegating resource management to individuals within the organisation who are as close to the point of resource use as feasibly possible should result in greater responsiveness. The impact on the decision-making processes should ensure that the match between resource acquisition and organisation, and learning and teaching becomes very tightly focused. Clearly this level of organisational management needs to comply with the overall aims and priorities of the school or college (Glover, 2000: 121). Additionally, some resources, due to their usage or financial complexity, are more appropriately managed from the centre rather than departmentally. However, the use of activity-based costing (ABC) within the organisation, can ensure that those who make the greatest calls on centrally maintained resources, such as library or ICT facilities, can be charged accordingly (for a more detailed examination of this approach, please see Goddard and Ooi, 1998).

McAleese (2000) emphasises the importance of managing resource expenditure at the point of use through the delegation of funds (see Unit 5.1):

> Heads of department found themselves with annual budgets for books and equipment which could actually be *managed*!
>
> (McAleese, 2000: 133)

Even in educational systems where devolved management has become the norm at institutional level, such as in the maintained sector in the UK, devolution of funding within schools is still relatively limited; latest indications suggest that in the region of 5 per cent of organisational funds are delegated to departmental level.

The cohesion between organisational and departmental priorities for learning outcomes needs to be assured through clearly defined planning structures. Departmental planning should reflect strategic institutional priorities in such a way that the flexibility of resource use devolved to departmental level is given direction by the school development plan. This process will involve the cooperation and coordination of senior and middle managers in evaluating past use of resources prior to planning the next round of resource acquisitions and organisation.

The extent to which resource evaluation and resource allocation is performed in the light of the departmental and organisational plan is brought into question by Glover (2000). A study of resource planning practice in 25 large UK secondary schools found a considerable degree of variation. Even where institutional planning was deemed to be a particular strength, prioritising resource utilisation in accordance with budgetary allocation, linking resources to particular learning initiatives, appeared to be problematic.

It is conceivable that departmental managers, who have had little or no input into setting the institutional priorities, are 'allocated some budgetary responsibility for implementing the consequences of these decisions' (Ainley and Bailey, 1997: 57). In many respects this imitates the situation that Headteachers may find themselves operating in, reliant upon gaining funding from the state which is attached to particular initiatives. In this way, the flexibility of the use to which resources can be put is seriously constrained by the outcomes that are expected or required.

Stoll and Fink acknowledge that 'it is neither manageable, possible nor a good use of teachers' time for everyone to be involved in the fine details of development planning' (1996: 63). A crucial element in ensuring the effectiveness of planning structures which involve input from all levels within the organisation is a clear and coherent communication system, which operates in both directions in the management hierarchy. It needs to be acknowledged that however successful the departmental acquisition and organisation of resources, the organisation as a whole must be correctly aligned with best educational practice, having set appropriate priorities.

Action point

- Undertake an audit of the resources available to your department.
- Consult with colleagues to discover what resources they would ideally like to have in order to improve teaching and learning.
- Cost these additional resources and attempt to draw up a strategic plan for the acquisition of these new items whilst still working within budget constraints.

MANAGEMENT OF THE LEARNING ENVIRONMENT

Expenditure on buildings is second only to expenditure on staffing in most educational institutions. Whilst staffing is the major element of recurrent expenditure, the acquisition of buildings and grounds represents the major capital assets of a school. The timescale involved in the management of the learning environment is such that it is more normally considered as a special project outside of the annual budgetary cycle. Unlike other major resource items, such as computing equipment, where renewal is budgeted for on an annual basis, renewal of buildings and grounds is almost certainly not. However, the maintenance of these resources certainly will need to be accounted for. Whilst expenditure on lighting, heating and décor may, at face value, appear to be a lower educational priority than say textbooks, it has a fundamental impact on the learning processes. If the learning environment is too cold (or hot), too dim (or bright), then the learning effectiveness will be reduced – basic levels of human comfort have to be achieved and maintained. Likewise the décor may not be prioritised from an educational perspective, but it is an essential element in marketing the school to both potential students and staff alike. A poorly maintained and undervalued learning environment will convey the perception that those who are required to work within it are also undervalued. A well maintained and cared for learning environment will instil a sense of pride and ownership in the fabric of the school or college. With this acknowledgement of the importance of properly maintaining school buildings and grounds many schools are now instituting the post of premises or estates manager, a strategic position going well beyond the scope of a 'caretaker' or 'janitor'.

At the operational level, the management of the learning environment will be within the control of individual teachers and departmental heads. Murphy (1994) suggests that this level of devolution may not be in the best, long term interests of the organisation. Notions of 'ownership' of particular rooms or teaching blocks may mean that any attempts at improving or rationalising the deployment of teaching accommodation could be construed as being 'politically sensitive'. This could easily result in an acceptance of the status quo and seriously impact on the potential for innovation.

With the aim of enhancing the quality of the learning environment for students and staff alike, senior and middle managers need to seriously consider the image that they are attempting to convey through the fabric of the building and surrounding grounds. This may be through a decision to present a 'corporate image' via a standardisation or thematic approach to the décor and underlying ethos, or by allowing departments who have been allocated adjoining rooms the flexibility to create their own individual ethos. This can be achieved by adopting a particular colour scheme or approach to display, or as the result of an investment in (or arrangement of) co-ordinated furniture, floor and window coverings, and wall and storage areas. Whether this is achieved through an allocation of the central budget or via funds delegated to individual departments is clearly dependent upon the school and the degree of corporate control and consistency that is required.

In order to maximise the potential of the curriculum that is taught and teaching strategies that are employed, it is clearly desirable for the actual teaching environment to be conducive to and supportive of this style of learning. In a practical learning environment, such as a lab or workshop, where an independent approach to learning is fostered, there will be a need for students to gain direct access to the equipment and materials that they require. For this to be achieved, within the bounds of health and safety and effective classroom management, the accommodation will need to be organised and equipped to make this possible. The use of environmental control and organisation is applied to support the development and maintenance of a desired learning culture.

These tools of cultural manipulation can also be employed to enhance the quality and ethos of the workspace used by staff. Brown and Rutherford (1998) have researched the ways in which departmental funds have been used to enhance accommodation for the benefit of staff:

> The department had its own staffroom for which the head of department had purchased a large oval table and matching chairs. ... we observed the collegium in action when members of the department gathered around the table in the staffroom during their free periods and at lunch.
>
> (Brown and Rutherford, 1998: 82)

This demonstrates how the thoughtful use of furniture and fittings can be employed to encourage a particular model of departmental teamwork. In another example, in order to create an environment where teaching staff would be more likely to perform planning and assessment tasks, one subject leader decided to establish a departmental staff office 'furnished with individual desks and workspaces for staff' and 'purchased good quality pictures to hang on the walls, to enhance and improve the appearance of what otherwise would have been a rather barren environment' (Brown and Rutherford, 1998: 82).

Although there may not be any way to clearly measure the impact on learning of these changes to staff accommodation, it is very likely that the morale of staff would be improved which would indirectly improve the student experience. Unit 5.3 will clearly demonstrate that the staff are the single most important resource in any school and their retention, professional development and deployment will need to be carefully considered in all other decisions that are made. However, there may be many 'micro-political' difficulties to overcome before changes can be made – with 'ownership' being at the root of the problem. Even accommodation that no longer appears to be in use or under the control of a particular department or group of departments can lead to territorial battles.

Five barriers to alterations in the deployment or innovative use of accommodation have been identified by Kelly and Kedney (1992: 146):

- Lack of accountability
- Lack of information
- Too much information
- Inappropriate territoriality
- Short-term thinking

Inertia, in thought or action, can be minimised where the ownership is undisputed. There may be dissenting voices from other departments on the grounds of perceived favourable funding towards that department initiating the improvement, but not for the improvements. Indeed it might be the case that the shared areas are prioritised in order to signal a specific message that can then be developed within individual departments. By beginning redecoration or refurbishment in a public or shared area of the school (possibly at the expense of buying text books or similarly obvious learning resources) the whole school can benefit from the initiative, hopefully stimulating more departmental initiatives as the benefits are recognised.

In summary, it can be said that the greater autonomy now enjoyed by schools has led to innovative use of the learning environment. It follows that by devolving some of that autonomy to departmental level schools could benefit from initiatives that make more effective use of the accommodation to better meet the specific learning needs within subject areas. In so doing the corporate and departmental cultures can be enhanced and developed to encourage and improve the quality of learning and teaching. New developments in learning technology encourage a re-examination of the traditional fabric of the school, with an increased emphasis on computer-based learning and individual educational planning. However, these developments need to take into account the inherent inertia of the school to invest in innovative learning space. One perhaps only needs to look towards the 'open-plan' approach to building primary schools in the 1970s to recognise the implications of making changes that may be very difficult to reverse. When considering the possibilities of making changes to the learning environment it would be advisable for the departmental leader to address the following questions:

- To what extent does the current accommodation support what and how we want the students to learn (and the teachers to teach)?
- How might the existing accommodation be reconfigured to be more effective?
- How might the appearance of the accommodation be improved?
- Could the acquisition of furnishings (more or different) have a tangible, positive impact?
- Does the structure of the accommodation need to be altered to enable improvements to be made?

Each subsequent question in the list suggests a greater degree of potential difficulty (and cost!) so it would be expedient to explore each level in turn.

MANAGEMENT OF LEARNING RESOURCES

Funding allocations for learning resources specific to the needs of particular subjects predate the more recent forms of devolved management. Capitation budgets for equipment and annually consumed resources have been devolved to departmental heads in all but the smallest schools for many years. Even where there has been no delegation of funding or purchasing power, there has usually been the delegation of responsibility for the organisation and maintenance of resources. In these cases senior management on the advice of the coordinator who has responsibilities in that area makes acquisitions.

Organisation and accessibility

Glover *et al.* (1998: 287) comment that 'in managing finances, producing lists and auditing stock, middle managers justify most of the pressures on their time'. Thus one of the primary responsibilities of a departmental head is to ensure that the existing resources are maintained in such a way as to make them accessible to staff and students as appropriate. For this to be successful, at the first level of access it is important to identify and record the existence and location of all appropriate resources, both those departmentally 'owned' and those shared more widely within the institution. An appropriate way to achieve this would be through some form of departmental induction pack. At the second level, it would be highly desirable to link resources, other than those which are used generally within the department or school, to those areas of the curriculum to which they specifically relate. In so doing, this would indicate the possible change of accessibility to the resource over the course of the teaching year. Force meters, for example, which are normally stored in the laboratory preparation room during most of the year, are brought into the lab and made accessible to students during a teaching unit on 'forces'. Clearly the issue of who has access and when and how will need to be decided within the department. The main determining factors will revolve around considerations of health and safety (both for staff and students), security, teaching and learning style (student led learning for instance requires a degree of resource flexibility), the flexibility of locating the resource (it is costly to relocate the computer suite) and space or the appropriate means to store the resources in the learning accommodation. To avoid the need to transport resources constantly around the school there will need to be a sympathetic organisation of the placing of teaching accommodation with similar resource requirements in the vicinity of where those resources are located. This also might mean the timetabling of teachers to particular rooms so that they are more able to manage their resource needs more effectively – i.e. they will not be expected to transport their teaching materials from room to room between classes.

The more flexible and accommodating the resource management system is, the more carefully it needs to be controlled. Whilst bureaucratic 'booking' systems may increase the level of security and knowledge of the system manager of the location of resources, they also have the potential to inhibit resource use and so might lead to a situation where the learning environment is becoming impoverished. At the other extreme, complete open access might quickly lead to a situation where the resources have effectively become 'lost', their location or even continued existence being in doubt. The system used must reflect the cost of the resource and the degree of accessibility expected, and be designed to maximise 'ease of use' within these constraints – the loss or destruction of a ruler might be acceptable, whilst for a laptop it would not be. Thus the issue of availability will be determined by perceptions of ownership and the degree of responsibility (especially financial!) that the user is willing to offer.

Acquisition and funding

The last point above, the possible disparity between 'ownership' and 'use' of resources, hints at one of the major problems for the management of learning resources – shared use. Those learning resources that are funded centrally by the school, such as reprographics and library services, can either be treated as 'free' to all users or departments can be charged on the basis of use. Each has its pros and cons – free use is fine if your department happens to be a heavy user; if it isn't, it could be perceived that other departments are being unfairly subsidised. Also it does not encourage efficient use of resources – there is no incentive to 'think before you copy' and consider other ways in which the resources available to you might be employed more effectively. Charging departments for use of centrally purchased resources is a very practical option for resources such as reprographics (where code programming is possible) or audio/visual equipment (daily charge via a booking system) but resources such as the library may be more problematic, especially where the pupils are given self-directed tasks.

Resources acquired by and for a particular department may be requested by another department for very occasional use. For example the science department may want to 'borrow' 50 of the PE department's tennis balls for a 10 minute demonstration of an aspect of molecular theory. It is hardly an efficient use of funds for science to buy (and store for the rest of the year) such a quantity of tennis balls – but where does the responsibility lie for them? In the reverse direction, PE might want to borrow remote sensing equipment from science to measure reaction times. Clearly the cost of these resources is considerably more, but how will it be treated? Fair swap? The borrower must take financial responsibility for non-return or damage? An inter-departmental fee is levied?

Beyond these bureaucratic niceties that will need to be debated and decided at an institutional level, one of the key responsibilities of the departmental head will be to acquire new and replacement learning resources to enable the agreed curriculum to be delivered as effectively as possible. Ensuring that the funding goes as far as possible can easily lead to an increase in other costs – the subject leader's time. The whole process of getting 'value-for-money' resources can be undermined if it leads to an excessive use of valuable time to find the 'best' resource from the 'best' supplier. Schools may find it more efficient to delegate such tasks, once the required resources are identified, to a member of the administrative team with specialist 'buyer' knowledge.

INFORMATION MANAGEMENT

This is quite properly recognised as a key resource in the drive to improve learning and teaching. Through the use of effective bureaucratic systems, almost certainly employing information technology, information such as scheme and lesson plans, and pupil assessments and targets can be more effectively stored, organised and recalled. Although setting up systems will be very time consuming, subsequent revisions will be made much more manageable. Just consider a system where the whole school is networked by a wireless system, and each teacher has a networked laptop. The teacher will have on their screen the lesson plan for the class entering the room along with a note of what happened in the preceding session. The class list will appear via the network, with students who were absent for the last session identified (as well as those not attending this one). Students with special needs statements or other special issues (e.g. need to attend a medical appointment at 10:30) will be highlighted, with dropdown menus providing the details. As the session progresses and learning objectives are met, the objectives can be dragged and dropped onto particular students to be included in their records. At the end of the session the teacher can make a brief note on progress as a reminder for the next session with this class – any issues with individual children or the class as a whole can be noted so that the teacher of their next session can be made aware.

Clearly very resource expensive to set up, but in a time where bureaucracy is seen as driving teachers from the classroom, the effective and efficient management of information might be seen as a vital component in ensuring staff retention. A subject leader who is able to initiate and maintain bureaucratic practices which enhance the flow of information and the proportion of the time teaching staff are required to devote to it, will be in a position to direct staff to pursuits that would be more beneficial to the students.

REFERENCES

Ainley, P. and Bailey, B. (1997) *The Business of Learning: Staff and Student Experiences of Further Education in the 1990s*, London: Cassell.

Brown, M. and Rutherford, D. (1998) 'Changing roles and raising standards: new challenges for heads of department', *School Leadership and Management*, 18, 1: 75–88.

Glover, D. (2000) 'Financial management and strategic planning', in M. Coleman and L. Anderson (eds) *Managing Finance and Resources in Education*, London: Paul Chapman.

Glover, D., Gleeson, D., Gough, G. and Johnson, M. (1998) 'The meaning of management: the development needs of middle managers in secondary schools', *Educational Management and Administration*, 26, 3: 279–92.

Goddard, A. and Ooi, K. (1998) 'Activity-based costing and central overhead cost allocation in universities: a case study', *Public Money and Management*, 18, 3: 31–8.

Kelly, R. and Kedney, J. (1992) 'Designing a college accommodation strategy', Mendip Papers, MP053, Bristol, The Staff College.

Levacic, R. (2000) 'Linking resources to learning outcomes', in M. Coleman and L. Anderson (eds) *Managing Finance and Resources in Education*, London: Paul Chapman.

McAleese, K. (2000) 'Budgeting in schools', in M. Coleman and L. Anderson (eds) *Managing Finance and Resources in Education*, London: Paul Chapman.

Murphy, M. (1994) 'Managing the use of space', in D. Warner and G. Kelly (eds) *Managing Educational Property: A Handbook for Schools, Colleges and Universities*, Buckingham: Society for Research into Higher Education and Open University Press.

Stoll, L. and Fink, D. (1996) *Changing Our Schools*, Buckingham: Open University Press.

FURTHER READING

Turner, C.K. (1996) 'The role and tasks of a subject head of department in secondary schools in England and Wales: a neglected area of research', *School Organisation*, 16: 203–17.

5.3 The Recruitment and Selection of Staff

Howard Stevenson

INTRODUCTION

OBJECTIVES

By the end of this Unit you should:

- Understand the labour market for school employees and how this impacts on recruitment and selection procedures;
- Understand how legislation impacts on the recruitment and selection process;
- Understand the key stages in a recruitment and selection process;
- Appreciate how effective recruitment and selection procedures should maximise staff quality and minimise the potential for discrimination.

It can been argued that a defining feature of the metamorphosis of personnel management into Human Resource Management (HRM) is a recognition of the central importance of people to organisational success. One of the philosophical foundations of HRM is the belief that people are the most important factor in creating successful organisations and therefore considerable organisational thought and resourcing should be devoted to both recruiting the best staff, and then seeking to develop them further. In a labour-intensive service industry, such as education, the contribution of the 'people factor' is pivotal. A key argument within this unit is that a strategic approach to recruitment and selection, supported by effective procedures, should be seen as the start of a process by which the organisation commits to investing in its most valuable asset – its staff.

The terms 'recruitment' and 'selection' are often rolled together, and little thought is given to their distinct meaning. However, it is important to recognise that the terms refer to two, quite different, concepts. Understanding this difference is likely to become increasingly important in the face of continued, and probably worsening, staff shortages. Recruitment refers to the process of trawling for applicants to fill a specific vacancy or vacancies. It embraces all the methods used to attract candidates to the job. Selection refers to the process of choosing the required number of potential employees from the pool of people willing and able to undertake the job.

Understanding the distinction between recruitment and selection is no simple case of being pedantic about terminology. Recognising that people have to offer themselves for work before any employer can have any choice over the selection of employees draws our attention to a crucial issue – all decisions relating to recruitment and selection take place within a context shaped decisively by the labour market. Understanding that labour market becomes a starting point for the strategic decisions any organisation has to make when assessing its personnel needs, and what steps it will take to meet those needs.

THE LABOUR MARKET FOR SCHOOL EMPLOYEES

A market is anywhere where buyers and sellers meet. In this case we are referring to people who are offering themselves for work (labour supply) and those who are seeking people to perform specific jobs (labour demand). At any one time what determines the supply and demand of labour, and therefore the relative balance between them, is the outcome of a multiplicity of complex factors (Seifert, 1996: 65). The supply of labour to schools hinges on both macro and micro factors. Macro factors might be considered to include overall population size, the number of people with appropriate skills and qualifications, e.g. Qualified Teacher Status, and the availability of alternative employment elsewhere in the economy. Micro factors will include the motivational factors that will affect each individual differently. Here pay is clearly a key issue, but other factors such as professional development opportunities or the proximity of the job to home will also intervene in the debate.

Labour demand is shaped by a similar range of complex macro and micro factors – public sector spending reviews, developments in curriculum policy (at national and school level) and decisions taken by neighbouring (and sometimes competing) institutions are just some of the issues that affect labour demand. It is against this background that schools must plan their personnel needs, identifying what staff they require and with what skills. In so doing they will be constantly weighing up difficult opportunity costs, for example, what should the balance be between teaching personnel and support staff?

Whatever the nature of these debates, what is now beyond refute is that the current labour market for employees in the school sector is very tight (White, 2002: 2). This is particularly the case for qualified teachers, and more so when specific subject specialisms, or geographical locations, are added to the equation. Furthermore, there is no suggestion that this situation will improve in the short to medium term. Indeed, demographic trends suggest it is likely to get worse before it gets better.

An inevitable consequence of the current, and future, labour market is that schools must think strategically about their recruitment and selection procedures, one feature of which will be to devote proportionately more resources to recruitment than has perhaps historically been the case. Arguably this strategic approach is best achieved when there is a clear understanding of the recruitment and selection process and an appreciation of how each element within that process contributes to the desired outcome – the appointment of the best available person for the job.

THE RECRUITMENT AND SELECTION PROCESS

The recruitment and selection process involves a number of integrated, but discrete, stages or activities. Understanding the role of each stage, and how each stage dovetails with the whole process, is central to developing the strategic approach required.

Recruitment, selection and the law

Recruitment and selection procedures are about matching the most suitable applicant to the available post. If this was always the result there would be no need to worry about discrimination in the process. However, there is considerable research evidence, and legal casework experience, to demonstrate that selection decisions can be, and are, shaped by discriminatory and prejudicial attitudes. Precisely because of this experience the state intervenes to provide legislative protection to employees, and potential employees, where discrimination on the grounds of sex, race or disability may have taken place. There is currently no statutory protection against discrimination on grounds of age, sexual orientation or political activity, although many schools would want to use their equal opportunities policy to attempt to prevent discrimination on these grounds.

Sex and race legislation (Sex Discrimination Act 1975, and Race Relations (Amendment) Act 2000) identifies two types of discrimination, direct and indirect. Direct discrimination exists where someone is treated less favourably on grounds of sex or race compared to others in comparable circumstances. Indirect discrimination is where a condition or practice is applied to both sexes, or all races, but it adversely affects a considerably larger proportion of one sex or race. The condition or practice cannot be justified within the law. Both these types of discrimination can feature in the recruitment and selection of staff in schools.

The Disability Discrimination Act 1995 prevents employers from unjustifiably discriminating against current, or prospective employees with disabilities, or those who have had disabilities in the past. This may require the employer to make suitable adjustments to their employment arrangements or premises if these substantially disadvantage a disabled individual compared to a non-disabled person.

Positive discrimination, for example, appointing someone because of their sex, is not permissible under current legislation. However, positive action is legal. This allows employers to take pro-active steps to encourage applications from under-represented groups. Given the under-representation of many key groups in positions of responsibility within schools this is an option many schools may want to consider.

In light of the above legislation it is vital that schools avoid any discrimination in their recruitment and selection procedures. However, this motivation should not be born out of a desire simply to avoid litigation, but out of a wider recognition of the moral need to ensure fairness and equality in employment practices. This is an important philosophical commitment that should be central to the school's values. It can be argued that the most effective way to demonstrate that recruitment and selection practices are transparent and fair, and therefore likely to minimise potential discrimination, is to ensure that there are robust and systematic procedures for dealing with the process. It is these, coupled with effective training for those involved in the procedures, which are likely to be the most effective guarantors against discrimination.

Identify the vacancy

The most common basis for recruiting a member of staff is to replace a departing member of staff, but it cannot be assumed that every staff departure automatically requires a replacement, let alone that the replacement should be a carbon copy of the post holder about to exit. Typically, the need for appointments arises from three sets of circumstances – a member of staff vacating a post, organisational expansion or an organisational restructuring which may require different skills to those that already exist.

It is important to recognise that any potential appointment must be integrated into the strategic and personnel plan of the school. A departing member of staff presents an opportunity to review the continued need for the post. Is a replacement required? Is there an opportunity to amend the post, or might the post be deleted entirely? Expansion or restructuring will trigger the same questions – does a vacancy exist? What is the vacancy for? How will the job be presented in terms of content and conditions of service/remuneration?

At this point the labour market context will already be shaping the answers to our questions. Will the post be able to attract a suitable pool of applicants? Is the pool of applicants to be restricted to existing employees, or will external applicants be sought? Whether to use only the internal labour market, or draw on the external labour market, will depend on the nature of the job itself and the availability of appropriate skills within the organisation. It is also worth considering whether flexibility needs to be built into the job design in order to maximise the number of applicants. Including this sort of flexibility can be important when trying to target specific sections of the labour market, for example, women returners.

Preparing the job description and personnel specification

Once the vacancy has been established it is important to clarify both precisely what the job entails, and what skills, experience and qualifications will be required by the post holder to perform the job described. Job content is presented in the form of a job description, whilst the statement of appropriate skills and experience is articulated in the personnel specification. Devoting time to the formulation of these documents can seem an administrative chore, especially when deadlines are tight for making an appointment. However, the production of a job description and personnel specification is not simply a bureaucratic exercise. It represents a crucial stage in the process in which those involved in selection share, and agree, thoughts about the post and the criteria to be used in selection. Time invested at this point makes later stages of the process both fairer and more time efficient, improving the chances of making the most appropriate appointment, and minimising the possibility of judgments being based on prejudicial or discriminatory views.

Job descriptions can vary considerably in their format and style. Most job descriptions consist of a narrative description of key tasks within the job, but other information will include job title, pay grading and scale, and an outline of important functional relationships to the post – for example, who is the line manager? Is the post holder responsible for other employees?

Many schools and colleges will have established procedures for drawing up job descriptions. It is important to ensure consistency across the organisation and therefore job descriptions will tend to have a common format, and in many cases, a high degree of common content. For example, the job description of a standard classroom teacher, without any additional management responsibilities, will in part reflect the duties of teachers set out in the *School Teachers' Pay and Conditions Document* (DfES, 2002 – updated and published annually). However, it will also reflect the expectations of staff that are specific to that institution, for example, a job description may specify an expectation that teachers act as form tutors and contribute to the pastoral curriculum through the delivery of PSHE.

Clear and consistent job descriptions not only perform an important function within the selection process, but they also make an important contribution to developing employment practices that are *seen* as transparent and fair. For example, job descriptions can perform an important function in ensuring equitable application of a school's pay policy. However, it is important to recognise that there is a need for flexibility, and therefore following any appointment there should be agreed procedures for reviewing job descriptions.

Once the job content has been clarified it is possible to prepare a personnel specification. This is a statement of the human characteristics required in order to perform the job. It is an absolutely crucial document because this provides the criteria on which a selection will be made. Typical content might include previous experience, qualifications, skills and personal attributes, and attitudes. The first important point to make at this stage is that the personnel specification must link clearly to the job description. A requirement within the personnel specification must be demonstrably linked to an appropriate element within the job description. If a requirement within the personnel specification has no obvious link to the job description then there is a potential argument for discrimination in the process.

Second, it is important to distinguish between those characteristics that are essential for performing the job, and those that are preferred. Technically, any applicant who does not meet any essential criteria should be eliminated early in the selection process as they lack a characteristic considered absolutely fundamental to execution of the post. However, the inclusion of preferred or desirable criteria can assist greatly in the selection of applicants by providing a mechanism to rank those who meet all the basic requirements.

The personnel specification is an important opportunity to ensure that the successful applicant will not just narrowly fit into the role, but will also integrate into the wider organisation. For example, a school committed to developing collaborative working will want to place a significant emphasis on teamwork skills, whilst a school may also want to ensure a philosophical commitment to important organisational values such as social inclusion. If these issues are important then they should feature within the selection process. Consideration must then be given to how candidates will be assessed against these criteria.

Action point

Work with your colleagues to draw up a job description and person specification. This can either be done for a completely imaginary post or can be undertaken by assuming that a current member of staff was about to leave. To avoid embarrassment it can be useful to focus this exercise on your own post rather than on that of a more junior member of staff (you may also find out a great deal about the way that you are perceived by colleagues and the range of duties that you actually perform).

Advertising the vacancy

Once details of the post and the personnel specification have been agreed the post can be advertised. Typically school posts for teaching personnel are advertised in the national educational press with non-teaching posts being advertised in the local press and through other agencies such as Job Centres and the Connexions service. Important issues to consider at this stage are which advertising media to use, and second, what information should be provided to applicants once an enquiry is made. Both these issues will reflect labour market considerations. Advertising for example is costly, but not as costly as having to re-advertise a post, and certainly not as costly as making a poor appointment due to an inadequate field of applicants. Considerable thought may need to be given to how the number of applicants can be maximised within cost constraints. Consideration should also be given to using advertising media which will encourage applications from sections of the community that might otherwise be under-represented in the school.

Once a potential applicant responds to the advertisement, then the school will want to provide details which will encourage the maximum number of applications from those suitable for the post. It is now widely accepted that applicants should be provided with a copy of the job description and the personnel specification. This helps create a level playing field in which all applicants can see what the job involves, and what the employer is looking for in a successful applicant. Candidates can submit applications tailored to the personnel specification and this allows them to present themselves most effectively. There is little to be gained from making it difficult for a good candidate to present their best application – there is no virtue in making applicants second-guess the selection criteria. Similarly, unsuitable applicants may decide not to proceed with an application on the basis of this information, saving the time of applicants and selectors alike.

However, it is also important to consider what other information will be provided to applicants. The recruitment pack is a vital opportunity to present the school to candidates so that candidates can assess their own suitability for the post. What is the student profile like? What are the distinctive values and ethos that the school seeks to promote? What are the school's strengths and achievements? What are the areas it is seeking to develop?

Comprehensive information, attractively presented, is an important opportunity to impress potential employees and encourage their applications. In a tight labour market, serious consideration must be given to how this is achieved. There is also evidence to indicate that candidates appreciate the opportunity to visit the school informally prior to any selection process. The provision of this offer is itself an important statement that the school values its staff and potential staff.

Selection

Careful thought about how the post is presented and advertised will maximise the chances of attracting a wide field of applicants. The task then becomes selecting the person(s) most suitable for the post advertised. The key here is to ensure that decisions about selection, and indeed rejection, because the selection process is effectively a process of elimination, are guided by the criteria laid out in the personnel specification. The task therefore is to draw on appropriate selection instruments that will effectively assess candidates' performance against the criteria. It is important to ensure that every criterion within the personnel specification is assessed somewhere in the selection process.

A range of selection instruments are available. Some are almost universally used, such as application forms and interviews, whereas others, psychometric tests for example, are used less widely, and rarely used within the education sector. The important principle is to ensure fitness for purpose – to select the methods that most effectively assess the candidate against the criteria within the resources available.

Application forms are usually standardised and the same form is used across the institution, and often the Local Education Authority, where appropriate. Where there are too many applicants for detailed assessment a short-listing process takes place in which the field of suitable candidates is reduced to a more manageable number. It is helpful if 'essential' criteria within the personnel specification can be assessed through the application form as this prevents applicants who lack these attributes from passing through to the next stage of the process.

Those candidates who are short-listed can then be assessed in more detail. Again, careful consideration must be given to how the candidates will be assessed. An ever-present in the selection process is the interview at which the selection panel can question the candidate on issues relating to the job description and personnel specification. There is also an opportunity for the candidate to ask questions of the panel. Interviews are almost certainly of some use, and it is difficult to envisage a selection process without an interview. Some selection processes involve more than one interview panel with 'sub-panels' feeding into the main panel. Deciding which panels to establish, and why, is an important consideration; for example, the use of student panels in schools is becoming increasingly common.

Despite the centrality of interviews in the selection process it is important to recognise their limitations. There are strong critics of the interview process and some have gone so far as to challenge whether interviews have any useful role to play.

> The bald conclusion from all the empirical evidence is that the interview as typically used is not much good as a selection device. Indeed, one might wonder, thinking rationally, why the interview was not, long ago, 'retired' from selection procedures.
>
> (Morgan, quoted in Torrington and Hall, 1991: 308)

Critics argue that interviewers have often made their mind up about a candidate within a few minutes of the interview commencing, and that the interview is then used to confirm judgments that have already been made on the basis of the application form and the candidate's appearance. There is also some evidence to suggest that interviewers place more emphasis on evidence that is unfavourable, than evidence that is favourable, in the interview process.

Part of the solution to this problem lies in the effective training of interviewers. An important principle in selection is that those involved should have received some training to prepare them for participation in the process. Such training, which should apply to all those involved (including school governors, for example), not only improves the quality of the process generally, but may make a decisive contribution to preventing discrimination.

Another compensation for the deficiencies of the interview is to ensure that a range of opportunities are provided to assess candidates. References provide one such opportunity, but these are widely recognised as of limited value. Questions as to their reliability mean they are generally used only in the most marginal of decisions. More important is the contribution of assessment activities such as presentations (to staff and/or students), simulations (such as in-tray exercises) and group activities (including role play). Precisely what candidates are expected to do will clearly depend on the job role and the personnel specification, with the nature of the tasks changing as the role shifts, for example, from that of classroom teacher to a post involving additional responsibilities.

The important principle to reiterate at this point is that the selection instruments should provide, within available resources, the best opportunities for candidates to demonstrate their aptitude against the personnel specification. Some criteria within the personnel specification will be harder to assess than others. For example, establishing whether an individual has Qualified Teacher Status is a relatively straight-forward task. Assessing someone's teamworking capability is more difficult. However, if teamworking is a criteria within the personnel specification, and within a school it is likely to be, then the selection panel must be clear about what they are looking for and how they will assess it.

Action point

Try writing an advertisement for a post at your school. Once again this can be completely imaginary or based on a current post. Remember that you need to be very accurate in your advertising, that the use of words costs money.

Try to take opportunities to become involved in the recruitment and interviewing of staff. Consider the kinds of questions you might ask and how they might be phrased in order to ensure equity and fairness in the interviewing process.

Making a decision

Once the process is completed, with all short-listed candidates having completed all elements within the selection process, the selection panel must make a decision. This involves weighing up all the evidence that has been gathered from across the selection process and judging each candidate against the criteria in the personnel specification. Many selection panels create grids and matrices in which they match candidates against the selection criteria, and some go so far as scoring them against each criteria. However, it is important to recognise that although scoring gives an air of objectivity to the process judgments are still fundamentally subjective. Clear and effective procedures can improve objectivity, but they cannot eliminate human judgment. Scoring systems therefore, where they are used, can only be a guide to judgment, and should not be used as a pseudo-scientific justification for picking the successful candidate.

Opportunities for all those involved in the selection process to feed into the final decision should be provided. Here the role of the selection panel is clearly important, and within that the pivotal role of the panel chair. The panel must not only draw on their own experience of the candidates, but must utilise the contributions of others who may have been involved in the process elsewhere. At this point it is important to generate serious and rigorous debate about the relative qualities of the candidates. The process of presenting and justifying the case for one candidate over another is a key element in ensuring that candidates are selected on the basis of the selection criteria, not on the personal preferences or prejudices of a key individual on the selection panel. Before making a final decision the panel must be convinced that it can proceed with an appointment at all.

Assuming the panel feels it can appoint, and a successful applicant has emerged from the group, the post can be offered. Effective procedures, which have provided opportunities for applicants to find out what they need to know about both the job and the organisation, should ensure that by this point an offer of employment will be accepted. However, this is not always the case, and if it is not, it is important to review why this might be so. Is it the case that the local labour market allows candidates to be highly selective, sometimes holding more than one job offer at a time? Or is it that a failure to adequately present the job or the school has proved a deterrent? In either case the school needs to reflect on the experience and identify appropriate strategic responses. Especially in a tight labour market, schools cannot be complacent about recruitment.

Assuming the successful candidate accepts the post two key tasks remain. First, opportunities should be provided to offer unsuccessful candidates quality feedback – clearly linking their performance in the selection process to the criteria in the personnel specification. Second, the school needs to consider the needs of the successful applicant – because their induction should start now.

CONCLUSION

People are pivotal to school success. This is not simply a reference to teachers, but to all staff employed within the institution. It follows that considerable care and attention should be invested in securing the best candidates for the posts available. Every appointment represents an opportunity to bring something new to the organisation, and to move it forward. Making a mistake represents more than a missed opportunity. It can prove to be a costly error for students, the member of staff concerned and colleagues. This Unit argues it is vital that schools approach the issue of recruitment and selection strategically and systematically. In a tight labour market, such as is likely to exist for teachers in particular for some time to come, this approach is imperative.

The hallmarks of this approach are robust and effective procedures, supported by a clear organisational commitment to equality of opportunity. This in turn needs to be supported with appropriate resourcing, a key element of which is training for all those involved in the recruitment and selection process. The benefits of such an approach are substantial – a high quality staff, functioning in an institution committed to fair treatment and staff development. These factors can then combine to create a powerful force for school improvement.

REFERENCES

DfES (2002) *School Teachers' Pay and Conditions Document*, Norwich: HMSO.

Seifert, R. (1996) *Human Resource Management in Schools*, London: Pitman Publishing.

Torrington, D. and Hall, L. (1991) *Personnel Management: A New Approach*, Hemel Hempstead: Prentice Hall.

White, P. (2002) 'Staff shortages are damaging pupils' learning', *Times Educational Supplement*, 22 November, 'News and Opinions': 2.

FURTHER READING

Seifert, R. (1996) *Human Resource Management in Schools*, London: Pitman Publishing

Torrington, D. and Hall, L. (1998) *Human Resource Management*, London: Prentice Hall.

WEBSITES

Commission for Racial Equality http://cre.gov.uk/

Disability Rights Commission http://www.drc-gb.org/

Equal Opportunities Commission http://eoc.org.uk/

5.4 Health, Safety and Welfare – Managing Stress

Howard Stevenson

INTRODUCTION

OBJECTIVES

By the end of this Unit you should:

- Understand what stress is, and its consequences for individuals and schools;
- Identify common symptoms associated with stress and the factors that generate stress in schools;
- Identify appropriate organisational strategies that seek to reduce stress risks to acceptable levels.

The first example of legislative protection for workers covered health and safety issues, and these matters continue to be a source of serious concern for employees in their working lives. Current legislation is framed by the Health and Safety at Work Act, 1974, which sets out the rights and responsibilities of both employers and employees in relation to health and safety issues. The enduring need for legislative protection derives from the inevitable conflict between capital and labour.

> There is always a conflict between the needs of the employer to push for increased output and efficiency, and for the needs of the employee to be protected from the hazards of the workplace.
>
> (Torrington and Hall, 1991: 329)

However, early health and safety legislation was designed to protect workers from very different hazards to those that now dominate workplaces in the twenty-first century. A recent survey of 5,300 safety representatives by the TUC indicated that stress was the major health and safety issue in 80 per cent of British workplaces; moreover this research indicated that education was one of the industrial sectors where stress was most likely to be a problem (TUC, 2002).

This assertion is supported by data relating to teacher sickness absence. Between 1999 and 2001 the percentage of teachers in England taking sickness absence increased from 54 per cent to 56 per cent, with each teacher taking sickness absence averaging 10 days off work in 2001. The total number of days taken in sickness absence was 2,799,000 in 2001; an increase of 296,600 days from 1999 (DfES, 2002a). Clearly this data will cover teacher sickness resulting from a multiplicity of causes. However, its upward trend points to increasing pressures within the system and therefore the need to understand the underlying reasons for these changes. It is data such as this, some of which has been accumulated over many years, which has focused attention on stress within the education sector generally, and amongst school teachers in particular. This Unit focuses on teacher stress by assessing definitions of stress, and identifying what the common sources of stress are within the teaching profession. It then discusses how, within an organisation, the risks of stress can be eliminated, or reduced to acceptable levels.

WHAT IS 'STRESS'? – DEFINING TERMS

Providing an acceptable definition of stress is not straightforward. The word is widely used in common parlance and can mean very different things in different circumstances. Travers and Cooper offer additional terms to provide clarification. For example, they distinguish between 'stressor' and 'strain' (1996: 12). A stressor is either a physical, psychological or behavioural stimulus, which in turn may generate a strain. Strain therefore becomes an indicator of stress, often showing in some form of ill-health. The implication of this analysis is that stress may be considered to have potentially positive, as well as negative, consequences – 'It can, up to a certain point, be a stimulant, and can have positive consequences ... but it is important that individuals can find their optimal stress levels' (Travers and Cooper, 1996: 13). This approach is common and echoed by other commentators (see Brown and Ralph, 1994: 15).

In contrast, the Health and Safety Executive, the government agency charged with promoting safety at work, argues that stress is an entirely negative phenomenon. They define stress as '... the natural reaction people have to excessive pressures or other types of demand placed on them' (HSE, 2000: 3). The same HSE publication rejects the notion of positive stress – it emphatically rejects the proposition that 'a little bit of stress is good for you'. Where stress becomes either intense or prolonged it is vital that remedial action is taken. This approach appears to echo Kyriacou and Sutcliffe, who specifically apply their definition to teachers. They define teacher stress as:

> A response syndrome of negative effect (such as anger and depression), usually accompanied by potentially pathogenic physiological changes (such as increased heart rate) resulting from aspects of the teacher's job and mediated

by the perception that the demands made upon the teacher constitute a threat to his (or her) self-esteem or well-being and by coping mechanisms activated to reduce that threat.

(Kyriacou and Sutcliffe, quoted in Travers and Cooper, 1996: 38)

This emphasis on the impact of stress draws our attention to the consequences of stress for both the individual concerned, and the organisation that employs them.

Individuals suffering from stress are likely to experience a number of mental, physical and behavioural symptoms. Examples of these are provided in Table 5.6.

Even a cursory look at this list will give some idea of the personal tragedy that is sometimes experienced by those who suffer from stress. Those experiencing stress can suffer profound depression as they become locked in a vicious circle of diminishing self-esteem and deteriorating professional performance. These problems are then compounded as personal and professional relationships decline similarly.

Clearly where these symptoms are significant they are likely to be accompanied by an increase in staff absence. If these difficulties persist then acute problems may develop. Some commentators identify 'burnout' as a distinct stressed state, in which individuals feel unable to ever overcome the problems they are experiencing (Gold and Roth, 1993: 30). At this point individuals often seek exit strategies from teaching – these might be changing employment, premature retirement or retirement on grounds of ill-health.

For individuals who have seen what might be a long career, and years of training, come to an ignominious end this is clearly a personal tragedy. Add to this the cost of strained, perhaps destroyed, family relationships and the personal costs become clear. These costs may be considered as internal to the teacher concerned, but if the full costs of stress are to be gauged then wider, external costs must also be taken into consideration.

An obvious cost is that experienced by students. Many symptoms associated with stress will impact, inevitably, on the quality of what the teacher can provide. Teaching is an intense job. Managing a classroom of 30 adolescents requires nothing less than a performance. Sustaining such a performance, often several times a day, when

Table 5.6 Stress symptoms

Physical symptoms	Mental health symptoms	Behavioural symptoms
Headaches/migraines	Depression	Excessive drinking
Palpitations	Low self-esteem	Excessive substance abuse
Lethargy	Withdrawal	Eating problems
Increased incidence of	Anxiety	Poor time keeping
minor ailments such as	Hypochondria	Making frequent mistakes
colds	Irritability	Increased accident rate
Asthmatic attacks	Tearfulness	Worsening personal
Increased cholesterol	Forgetfulness	relationships
levels	Poor concentration	
Digestive problems		
Raised blood pressure		
Menstrual disorders		
Insomnia		

experiencing stress symptoms is almost impossible. There will almost certainly be a diminution in the quality of what students experience. If stress symptoms are accompanied by an increase in sickness absence these problems will be compounded.

However, the wider costs of teacher stress are not restricted to students. Fellow team members and close colleagues experience an increase in their own pressures. Sometimes these are physical pressures – the need to set up additional classes, or to provide extra cover. In other cases, the pressures are emotional – arising from providing support to a struggling colleague. Whatever the issue, it will be increasingly difficult to maintain quality provision.

Even beyond this, there are more, hidden, costs of stress. At an institutional level there will be increased supply cover costs, together with problems associated with high rates of labour turnover. In the current climate, a combination of staff instability and teacher shortages is a recipe for major problems. There may also, in some cases, be costs of litigation. Beyond the school there are the costs of health care to consider, plus the investment in training teachers which may subsequently prove to be wasted.

For all these reasons, personal, institutional and societal, it is vital that the issue of stress within teaching is tackled strategically. This must be approached by identifying the sources of stress, and then systematically ensuring they are reduced to acceptable levels.

SOURCES OF STRESS

The individual

A common approach to stress management is to begin to analyse why some individuals appear to be more 'stress prone' than others. Why is it that when faced with the same circumstances and pressures some people cope, whilst others crumple?

Part of the explanation may lie in individual's lives outside of school. We know that individuals can be exposed to hugely stressful situations in their personal lives, which may make it more difficult to cope with pressures in their work life. Family problems, including illness, divorce, or bereavement, financial problems, or other factors such as negotiating a house move can all play their part.

Whilst these individual circumstances are clearly important Friedman and Rosenman (1974) went beyond this to identify whether different personality types were more or less prone to stress. They distinguished between 'Type A' and 'Type B' personalities. Friedman and Rosenman's work argued that A and B personalities responded to stress pressures in different ways, A personalities with heightened stress levels, whilst B personalities appeared to absorb stress more effectively. Friedman and Rosenman's study linked type A behaviour to increased incidences of stress illnesses such as heart disease. Characteristics of type A and B behaviour are summarised in Table 5.7.

Analyses such as Friedman and Rosenman's are particularly useful for two reasons. First, they highlight the importance of the individual in stress incidence. It is important to recognise that different people respond in different ways to the same stressor. An effective approach to stress management within an institution will inevitably focus on systems, but it must not lose sight of the individual. An organisation that is sensitive

Table 5.7 Characteristics of type A and B behaviour

Type A behaviours	Type B behaviours
Fastidious about punctuality	Relaxed and easy-going
Poor listener	Good listener
Competitive	Manages workload effectively –
Always rushed	focuses on one activity at a time
Attempts to cope with several tasks	Satisfied with meeting own objectives
simultaneously	Expresses feelings
Seeks recognition from others	Wide range of interests
Eats and walks quickly	Sociable
Ambitious for self and others	Good work–life balance
Reluctant to share feelings	
Interests dominated by work and home	
Works long hours	
Has difficulty relaxing	

and responsive to the needs of its individual employees will almost certainly be rewarded with improved staff loyalty and commitment.

Second, Friedman and Rosenman's analysis draws our attention to organisational sources of stress. There is nothing fixed about type A and B behaviour – we are not pre-ordained A or B at birth. A and B characteristics are behaviours that are shaped by external factors. For example, focusing on one task at a time may be manageable in some circumstances, but when pressures of workload demand an employee juggles several tasks simultaneously, it may be that an employee more naturally disposed to type B behaviour increasingly begins to take on type A characteristics.

The organisation

Travers and Cooper identify several sources of stress which they associate with the ethos, structure and management of the organisation (1996: 36–74). In this case the organisational stress factors might be considered to embrace both institutional (school-based) factors and wider system issues relating to the implementation of state policy. Factors identified by Travers and Cooper include stressors intrinsic to the job, the teacher's role, relationships at work, career development and organisational structure and climate.

Stressors intrinsic to the job include a number of issues such as physical working conditions and workload. Teachers' physical working conditions have often been considered to be poor – a point acknowledged in the government's Green Paper for reform of the teaching profession (DfES, 1998). This same document makes the case for improved staffroom facilities as part of a programme of environmental improvement. Such developments are clearly welcome, although they appear to be slow to materialise. At the same time, wider issues such as large class sizes, present teachers with major problems. Class sizes are just one manifestation of the rising workload pressures for teachers. These pressures represent an increasing intensification of the labour process of teaching, in both quantitative and qualitative terms. Successive reports of the School

Teachers' Review Body have recorded increases in teachers' working hours, with the most recent report acknowledging that teachers' term time hours are 52 per week (DfES, 2002b: 5). It is also acknowledged that at particular times of the year working hours may rise well above even these levels. This evidence suggests that in response to external pressures, teachers are increasingly exhibiting type A behaviour.

Stress levels in teaching may also be rising due to the changing nature of the teacher's role. This can take many forms. For example, increasing concern relating to a range of social issues has focused attention on schools to provide solutions. Hence, in addition to improving standards in national tests teachers are expected to educate youngsters to deal with complex social issues, such as substance abuse or sexual health. As young people appear disengaged from the political process, teachers are expected to reconnect them through citizenship education. All these aims are laudable, but they can give rise to unrealistic and unattainable expectations. Where teachers are inadequately prepared to deal with these issues, the sense of overload and inadequacy can increase.

Travers and Cooper identify work relationships as a key source of stress for employees (1996: 51–5). Within a school the network of relationships are many and complex. Clearly a key relationship is that which exists between teachers and senior managers. This has long been recognised as a major source of stress in cases where staff feel they are misunderstood, under-valued, not involved in decision-making or even bullied and intimidated. The danger is that as increasing pressures are applied to schools to deliver performance improvements management's response may be more inclined to become blunt and unrealistic. In such situations relationships fracture and stress levels rise. This pressure can be particularly acute for those in middle management posts. Management of people (as opposed to 'things') is a key stressor, and middle managers can often feel caught in the middle between the demands of senior management and the expectations of team members. Where middle managers are trying to cope with a significant teaching commitment these tensions are exacerbated.

Much attention has focused recently on the changing nature of relationships between teachers and students. Whilst it is difficult to test empirically whether student behaviour is indeed any worse than it was at some point in the past, there is clear circumstantial evidence (such as the increase in industrial disputes relating to this issue) to suggest that teachers see this as a worsening problem.

Travers and Cooper identify several other factors which contribute to rising stress levels – a lack of job security, a blame culture in which the teaching profession is frequently denigrated by the media and politicians and a raft of reforms, such as appraisal and performance management, which raise pressure and expectations often without any corresponding increase in resources.

These sources of stress are in large part reflected in research undertaken by the National Union of Teachers (NUT, 2000). The NUT research clusters stressors into four general areas – workload, student behaviour, school management and specific pressures relating to OFSTED inspection. Their report goes on to assert:

> The major underlying sources of stress are organisational in nature. Stress is rooted in the way teaching and schools are organised. The solutions, therefore, must rest with employers. Stress cannot be eliminated by individual teachers 'taking up hobbies' or adopting 'coping strategies' as is sometimes suggested.
>
> (NUT, 2000)

What does appear clear is that there are a number of structural issues within school sector education that are contributing to rising levels of teacher stress. Ever since the 1988 Education Reform Act teachers have had to adjust to a state of permanent revolution and restructuring. These changes have often been substantial, including, for example, introduction of the National Curriculum. Moreover, reforms have frequently been introduced without the professional advice of teachers, indeed sometimes in opposition to such advice. Teachers, and their representative organisations, have often been deliberately excluded from the process of policy development – they have found themselves portrayed as the cause, not the solution, to problems within the system. More recently, the emphasis on meeting centrally determined performance targets has added to the pressure. This lack of control and influence, at both institutional and national level, has almost certainly compounded the problems. Hence there is little evidence to suggest that since 1988 pressures have in any significant way reduced. For these reasons it is vital to ensure that there is an appropriate organisational response to a significant, and continuing, problem.

STRATEGIC STRESS MANAGEMENT – AN ORGANISATIONAL RESPONSE

Employers have a legal obligation, under the Health and Safety at Work Act 1974 (HSWA), to take action on stress. This was reinforced in 1992, following the introduction of the Management of Health and Safety at Work Regulations. These regulations marked an important shift in health and safety culture from being reactive to problems in order to protect the status quo, to being proactive to prevent their occurrence in the first place. A fundamental element in the shift towards prevention was the notion of 'risk assessment'.

Risk assessment involves a number of distinct activities:

1   Identify hazards
2   Identify people at risk
3   Evaluate risks and identify control measures
4   Implement control measures
5   Monitor and review control measures – revising where necessary.

Stress is an occupational risk for teachers and one that requires a formal risk assessment. Schools are often well used to carrying out risk assessments for physical dangers, especially in laboratories and workshops. However, evidence that risk assessments are carried out with regard to stress is less prevalent. It is important that schools create the cultural climate that encourages a proactive approach to stress management – this involves a shift away from emphasising individual treatment to prioritising organisational prevention. This whole school approach requires full staff discussion of the issues, in a climate where discussion of stress issues is not seen as an issue of personal inadequacy. Here the involvement of official safety representatives is vital. The HSWA provides for site safety representatives, nominated by recognised trade unions. Such representatives are relatively rare in primary schools, but much more common in secondary schools. They can make an important contribution to creating the conditions in which issues such as stress are discussed openly and constructively. The outcome of such discussions should be a framework in which the organisation has clear policies covering health and safety, stress and related issues. There should also be agreed procedures for monitoring and evaluating these policies. In schools policy development and review is the responsibility of the governing body. Many governing bodies have designated health and safety committees which are able to co-opt non-governors, such as the safety representative, into their membership.

It is difficult to take any action on stress unless there is a clear picture of the extent of the risk. An important feature therefore of being 'stress aware' is that a school knows its pressure points. Only when risks are identified, and to a degree quantified, can action be taken to eliminate or minimise the stressor. One widely used tool is a 'stress audit'. These come in a range of forms, but the function is largely the same. Questionnaires are used to identify both sources of stress at the workplace (the stressors), and the prevalence of stress. Those factors which appear to be giving rise to the most stress can then be quickly tackled, with an action plan for tackling other issues on a longer term basis. Stress audits are widely available (one can be downloaded from the TUC website – http://www.tuc.org.uk/), with several being adapted for use in schools. Many Local Education Authorities and teacher unions have exemplars that can be used or customised for individual schools.

Stress audits perform a useful function in raising the profile of stress as an issue (although unfortunately this is sometimes provided as a reason for not undertaking such an exercise!). When used over a period of time they become a rich source of data, and a powerful lever for change. They can then be used to support a wide range of individualised and organisational responses. Indeed, stress management solutions will be driven by the process of risk assessment, and the results of stress audits where these are used. For this reason it is difficult to specify 'off-the-shelf' solutions to stress problems. For example, in one school the major source of stress might be student behaviour, whereas in another school it may be the number of new initiatives expected by senior management. Clearly in each case the policy response will be different.

Schools should also generate on-going data that may give some indication of the prevalance of stress within the institution. The monitoring of staff sickness data, and the benchmarking of this data against comparable schools is an important exercise.

However effective organisational responses are this will never prevent individuals, at certain times, suffering from stress. For this reason many schools offer access to counselling services, and national organisations, such as the Teacher Support Network, exist which provide a high quality service. These services are clearly important, and can be invaluable for particular individuals. But it is important to remember that this solution is about treatment and not prevention, and therefore its provision is about complementing, not substituting, a more systematic approach. Prevention requires wider cultural and organisational changes.

Ultimately, comprehensive prevention is likely to involve significant changes in teachers' contracts and their conditions of service. The government is currently considering proposals to remodel the school workforce, with a view to 'freeing teachers to teach' (DfES, 2002b). However, the outcome of these reforms is far from certain, and it is likely that they will be phased in over many years. Hence, it is important for teachers, through their professional associations, to maintain the momentum for change. However, until and unless significant reform is achieved, it will fall to the management in schools to ensure that stress risks, from whatever source, are eliminated, or at least reduced to acceptable levels.

Action point

> Undertake a risk assessment for your own department if you have not already done so. Identify key hazards and those at risk and then identify and implement any required control measures. Monitor the situation systematically.
>
> As part of a staff development activity try to identify the key things that cause stress to you and your staff. Brainstorm what measures can be taken to alleviate the situation (the mere discussion of these issues is often the most important step).

CONCLUSION

There is considerable evidence to suggest that stress levels within the teaching profession are unacceptable. The consequences of this impose huge costs on individual teachers and their families, students and colleagues. Evidence also suggests that the sources of this stress are many and complex. In some cases stressors are bound up with the realities of modern day teaching – the relentless drive to raise performance in national tests, often against a backdrop of inadequate resources. This is now coupled with a complex web of accountability mechanisms that intensify pressures and heighten anxieties. However, not all stressors result from external sources. Many derive from within the context of individual institutions, and we know that similar schools, facing similar circumstances, can often generate very different stress levels amongst their staff.

What is clear is that regardless of the source of stress, it falls to the individual employer to ensure that the risks arising from stress are eliminated, or maintained at acceptably low levels. This can only be achieved when institutions are proactive in dealing with this issue. Current legislation places a premium on prevention rather than cure and it is vital that this approach informs school practice. It is incumbent on those in leadership positions in schools to identify the nature of stress-related hazards and to take appropriate action. This requires the school to systematically identify hazards through effective monitoring procedures and the use of risk assessments. Equally important, however, is the creation of an organisational culture that challenges the notion that stress is 'part of the job'. When teachers refuse to accept this fatalistic notion, significant progress will have been made.

REFERENCES

Brown, M. and Ralph, S. (1994) *Managing Stress in Schools*, Plymouth: Northcote House.

DfES (1998) *Teachers: Meeting the Challenge of Change*, London: HMSO.

DfES (2002a) *Teacher Sickness Absence in 2001 (Provisional)*, 30 May, available online at http://www.dfes.gov.uk/statistics/DB/SFR/s0335/sfr13-2002.do.

DfES (2002b) 'Special report – the government's proposals to reduce teacher workload and raise standards', *Teachers*, November, available online at http://www.teachernet.gov.uk/management/remodelling/specialreportnovember2002/.

Friedman, M. and Rosenman, R. (1974) *Type A Behaviour and Your Heart*, London: Wildwood House.

Gold, Y. and Roth, R.A. (1993) *Teachers Managing Stress and Preventing Burnout. The Professional Health Solution*, London: Falmer Press.

HSE (2000) *Stress Fact Sheet, No 1*, London: HSE.

NUT (2000) *Tackling Stress*, available online at http://www.data.teachers.org.uk/pdfs/stress2000.pdf.

Torrington, D. and Hall, L. (1991) *Personnel Management: A New Approach*, Hemel Hempstead: Prentice Hall.

Travers, C.J. and Cooper, C.L. (1996) *Teachers Under Pressure: Stress in the Teaching Profession*, London: Routledge.

TUC (2002) *Work Overload is Main Cause of Stress at Work*, 4 November, available online at http://www.tuc.org.uk.

FURTHER READING

Travers, C.J. and Cooper, C.L. (1996) *Teachers Under Pressure: Stress in the Teaching Profession*, London: Routledge.

WEBSITES

The Health and Safety Executive at http://www.hse.gov.uk/

Trades Union Congress at http://www.tuc.org.uk (Several interesting items on stress, reflecting the increased concern with this issue in the workplace. Contains a useful downloadable stress audit.)

Section 6

Managing Your Own Performance and Development

6.1 Self Management for the Subject Leader

Ian Terrell and Kathryn Terrell

INTRODUCTION

OBJECTIVES

By the end of this Unit you should:

- Be able to evaluate and reflect upon your own performance;
- Understand how to establish strategies for your personal improvement.

Middle managers are expected to take responsibility for their personal effectiveness and development. This involves being effective while continuing to work for improvement. Your satisfaction in your job depends on a number of factors. You may consider the following:

- you are successful in your job
- you know exactly what is expected of you
- you concentrate explicitly on those things
- you are in control of what you do
- you are productive
- you are secure in your job
- you can plan and move into job areas that you enjoy
- you can avoid staying late at work
- you give yourself quality time to relax and enjoy life outside work.

Being personally effective has a number of elements including:

- Showing a sense of purpose
- Dealing with emotions and pressures
- Being responsible for your own development and learning.

The Unit deals with some of the important self-management issues facing the subject leader. These include:

- Showing a sense of purpose
- Dealing with emotions and pressures
- Being assertive
- Building collaboration
- Organising and leading effective meetings
- Managing time as a subject leader.

SHOWING A SENSE OF PURPOSE

Showing a sense of purpose is based upon trying to make things better, being clear about your vision for the subject and working well with people. Planning, based upon priorities, is key to this. A sense of purpose is key to being a positive role model as leader but more importantly, in self-management terms, it is key to your own motivation.

Fundamental to your sense of purpose are, your beliefs and values concerned with what is important, your vision for the subject area and your personal goals. You might ask yourself have you got this clear in your own mind. How far can you stick to these goals or do they change frequently? Some find it helpful to make their goals public.

Certainly reviewing your achievements and celebrating your success can be key to maintaining that sense of purpose. Using a mentor or colleague to work with, if it is not part of your performance management review, can be helpful.

DEALING WITH EMOTIONS AND PRESSURES

Stress appears to be endemic in teaching. The management of stress is your own personal responsibility and as a middle manager you are responsible for making sure that your colleagues are not too stressed. Stress causes health problems and absenteeism and ultimately leads to 'burn out'.

You may wish to consider five strategies for coping with stress, these include:

- Identify sources of stress for yourself and others
- Develop effective behavioural skills
- Use your peer groups for support
- Keep a focus on where you are going
- Maintain your health.

Knowing what causes you stress and anticipating and planning for it helps you take control and thereby reduces stress. For example, pressure of work may be a problem alleviated by prioritising, delegating some tasks, and even choosing not to do some things that are unimportant. Planning for stressful meetings can help. It is important to manage stress and not to become its victim.

You might wish to identify with whom you might talk things over. This may be a colleague or a peer, a friend or a partner. A problem shared is a problem halved and you will feel better for unloading your feelings. Believe in your abilities and surround yourself with those that believe in you too.

Some colleagues and managers are 'drains' in this world who sap confidence and are often negative or critical. They cast a dark cloud over your enthusiasms and triumphs. They are a negative influence. Often they masquerade as the voice of authority and the guardians of standards. Do not be deceived, for 'drains' are not helpful to motivation or improvement. Avoid them!

Surround yourself with 'radiators', who warm you with enthusiasm, direction and positive thoughts. Lively warm people are more useful. Encourage them in return. Make sure that smiles and laughter are the tone of your department. Make yourselves students of 'jollyology' for it makes the tough times much more of a breeze. Have fun!

Take praise well. Lap it up and thank those that praise you for their kindness in mentioning your qualities. Praise others.

Keep an eye on the vision and where you are going. This helps to prioritise and deal with what is important. Much of what stresses people is forgotten within a short period of time. Think about where you will be in a year's time.

BEING ASSERTIVE

A key management skill is assertiveness. This is about expressing your own point of view, how you feel, your values and your agenda. It is about making where you are coming from clear to everyone. It is not aggressive, nor manipulative.

Assertive language is clear. It uses phrases that are unambiguous and show desires, wants and feelings clearly, such as:

- I want …
- I can …
- I cannot …
- I would like …
- I am very …
- My preference is …
- I want to …
- My view is …

Assertiveness is not about putting other people down, scoring points, or criticising others. It is as much about leaving others feeling good as it is about making sure that you feel all right yourself.

The key to assertiveness is often one word: 'No'. However, you might like to think of how you say no clearly, unambiguously and certainly. How might you say no without upsetting the people that you work with? You may wish to consider how people have said no to you effectively.

Consider, for example, how you might say no in the following instances:

- A Year Head wants you to run assembly next week
- The Headteacher wants you to organise the mock examinations
- A pupil wants you to organise a trip.

Saying no becomes easier if you know your priorities and commitments, and agree that the offer is a wonderful one but one that on this occasion you wish to turn down because it is not right for you at the moment. At least it is clear.

But are you personally sure? You need to be clear if others are to be clear what you want:

- Do you know what you want?
- Do you know your priorities?
- What is your agenda?
- How do you feel?

BUILDING COLLABORATION

The work of Thomas-Kilmann is useful in reflecting on the balance between assertion and co-operation (see http://www.businesspotential.com). It is suggested that distinguishing behaviour that is accommodating from collaborating or compromising is helpful. The desired state is one where there are high degrees of co-operation but also high degrees of assertiveness displayed by all participants in the group.

Building collaboration requires being flexible, discussing alternatives, and airing different perspectives. The desire is to build situations where everyone feels that they have 'won' and no one feels that they have lost. This is building consensus and is not achieved by majority voting, which simply leaves a minority who are out-voted.

Collaboration is built by seeking common ground. Understanding the differences between positions and being empathetic to them is a good second step. This requires a great deal of clarification seeking on the part of the middle manager. Listening is an essential skill in resolving differences. Reinforcing the common ground and focusing on common goals enables collaboration to be built. A number of alternative solutions may need to be considered and this illustrates flexibility.

ORGANISING AND LEADING EFFECTIVE MEETINGS

Organising for meetings is about being in the right place at the right time and being well prepared with the right material. Middle managers need to hold meetings in comfortable surroundings. Tea, coffee and cake are not luxuries but part of providing the right environment for a professional discussion. Try occasionally holding some meetings at venues other than the school.

Planning an agenda, sticking to it and allowing time for each item is essential for running the meeting. However, some issues need your flexibility to allow you to let people discuss and run with ideas. No one said middle management was easy or did not have these impossible contradictions.

Make sure that everyone has a chance to speak. This may mean asking each person in a sensitive but insistent way. Passive resistance is the most damaging feature of a team effort. However, everyone's ideas must be expressed without personal criticism or ridicule. Chairing a meeting is not dissimilar to holding a classroom discussion with pupils. Thinking of it in these terms might help.

Make sure decisions are recorded and notes are made of who is going to do what. Lengthy minutes are frequently not required. Getting someone to take notes during the department meeting is often helpful and these can be photocopied instantly at the end of the meeting. Using a laptop for action points and emailing them to the group is instant and saves paper but allows access to the record of who is going to do what.

Always finish meetings in a positive and upbeat way. Celebrate the success. Remind everyone of the vision. Keep meetings fun.

MANAGING TIME AS A SUBJECT LEADER

Subject leaders are like most teachers pressed for time. Indeed, most would recognise the pressure of time. Some work long hours; probably many do so to compensate for a lack of time. Some have suggested that people do not use time management effectively because:

- They don't know about it
- They are too lazy to plan
- They enjoy the adrenaline buzz of meeting tight deadlines
- They enjoy crisis management.

Time management is a continuous struggle between demands and available time. Leask and Terrell (1997) use a three-point model concerned with time management. Their three components include:

- Time effectiveness techniques and skills
- Working with people
- Dealing with your own feelings about time and tasks.

In proposing this model they assume that people can manage time but that simple management techniques are not enough without dealing with the most time draining issues of working with people and dealing with your own feelings and attitudes. Techniques are not that useful in handling emergencies or sudden unexpected time demands. Keeping a diary well does not help to deal with the personal relations, motivational, and other issues that can be time consuming in middle management.

Time effectiveness techniques and skills

In the first category there are standard techniques and skills in planning the use of time, and in prioritising. They include:

- Do a time audit of how you currently use time as subject leader.
- Identify priorities on how you would like to spend time.
- Budget activities within a reasonable working week.
- Streamline activities to fit time; do not extend time to fit action.

- Use proformas as short cuts, e.g. for classroom observation, ordering materials, sending messages and so on.
- Chair meetings recognising time limits for discussion.
- Use waiting time effectively.

Working with people

Working with people is time demanding. People need time to discuss, to connect socially and to negotiate. Subject leaders are in a pastoral role as well as being managers of tasks. Time for people needs to be planned into the working week.

Listening carefully to people's concerns requires time and effort. Listening is best done in an appropriate venue. Staff need time to express their feelings. Good managers invite staff to talk about their emotions as well as plan strategies. Listen to the subtexts and the other agendas. People are not always able to express what lies behind what they say.

Three strategies might be suggested for working with people:

- Planning time for working with people.
- Saying 'No' sometimes.
- Delegating tasks to people.

The subject leader will need to know what tasks can be delegated and who it might be appropriate to delegate to. This corresponds with what has been said about stimulating distributed leadership (see page 9–10). Members of the department can and may wish to take responsibility for a key stage, writing a document, preparing materials, for resources and so on. Taking responsibility can be seen as a staff development function.

It should be clear that delegation is of a whole job. People need space to approach tasks the way they want to, with support and guidance. There is nothing so irritating as to be delegated a task and to be supervised so closely that nothing remains to be done.

Delegation is best done through establishing outcomes and criteria for success. For example, in the case of delegating the task of creating a resources inventory, the outcome would be an inventory that can be accessed by all staff and pupils, can be easily updated, and would promote the use of resources by staff and students. Credit, praise and celebration of success are essential parts of delegation.

Dealing with your own feelings about time and tasks

The third area is dealing with your own feelings about the use of time. You may feel guilt for not doing more, or for saying no. You may feel stressed or pressured, or that you are not really coping in the job.

These feelings are associated with your views on the use of time, including, for example:

- Saying 'No', 'I can't' or 'I won't be able to' is a sign of weakness.

- If I do more it will produce better work.
- If I delegate it will not be perfect.
- Not doing things is a sign of incompetence.

The fact is that the working week should not be excessive. Analysing your feelings is as much a part of time management as effective time planning.

REFERENCES

Leask, M. and Terrell, I. (1997) *Development Planning and School Improvement for Middle Management*, London: Kogan Page.

FURTHER READING

Allcock, D. (2002) *Time Management*, London: Spiro.

Pearson, B. (2002) *Common-Sense Time Management*, London: Chalford Management Books.

Thompson, N. (1996) *People Skills*, London: Macmillan.

Tyler, D.A. (2001) *Managing Time*, London: Industrial Society.

Whetton, D.A., Cameron, K. and Woods, M. (1996) *Effective Stress Management*, London: Harper Collins.

6.2 Your Own Professional Development

Ian Terrell and Geraint Lang

INTRODUCTION

OBJECTIVES

By the end of this Unit you should:

- Be able to identify strategies for your own professional development as a subject leader;
- Be aware of sources of further information for your own professional development.

As a greater emphasis is placed upon continuous professional development, senior and middle managers in schools are encouraging staff to regularly update their knowledge base and skills, and subsequently disseminate learning amongst their colleagues.

The National College for School Leadership maintains:

> Leaders have a responsibility for the learning of their adult colleagues. We will encourage them to develop every school as a professional learning community.

> (NCSL, 2000: 6)

Hopefully regularly updated professional knowledge should inform and extend good practice such that pupils become the ultimate beneficiaries. The TTA standards for subject leaders emphasise that you are to take responsibility for your own professional development.

Clearly, the reflective subject leader must be able to review their own work and establish clear goals for their own development. Not least they may wish to do this in collaboration with both the department and others and in addition to other CPD activities covered elsewhere in this book.

YOUR PORTFOLIO OF PROFESSIONAL DEVELOPMENT

There are a number of benefits in having a professional development portfolio as an aid to planning and recording professional development. As a role model, the subject leader may wish to develop this strategy for their own development. This underpins the importance of this approach in the eyes of members of the department.

Working with your own mentor

If a mentor has not been appointed by the school, consider approaching people to take on this role for yourself. You may wish to approach a more experienced subject leader, particularly one who leads a successful department. Alternatively your mentor may be from outside the school.

This is a person that you can talk through your work with, the achievements and the difficulties you face. They need not offer advice but will be good listeners and good at getting you to talk things through.

Online communities for professional development

Increasingly, opportunities to share knowledge with a wider audience of teachers in similar professional circumstances (such as science teachers within secondary schools) are becoming greater through the increase in specific professionally related websites and online communities.

Sometimes these are provided via local education authority 'learning grids', the DfES website, BECTa, professional associations and the NCSL. The ability to access shared information is enabled via the World Wide Web. The following may be useful sources of information about professional development:

www. ngfl.gov.uk	The National Grid for Learning
www.mirandanet.com	Mirandanet: an online community
www.becta.org.uk	The British educational technology site
http://teachernetuk.org.uk	A teachers' network online
www.naace.org/	The National Association for Advisers in ICT
www.teachersweb.co.uk	Teachers website for teachers

(A number of other useful websites can be found in the Appendix.)

The National College for School Leadership (www.ncsl.org.uk) recognises the role of the middle manager in school, and acknowledges that particular position as one of the five stages within the Leadership Development Framework, referring to it as

'Emergent Leadership' (see http://www.ncsl.org.uk/index.cfm?pageid=ldev-emergent-index).

The NCSL is currently developing specific programmes for this group of school managers. As part of this process, the NCSL provides 'online tools', one of which can assist school managers to focus specifically on reviewing numeracy strategies within their school (http://www.ncsl.org.uk/index.cfm?pageID=managing-tools-index points to the source of those online tools).

The *A to Z' of School Leadership and Management* is another online tool. This is found within the Teacher*net* section of the DfES website. This index features a diverse and extensive range of topics from absence management, head lice, and multicultural education, through to working with governors and youth offending teams – to mention but a fraction of the subjects included therein.

Exploring this site further, specifically the *Category Index* (http://www.dfes.gov.uk/a-z/catindex.html), reveals a myriad of topics, where teachers may discover schemes of work specific to their subject or phase under the *Curriculum and Standards* button, then having reached the specific web page, scrolling down to reveal *Schemes of Work*.

A cautionary note here though. The link to the actual schemes of work is unclear, and requires the reader to first go to the QCA site, where a graphical link to the DfES *Schemes of Work* may be found within the right-hand margin.

At last the reader is directed to the DfES Standards Site, at http://www.standards.dfee.gov.uk/schemes.

At this juncture, however, the genuine concerns of teacher organisations must be reflected on, as these additional points of reference so far highlighted may be perceived by some as adding to the large workload already facing the teaching profession. With this in mind, teachers may wish to view the DfES site, specifically focusing on Cutting Burdens (at http://www.dfes.gov.uk/cuttingburdens/index.shtml). The advice contained within, complete with an exemplar-planning framework, is worth considering. If it is no match for the reader's current planning strategy, then at least a certain degree of reassurance and personal satisfaction is derived from discovering that fact!

The need to embrace ICT both for increasing personal productivity (and thus reducing workload) and improving the overall record-keeping and target-setting practices of individuals and the school as a whole is a constantly recurring theme, and perhaps fittingly, BECTa launched its ICT Advisory site in March 2002 specifically to address the ICT needs of all teachers, from the classroom specialist and the middle manager, right through to the senior manager:

- http://www.becta.org.uk/teachers/index.cfm (for classroom teachers)
- http://www.becta.org.uk/leaders/index.cfm (for school leaders)

Gradually, however, the next generation of internet sites, particularly those that permit the formation of professional online communities, which may be accessed from virtually any online computer, has opened up virtual world wide audiences of teachers who may be able to share and discuss good practice and essential specific professional guidance with one another, pertinent to their own subject-specific field.

The asynchronous nature of online communities and the ability to access them without the need to travel vast distances, enable an individual to participate within a particular discussion. The establishment of online, facilitated professional communities within the UK education sector during the last three years has made possible the development of online learning opportunities for school leaders.

Bradshaw *et al.* (2002) reported on the development of the Talking Heads, Virtual Heads and Bursars Count online communities, with certain references to CPD. They reported that the concept of asynchronous online contribution enables time for learners to reflect, and more importantly, contribute their workplace experiences to the overall learning process.

Bradshaw *et al.* (2002) also found that successful school leaders' learning was both self-directed and participatory, underpinning the theory that the best learning was self-directed (Knowles 1984). They stated that the online community environment provided the opportunity for participants in the learning process to progress in their own time, which was described as a liberating experience. This fact ties in well with one of the main essential qualities ascribed to a middle manager in a school, namely that *you are in control of what you do.*

REFERENCES

Bradshaw, P., Powell, C. and Terrell, I. (2002) *The Development of Online Communities for Professional Learning*, available online at www.ultralab.net.

Knowles, C. (1984) *The Adult Learner: A Neglected Species*, 4th edition, Houston: Gulf Publishing.

NCSL (2000) *Leadership Development Framework – 6: Principles of Learning*, Nottingham: NCSL.

FURTHER READING

NCSL (2000) *Leadership Development Framework – 6: Principles of Learning*, Nottingham: NCSL.

WEBSITES

BECTa at http://www.becta.org.uk

DfES A–Z of Management at http://www.dfes.gov.uk/a-z/catindex.html

DfES Standards at http://www.standards.dfee.gov.uk/schemes

National College of School Leadership at www.ncsl.org.uk

6.3 Moving Towards Senior Management

Ian Terrell and Kathryn Terrell

INTRODUCTION

OBJECTIVES

By the end of this Unit you should:

- Be able to identify areas of development in preparation for senior management positions;
- Have a clear understanding of the strategies needed for you to develop the knowledge, skills and experience for senior management roles.

Most of this book has been aimed towards the new middle manager or head of department. We have explored the role and identified key areas of work and responsibility. Practical strategies have been suggested for leading the department and the subject. Underpinning the work has been improvement through critical reflection, analysis and problem solving.

This section has a different focus and addresses a potential next career stage after gaining some experience as a middle manager. Again the basis is critical reflection.

Not everyone will be interested in taking on senior management positions. The extra responsibility of the role in taking a whole school perspective may have some disadvantages for some people. Emphasising management or lessening focus on classroom teaching may be too high a cost relative to the status or financial reward that may be gained. However, this chapter is for those who may wish to consider a senior management position at some stage.

The Unit opens with a discussion on the difference between senior management and middle management in schools. There follow some suggested development strategies you may wish to adopt. Included in this are the following:

- Leading whole school initiatives
- Working beyond the school boundaries
- Work shadowing and placement
- Learning visits
- Training and qualification
- Journals and associations.

MIDDLE MANAGEMENT AND SENIOR MANAGEMENT: WHAT IS THE DIFFERENCE?

At first sight there may be no marked difference between middle management and senior management roles. Practice and roles vary in schools. There are many middle managers who undertake senior management roles anyway. For example, a manager of a large department or faculty would probably have a similar administrative, leadership and staffing role that an assistant headteacher might have. Any difference, therefore, is one of focus and priority.

First and foremost senior management roles are usually about whole school issues. In contrast, this means being aware of more than one curriculum area.

Senior management is and ought to be about strategic decision-making. This is decision-making that affects the long term. It is about the overall direction of the school. It is built upon a vision of where the school is going and what the school is trying to achieve. Values and beliefs about education are at its heart. To achieve career progression to headship, you will be expected to have views about these issues and a track record in having some involvement in strategic planning and management.

Issues in strategic decision-making include, for example, how the school is going to develop the following over the next five years:

- Information and Communication Technology across the whole curriculum
- Specialist school status
- Buildings and classrooms
- Staffing structure.

These decisions affect all subjects and staffs. The concerns of any one area need to be understood in relationship to the concerns of other areas and to the whole school. Partiality of perspective or knowledge is clearly dangerous.

Working as part of a senior management team is also important here. Building mutual trust, taking collective responsibility and acting as a team are important and difficult aspects of the role. They are also different even in the most collaborative of schools too.

Hence, taking on a senior management role may create personal difficulties in how you relate to colleagues who you may have worked with for some time.

Improvement is the central focus of senior management roles. Improvement has two facets. First, there is the achievement of the qualities and standards expected of teachers and schools. This is emphasised by the Ofsted Inspection, the annual performance and assessment (PANDA) and the DfES standards. Much of this is derived from studying effective schools and hence is termed the 'effective school movement' (see, for instance, Teddlie and Reynolds, 2000).

Then there is improvement as a long-term continuous effort to build the capacity of the school to adapt and change to raise the attainment of all children (Hopkins *et al.*, 1994; NCSL, 2001). Not that this view of improvement is about all children and all achievements and simple measures of GCSE results. This view recognises that conditions, expectations and values change. Schools over the long term are expected to achieve different things. Citizenship, AS levels, and ICT are but three recent and emerging issues.

There can be no expectation that schools will not continue to face pressures to change. The external environment of the school is also changing with changing demography, and economic and social conditions. Schools continue to face new agendas of coping with changing attitudes to life, crime, work, health, the family and so on. Change is endemic (Hopkins *et al.*, 1994; Whitaker, 1993; Fullan, 1991).

Thus, focusing upon effectiveness now and continuous improvement in the future is a central concern of the good senior manager. Hence knowledge of the management of change, the building of the capacity of the school to change and the creation of the school as a learning organisation is essential for the modern member of the senior team.

So, after an appropriate period of time the middle manager may wish to take on new responsibilities in preparation for a senior management position. We turn now to consider how. In this discussion we are assuming that the ideas in Section 3 dealing with developing staff have been applied to your own development. In particular that you plan your development goals and record your success in some form of professional portfolio.

You may have already considered working with someone as a mentor on your portfolio of goals and your record of success. Your mentor may also support and advise you in preparation for senior management.

Clearly, your involvement in staff development and reflective practitioner research projects will contribute to your experience in leading staff and be good preparation for a senior management role. Other activities might be considered and these are outlined below.

LEADING WHOLE SCHOOL INITIATIVES

One strategy might be to offer to lead, or work with a senior manager who is leading a whole school initiative. Such initiatives will vary with time and with different contexts. Some examples might include:

- Literacy
- Numeracy
- ICT
- Citizenship
- Teaching and learning

- Assessment
- Examinations
- School self-evaluation
- 14–19 curriculum
- Excellence challenge.

Leading the initiative will give you the opportunity to work across the whole school. You will encounter a larger cross section of staff. You will need to plan, develop their knowledge and skills, and monitor and evaluate progress.

WORKING BEYOND THE SCHOOL BOUNDARIES

Similarly, you may volunteer to take on a whole school role on an issue beyond the boundaries of the school and its staff. Such a role might be:

- Partnership with primary feeder schools
- Business partnership
- Partnership and liaison with LEAs
- Working with parents on specific projects or as the key contact with parent-teacher groups.

Again working with agencies outside of the school is good experience. Crow (2002) argues that such experience is important in understanding the school from the perspective of 'outsiders'. Such a view is important for senior management and future headship.

WORK SHADOWING AND PLACEMENT

You may be able to negotiate and plan a short period of time shadowing a senior manager or being 'placed' in a senior management work environment. Such an arrangement may last for short periods of time, for example a day, or for longer.

This may be an internal arrangement. For example, you may work with a senior manager on timetabling or preparing the daily cover list. External shadowing and placements are of considerable value. For example, you might arrange to visit the manager of a small or medium enterprise. You could arrange to shadow staff appointment procedures, Human Resources discussions or strategic planning meetings. Although Crow (2002) suggests that educational management is too different and complex to learn much from traditional industrial models, the cautious and evaluative practitioner can find useful practical ideas in seeing management and leadership in a different context.

LEARNING VISITS

Knowledge of different school management systems can be most easily gained by arranging exchange visits with other institutions. By planning an agenda and negotiating a focused visit you can plan your own professional development.

You might, for example, meet with senior managers to ask how they are developing their strategies, what their plans look like, how they work with the staff and so on. Reciprocal visits might be offered.

TRAINING AND QUALIFICATION

You may wish to undertake programmes of training for senior management positions. Such training may be available from the LEA, from Higher Education Institutions or from other agencies. You might, for instance, consider undertaking a degree in Education or Educational Management. In a survey of twenty Headteachers, nineteen agreed that having a postgraduate qualification was an important factor in gaining a senior management position. Practical experience was important but an additional qualification in a relevant area displayed a commitment to long-term professional development and learning at a significant level. Candidates were also likely to have in-depth knowledge of an aspect of schoolwork.

Often these training opportunities are modular and credit bearing. This means that you frequently get a choice of which modules you wish to undertake. Each module, on successful completion, allows you to accumulate 'credit' or points. These can be collected for a variety of awards at graduate or postgraduate level:

- Postgraduate Certificate – 60 credits at level 4
- Postgraduate Diploma – 120 credits at level 4
- MA in Education – 180 credits at level 4.

Clearly the knowledge, skills and expertise in topics such as learning, raising achievement, school improvement and leadership encompassed within these programmes is a valuable commodity. Most programmes these days combine discussion of key ideas with practical experiences and reflection on what you do in school. Practitioner enquiry and reflection is often central. Details of courses at your local HEI may be obtained on application and are usually available via their website.

A further, and key, recent development for those seeking to gain qualifications as school leaders is the creation of the National College for School Leadership which was discussed right at the start of this text (pp. 10–11). Details of their current programmes can be obtained from their website at www.ncsl.org.uk. Current NCSL programmes include 'Leadership from the Middle' and 'Emergent Leadership'.

JOURNALS AND ASSOCIATIONS

Keeping abreast of management issues can be achieved by reading journals. *Management in Education* and *Professional Development Today*, for example, are two practice-focused journals. These can be useful supplements to the regular reading of the TES. These will keep you abreast of the in-depth debates and developments in leadership.

The British Educational Leadership, Management and Administration Society (BELMAS) and the In-service and Professional Development Association (IPDA) may also be good sources of contacts and information. Professional associations are another good source of information and this can often be accessed from their websites.

Keeping a box folder or file of useful information can be helpful in keeping important documents to hand, especially if preparing for your interview for a senior management position.

CONCLUSION

It is delightful to be able to say that there is now a wider range of opportunity for structured professional development for those aspiring to school leadership posts than has ever existed in the past. Such opportunities are offered by a wide variety of organisations including individual schools, private organisations, Local Education Authorities, and Higher Education Institutions. The development of the National College for School Leadership in the UK has revealed a strong governmental commitment to offering nationally recognised programmes of study for school leaders and this development is mirrored in similar national initiatives in other countries.

The key issue for the middle manager who aspires to a senior position in schools is to make the most of such opportunities by seeking out all of the available opportunities in order to find programmes that are especially suitable to individual ambitions and personal circumstances.

REFERENCES

Crow, G.M. (2002) *School Leader Preparation: A Short Review of the Knowledge Base*, available online at www.ncsl.org.uk.

Fullan, M. (1991) *The New Meaning of Educational Change*, London: Cassell.

Hopkins, D., Ainscow, M. and West, M. (1994) *School Improvement in an Era of Change*, London: Cassell.

NCSL (2001) *A Prospectus*, Nottingham: NCSL.

Teddlie, C. and Reynolds, D. (2000) *The International Handbook of School Effectiveness Research*, London: Falmer Press.

Whitaker, P. (1993) *The Management of Change*, Buckingham: Open University Press.

FURTHER READING

Educational Management and Administration, Published for the British Educational Leadership, Management and Administration Society, London: Sage Publications.

Management in Education, Published for the British Educational Leadership, Management and Administration Society, Crediton: The Education Publishing Company Limited.

School Leadership and Management, Oxford: Carfax Publishing.

Appendix
Websites of Interest to School Leaders and Subject Leaders

AERA: American Education Research Association http://www.aera.net/

Australia Educational Leadership Development Unit http://tdd.nsw.edu.au/leadership/index.htm

Bath Department of Education Centre for Educational Leadership, Learning and Change http://www.bath.ac.uk/education/cellc/

Becta: British Educational Communications and Technology Agency http://www.becta.org.uk/

BELMAS: British Educational Leadership, Management and Administration Society http://www.shu.ac.uk/belmas/

BERA: British Educational Research Association http://bera.ac.uk/

British Library – guide to resources for school and colleges http://www.bl.uk/schools/index.html

Cambridge School of Education http://www.educam.ac.uk/links.html

Centre for Educational Leadership, Faculty of Education, University of Hong Kong http://www.hku/hk/educel/

Centre for Leadership Development, Ontario Institute for Studies in Education, University of Toronto http://www.oiseutoronto.ca/

Chicago Academies for Supporting Success (CLASS), Chicago, USA http://www.cpaa-class.org/CLASSpg/classhome.htm

DfES A-Z of School Leadership and Management http://www.dfes.gov.uk/a-z/atozindex_ba.html

DfES CPD page http://www.dfes.gov.uk/teachers/Professional_Development

DfES http://www.dfes.gov.uk/

DfES Publications http://www.dfes.gov.uk/circula.shtml

DfES School Performance Tables http://www.dfes.gov.uk/performancetables/

DfES Standards and Effectiveness Unit http://www.dfes.gov.uk/seu/

DfES Statistics http://www.dfes.gov.uk/statistics/index.html

DfES Teacher*net* – for the school management part of Teacher*net*, go to http://www.dfes.gov.uk/teachers/Management

Educational Leadership http://www.ascd.org/readingroom.html

ERIC database – clearing house for Educational Management http://eric.uoregon.edu/

EURYDICE (Information Network on Education in Europe) http://www.eurydice.org/

General Teaching Council http://www.gtce.org.uk/

Hay McBer http://www.transforminglearning.co.uk/

Headmasters' Conference http://www.rmplc.co.uk/orgs/hmc/brochure.html

Hull Institute for Learning International Leadership Centre http://www.hull.ac.uk/ILC/

ICSEI: International Congress for School Effectiveness and Improvement http://www.edu/icsei/index.html

Improving the Quality of Education for All http://www.nottingham.ac.uk/education/crtsd.iqea

Independent Schools http://www.isis.org.uk/

London Institute of Education London Leadership Centre http://www.ioe.ac.uk/llc/index.html

Manchester Faculty of Education Centre for Educational Leadership http://www.man.ac.uk/leadership/

NAHT: National Association of Headteachers http://www.naht.org.uk/

NAPE: National Association for Primary Education http://www.nape.org.uk/

National College for School Leadership http://www.ncsl.org.uk

National Curriculum Online http://www.nc.uk.net/home.html

National Grid for Learning http://www.ngfl.gov.uk/

National Institute for Urban School Improvement (US) http://edc.org/urban/index.htm

National Institute of Education, Nanyang Technological University, Singapore http://www.nie.edu.sg/

National Library of Education (US) http://www.ed.gov/NLE/

New Zealand Principal and Leadership Centre, College of Education, Massey University, North Palmerston, New Zealand http://ssinet.massey.ac.nz/

Nottingham School of Education http://www.nottingham.ac.uk/education/

NPHA: National Primary Headteachers Association http://www.primaryheads. org.uk/

OFSTED http://www.ofsted.gov.uk

Pathways to School Improvement http://www.ncrel.org/sdrs/

Principals' Executive Programme, University of North Carolina, USA http://www.ga.unc.edu/pep/

Principals' Qualification Programme, York University, Toronto http://www.edu.yorku.ca/FieldDev/PQP/

Qualifications and Curriculum Authority http://qca.org.uk/

Reading School of Education School Improvement and Leadership Centre http://www.soews.rdg.ac.uk/silc/default.html/

School Improvement UK http://www.school-improvement.co.uk/

School Manager.net http://www.schoolmanager.net/

SHA: Secondary Heads Association http://www.sha.org.uk/

TES: Times Educational Supplement http://www.tes.co.uk

The Australian Principals' Centre http://www.apcentre.edu.au/

The Educational Leadership Centre, School of Education, University of Waikato, New Zealand http://www.waikato.ac.nz/education/elc/

The Institute for Learning, Learning Research and Development Center, University of Pittsburgh, USA http://www.instituteforlearning.org/

TTA http://www.canteach.gov.uk

University of Leicester Centre for Educational Leadership and Management http://www.le.ac.uk/se/centres/celm.home.html

US Department of Education http://www.ed.gov/

US Department of Education, Office of Educational Research and Improvement http://www.ed.gov/offices/OERI/

Warwick Institute of Education http://warwick.ac.uk/wie/

Index